THE WRONG KIND OF WOMEN

THE WRONG KIND OF WOMEN

INSIDE OUR REVOLUTION TO DISMANTLE THE GODS OF HOLLYWOOD

NAOMI MCDOUGALL JONES

BEACON PRESS
BOSTON

BEACON PRESS
Boston, Massachusetts
www.beacon.org

Beacon Press books
are published under the auspices of
the Unitarian Universalist Association of Congregations.

23 22 21 20   8 7 6 5 4 3 2 1

This book is printed on acid-free paper that meets the uncoated paper
ANSI/NISO specifications for permanence as revised in 1992.

Text design and composition by Kim Arney

Library of Congress Cataloging-in-Publication Data

Names: Jones, Naomi McDougall, author.
Title: The wrong kind of women : inside our revolution to dismantle the gods
of hollywood/ Naomi McDougall Jones.
Description: Boston : Beacon Press, 2020. | Includes bibliographical references.
Identifiers: LCCN 2019026267 (print) | LCCN 2019026268 (ebook) |
    ISBN 9780807033456 (hardcover) | ISBN 9780807033463 (ebook)
Subjects: LCSH: Women in the motion picture industry. | Women in motion
    pictures. | Minority women—Employment. | Sex discrimination against women.
Classification: LCC PN1995.9.W6 J64 2020 (print) | LCC PN1995.9.W6
    (ebook) | DDC 384.8082—dc23
LC record available at https://lccn.loc.gov/2019026267
LC ebook record available at https://lccn.loc.gov/2019026268

To our mothers,
on the foundation of whose struggle
our work is possible: thank you.

To my sisters, beside whom I work:
your courage, passion, and hope for a
different future inspires me in all that we do.

To our daughters:
may this all be better for you.
Don't you dare take your eyes off the ball.

CONTENTS

AUTHOR'S NOTE

The term "women" in movements and in books such as this one tends to address disproportionately the experiences and struggles of white, straight, cis, able-bodied women. As a white, straight, cis, able-bodied woman myself, who now has a platform, I am perpetually in danger of contributing to this problem. That was front of mind during the researching and writing of *The Wrong Kind of Women*. I have included voices and stories from different perspectives than my own. And yet the unique and nuanced difficulties of women who do not look like me or have my access to privilege cannot wholly be captured by me, nor in the space of this book. What these pages present is the broad, disturbingly consistent barriers that hinder women. Where an interviewee or where research and data shed light on specific demographics of women—that is, women of color, women of a certain age, women of certain abilities—I shine my flashlight there. But I do not go beyond what I know. My hope is that by sharing what I do know, it creates space for more women's stories. The more inclusive, the better, as it is my deep belief that our work cannot be considered successful unless it elevates the voices of every kind of woman.

BEYOND THE LIGHTS*

On October 5, 2017, the *New York Times* published an article detailing decades of allegations against superstar film producer Harvey Weinstein, including horrific on-the-record accounts from Rose McGowan and Ashley Judd. Similar stories from Hollywood heavyweights Angelina Jolie, Gwyneth Paltrow, Lupita Nyong'o, Salma Hayek, Terry Crews, and Uma Thurman quickly followed. So did allegations against other Hollywood juggernauts, including Kevin Spacey, Louis C.K., and Les Moonves. The aftershocks of these revelations were nothing short of seismic. What started as an isolated Hollywood scandal reverberated in other industries (politics and the media, most memorably), unleashing a full-throated roar of long-silenced pain. Powerful man after seemingly untouchable powerful man was felled by histories of abuse and harassment. Women and men who had suffered in private, cleaved open by the scale of it all, picked up on Tarana Burke's #MeToo hashtag and painted the internet with rage and indignation.

It was a moment of deep cultural reckoning.

There were many overblown hot takes in the immediate aftermath, with *Forbes* heralding "the end of patriarchy."[1] Not quite—but there is no question that something fundamental shifted in the months after Weinstein's abuse was finally taken seriously.

---

* *Beyond the Lights* (2014), dir. Gina Prince-Bythewood.

Journalists, tweeters, and op-ed writers began to ask bigger questions about both Hollywood and society at large: How did this happen for so long? What kind of culture exists that allowed for so much unchecked behavior?

In Hollywood, those of us who had already been women in film activists worked to shift the conversation toward the deeper cause: namely, the chronic lack of representation of women in front of and behind the camera. Since almost the beginning of cinema, the near absolute exclusion of women from positions of power on set and in the studios has allowed for a culture to develop in which women working in the industry are seen as mostly inconsequential, sometimes bothersome, and, at worst, props to be used to the satisfaction of the men in power. Behind the most visible stories of sexual assault and abuse is a much more complicated one. The worst behaviors of Weinstein, Moonves, and the rest, revealed by a handful of high-profile actresses, were not a pernicious outgrowth of a "casting couch" mode of business, in which desperately ambitious actresses would do anything to become stars, but rather the result of an industry that has systematically ignored, undermined, and excluded women's voices for the better part of a century.

I understood none of this originally. I didn't understand it growing up when, on that special night each year, I got to stay up late in my pajamas to watch the Oscars, measuring the outcomes against my own projections, weeping, heart swollen as the winners accepted their little gold men triumphantly, often tearfully, and the losers smiled and applauded. I didn't understand it when, many other nights of the year, I practiced my own future Oscar speech in the bathtub, as I got dressed in the morning, or lay in bed at night. I didn't understand it when, flush with the giddy joy of telling stories, I set my sights, hell-bent, on becoming an actress myself. I didn't even understand it by the time I graduated the American Academy of Dramatic Arts (AADA) in 2008, gasping with eagerness to get to work and take my rightful place as the next Meryl Streep.

Like many women before me, I had swallowed the myth of the glittering gowns, tearful speeches, and media-fueled fairy tale of a meritocracy. As a young, white woman, raised in the 1990s and early 2000s by a feminist mother and father in Colorado, I had the privilege of stepping out into the world on seemingly strong footing. I was smart, capable, talented, ambitious, unafraid of hard work and sacrifice, and, I imagined, entirely unstoppable.

I moved to New York City on my nineteenth birthday—May 19, 2006— on a bus clutching two suitcases that held the bulk of what I owned, like something out of a goddamn 1940s musical. I had been pulled there by a pure desire to participate in that particular magic of telling stories and having those stories affect the lives, minds, and hearts of people watching. That's what the film industry held the promise of. That's what so many people headed to New York or Los Angeles are seeking.

Two years later, I graduated from acting school and began pounding the pavement. Quickly, I was informed over and over again that I was the wrong kind of woman to be an actress—not pretty enough or thin enough, teeth not straight enough, hair too frizzy, my intelligence a little too much at the fore.

Eventually, I began to think, Perhaps it's the roles for women that are wrong. So, I became a writer and a filmmaker, determined to write roles for myself and other women that more fully matched the real women I knew.

No one wants to see films like that, the powers that be told me. *Who, precisely, do you think will want to watch these films about women and their experiences? Isn't there a lesbian sex angle you could explore? Could the film have some more blood?*

To the gatekeepers dictating access to those hallowed means of shaping culture, I was maybe working hard but not in the right way. I didn't have enough experience to deserve power in the form of a voice.

Like nearly every woman who has walked these roads before me or beside me, there were years when I believed what I was hearing, when I strained to twist myself to fit the mold that they promised would make me the kind of woman who would get plucked up and welcomed into their glittering fold—whose wildest dreams they would make come true.

Except that as the years went by and I pretzeled myself painfully, as I watched my male peers begin to travel up the ladder in a way that neither I nor my female peers seemed to be able to, as I began whispering and then speaking and then bellowing the truth of my experiences, as I heard my fellow women resonating the same truths back—I came to understand the truth: all that wrongness was not about me in particular but in me being a woman at all.

My story is not remarkable. It is the story of every woman who has ever dared to dance with the industry known as Hollywood.

Generation after generation, for nearly one hundred years now, each of us has cycled through belief, brutality, gaslighting, blaming ourselves, and, eventually, facing the devastating reality that Hollywood is a system built to keep us out. Many of my peers of color, forced to live with a far more present awareness of the mechanisms of oppression, arrive with their understanding already mature. For my part, it took a long time. Longer than it should have. Even once I was a real, working, struggling actress—even a little ways beyond that—I kept watching the Oscars, year after year, seeing how happy and free and fulfilled Meryl and Kate and Cate seemed to be. Surely, I thought, surely if they were experiencing what I was experiencing, they would say something, or at least look less fabulously happy.

So, I persisted. We persisted.

Although to many, October 5, 2017, felt like the beginning of a new era or a thunderclap to kick off a brand-new conversation, it was only the latest opener in a cyclical conversation about the lack of women in film, which has happened nearly once a generation since the industry began. Every time some newsworthy event sets people yelling at Hollywood, the industry makes a few flashy, short-term moves and vows to do better. A handful of mostly white women get through the golden gates, are hired, and are given opportunities. The news cycle fades. Within five years, the data points stagnate, there is a backslide, and the white men who control this business continue to make movies that go out into the world and shape narratives about everyone's lives.

The truth of what is actually happening to women in Hollywood has remained veiled due to the silence of the women and men who work there. It is a silence continually purchased by Hollywood and the ever-dangling carrot of a dream career, a silence that has been an accomplice to the secret sexual and physical abuse of women but also the near total exclusion of women's voices and stories from cinema.

That silence has resulted in a culture in which the films and television that we consume—in spite of the fact that they demonstrably shape everything from our career choices to our brain chemistry—come almost exclusively from the white, male perspective.

With *The Wrong Kind of Women*, I am far from the first person to try to break that silence, but I come armed not only with facts but as a harbinger of a kind of transformation that has never before been possible.

I write this book as an actress, a writer, a producer, and an activist, bringing my experiences and personal stories into the mix. But I come armed, too, with over a hundred hours of interviews with women and men from every corner of the industry—the famous and the obscure, the powerful and those who do not even register at all—as well as research and data pulled from hundreds of articles, books, and scholarly papers.

This book is an attempt to help uncover the personal, collective, systemic, and data-driven mechanisms by which women have been historically kept out of key roles in Hollywood, even as 50 percent of film school graduates are women. Most importantly, I want to address the impact the absence of women in cinematic storytelling is having on our individual and collective psyches, because the stories we consume—in greater volume than ever now—are told almost exclusively from the monolith of the white, male perspective.

The stories you have heard over the past two years in the wake of Weinstein and #MeToo are only the most visible outcroppings of a system of oppression and exclusion that, to this day, even post-#MeToo, will get women blacklisted for speaking out. Behind the courageous actresses who did speak out is a much longer list of women, many of them the world's most famous actresses and filmmakers, who remain silent. This is a book about the stories you have not heard, from the famous ones, yes, but also from the women who did not make it, have not made it yet, and whose careers and lives have been laid waste by the sparkling promise of Hollywood.

But this story is also one of hope, courage, and revolution. The confluence of the internet, streaming, technological advances, and social media has ignited a once small but now rapidly growing movement of women, people of color (POC), disabled people, LGBTQ+ folks, and other historically marginalized voices who are finding alternative ways to tell their stories and deliver them to audiences who are, amidst Hollywood's endless remakes and franchises, craving fresh and unheard perspectives. It is the story of a growing insurgency facing off against a century-old behemoth of an industry.

It is time, once and for all, to dismantle the gods of Hollywood to whom we have all sacrificed too much for far too long. It is time to think and act radically about building a different kind of future for the industry that shapes our culture—not only for the women being actively hurt inside the film industry but also for those outside it, whose careers, relationships, purchasing decisions, and sense of self are shaped by the stories our industry is feeding them.

If I have done my job, by the time you have finished reading this book, you will never again be able to sit down and watch a film or TV series without questioning who created it and what cultural dynamics it is working to disrupt or reinforce; you will understand the subtle and not-so-subtle ways in which women and other groups can be systematically excluded from a system that claims to be the height of forward-thinking liberalism; and you will be prepared to take up the fight for the most hopeful piece in all of this: the surging, grassroots, internet- and women-driven revolution in filmmaking that is quietly catching fire.

CHAPTER 1

IT FELT LIKE LOVE*

Most people assume that rejection following an audition is the hardest part of being an actor,† but that has never been my experience. In fact, the opportunity to be rejected actually becomes a goal—particularly when you are a doe-eyed acting school graduate—because it means you managed to get into the audition room at all.

To truly understand what happens to women in Hollywood, you need to understand what it's like for anyone first entering the business, so cycle back with me to my earliest, greenest days fresh out of acting school.

When I was that young, starry-eyed actress, getting into the audition room felt next to impossible. I understood that until I was represented by an agent or was well known among casting directors, I would not get the opportunity to audition for projects that actually pay actors money, have prestige, and feature the established and talented creative teams that an actor would most want to work with.

Luckily, or unluckily, for all starry-eyed young actors, there is, below that seam of Serious and Respectable projects, a vast sea of theater (off-off Broadway, "downtown" theater), web series, and film projects (student films, some lower-end short films, and micro-budget feature films) that don't have enough money to hire a casting director and, therefore, put

---

* *It Felt Like Love* (2013), dir. Eliza Hittman.
† In this book, I use the term "actor" when I am referring to both men and women and "actress" when I am referring only to the female members of the profession. This is for ease of understanding when I speak of experiences that apply specifically to women.

the word out directly to actors to apply for roles. As you might imagine, the range of quality of these projects is considerable, as is the caliber, talent, and emotional stability of the creative teams behind them.

It is from this land that most young actors spend many, many years—sometimes their entire careers—trying to break free. This teeming land is what I like to call Purgatory.

When you are an actor in Purgatory, because you have no agent and, therefore, no access to Non-Purgatory projects, you spend your days submitting your materials to hundreds of these lower-level projects, alongside at least several thousand other actors, hoping against all logic that your headshot and resume will somehow be noticed. If you get noticed, you get your golden opportunity to audition.

When you get that magical call (or email, as it mostly is these days), it is generally for an audition slot the very next day, or even that afternoon. The project's creative team generally sends you three to ten pages from the script, or *sides*, from which you must prepare. You then make some quick hair, makeup, wardrobe choices and show up for the audition, where you are now competing against a much smaller pool of somewhere between thirty and several hundred actors for the role.

As you might imagine, this lifestyle makes holding down a side job (so you can do things like pay your rent) outstandingly difficult, as there's not a huge amount of negotiating room with times or dates of audition slots. You are given a slot, and you're expected to be there. If you are not, someone else will be.

But in exchange for that difficulty, you do get the opportunity, maybe once or twice a week, to do the thing that you moved to this place and made sacrifices to do: act. For three or five or, if you're very lucky, ten minutes of time, in this audition room, in front of strangers, you are an actor.

Unlike most industries in which you might participate in a difficult, competitive, and stressful hiring process every once in a great while when you're starting out or switching jobs, being an actor is mostly a business of furiously battling to get auditions, going in for some auditions if you are lucky, interrupted by extremely brief moments of actually getting hired for a job, before you are back on the streets hustling again.

According to my notes, from May through December in 2008—the eight months immediately after graduating acting school—I went on eighty-six auditions, somewhere between two and three each week. In the following years, once my resume was a bit more robust with a few higher-profile credits on it, I averaged more like six to eight each week, 3 to 6 percent of the hundred or so projects I would submit to. I believe I booked about four Purgatory-level jobs during those first eight months. I was paid for none of them.

I realize that to anyone who has never participated in the entertainment industry this may sound like a ridiculous way to live, and believe me, it is. But you have to understand that, particularly at first, these difficulties feel amazing—like your muscles shaking during a workout. You are suffering, but you are suffering *for a dream*, and not just any dream but, for most people entering the business, as it was for me, a dream that you have held since childhood and which feels so urgent that you think you will never find happiness at all if it is unfulfilled.

Each hardship is an opportunity to pay your dues. Every week I used to receive my issue of *Entertainment Weekly* and read the interviews with my idols, famous actors and actresses, wryly telling stories of *their* days in shitty, Brooklyn basement apartments, the time that sleazy director made them get naked in front of a crew. Enduring these things wasn't a problem; it was the *point*. Otherwise, what on earth were we going to talk about with the *Entertainment Weekly* reporter?

Aside from the lightly deranged quality of all of this, the true pitfalls of Purgatory, most especially if you are a woman, arise from the level of amateur-occasionally-bordering-on-professional work, in which anyone can throw together a project and call themselves a director. Young actors are so desperate to build their resumes that most will put up with almost anything for the chance to work, and there is nary a casting director nor agent nor union in sight to vet anyone on either side of this process.

The tamest, although thoroughly demoralizing, consequences of this situation are subjecting oneself to the most ridiculous or offensive impulses of the usually-quite-young, usually-quite-male directors, who have little training or experience but who wield the ultimate power of being able to cast you, because they have somehow convinced someone with resources of their burgeoning brilliance.

Frequently, however, the most pernicious circumstances occur when you actually book the job.

At one particular low point, I got cast in a play in a seedy theater in midtown that was run by a nasty individual who remained vertical most days while hopped up on an impressive array of cocaine, alcohol, and goodness knows what else. Like so many mediocre white male directors, this man had inexplicably managed to build a cult of genius around himself, such that he perpetually managed to dupe a never-ending parade of young actors and actresses to participate in his shows for free, in spite of a penchant for spending most rehearsal time screaming frequently misogynistic abuses at them.

My job in this show was to participate in a two-person sketch in which a man sat in a chair and delivered a monologue to the audience, while I gave him a lap dance. The big joke was that the monologue had absolutely nothing to do with the lap dance and, throughout the entire sketch, the man never once acknowledged my presence nor the fact that he was receiving a lap dance. Hysterical, right?

But I agreed to that—through two weeks of rehearsal and then six times in front of an audience, before I finally worked up the self-respect to quit the show.

Each time I performed that lap dance—or any of the sundry other humiliating and degrading things I let myself get talked into in those early years—even as fifty or so drunk audience members guffawed, heckled at, and ogled me, I gritted my teeth and proudly reminded myself that we all have to pay our dues.

My experience as an actress in Purgatory was so commonplace that, I can promise you, it wouldn't raise an eyebrow in actor circles. I readily, even proudly, accepted it as part of the deal. I figured that if I could just hang on long enough and be tough enough to endure whatever directors and producers threw my way, I would rise with the cream and eventually get to be part of telling beautiful, important, daring stories. I would get to play the kinds of complex, strong, messy, vulnerable women that Meryl plays.

For that dream, I reminded myself, I could endure anything. No number of lap dances or grandiose assholes on cocaine were going to keep me from that future I could see so clearly for myself. I was tough. I was singularly focused. I was ambitious.

My fellow actress-turned-creator Sonja O'Hara told me that she had a mantra through those early years in Purgatory: "Act or die."

For my part, it never occurred to me that I would die. I had been practicing my Oscar speech for too long.

As desperate as actors are to get jobs *in* Purgatory, that has nothing on the level of desperation to get *out* of Purgatory. Like every one of my peers, I was hell-bent on a mission to earn my ticket up. The means of doing this were, at best, murky. Career progress in the entertainment industry has more in common with a pinball machine than a ladder. But the ever-present goal was to get agents, managers, and casting directors to notice me out of the vast sea of other actors, which involved hounding these gatekeepers by every available method.

During this period of my career, I had a genuinely impressive set of spreadsheets with the name of every agent, manager, and casting director in New York, along with notes of progress or actions in my pursuit. Initially, I would mail each of them a headshot and resume with the precise font that I had obsessively chosen as the perfect representation of myself, along with a personalized and witty, cover letter that might catch the attention of an assistant and be put forward for further consideration. For a full four years, I then sent postcards with a photo and any "news" or "updates" mailed once a month like clockwork. I paid for auditions—through a morally dubious cottage industry common in New York and Los Angeles and made vaguely legal only under the auspices of studios offering them as "classes"*—with these same people so that they would see and learn my face, after which, I followed up with more postcards. Had I applied the level of industriousness toward some sort of normal career, I would probably be running a large company by now, possibly a country. But, as Hollywood is no normal industry, the return on all this effort was unimpressive.

Still I slogged on in Purgatory, living, like all of us poor-sod actors without trust funds, off of a numerous, and ever stranger, hodgepodge of side hustles, never making more than $18,000 in a single year. My personal side-hustle strategy was to take jobs that paid relatively good hourly rates, had flexible schedules, and were just weird enough that not many other people would want to do them. I de-liced kids' hair, was a test subject at a medical school, and worked as an assistant (read: glorified cleaning lady) for a professor at a major NY university who had such severe epilepsy that he couldn't go out in sunlight or go outside

---

* California's Krekorian Talent Scam Prevention Act has made them actually illegal, though the law is murky and ill-enforced.

very much at all, and, therefore, slept during the day and was awake all night. He chain-smoked and had Tourette's that manifested specifically if I slammed a cabinet door even slightly too loudly, in which case he would come screaming into the living room cursing his head off and making me keenly aware of how many seconds it would take to get to the front door if necessary. I discovered after the fact that he had on at least one occasion kept a student, bound and gagged, locked over the weekend in the bathroom that I regularly cleaned.

I worked at that last job for two years. The money was good.

Purgatory is a hard-knocks existence for actors of all genders. No one who succeeds as an actor does so without depths of determination, talent, grit, and hard work. That said, Purgatory is much, much worse for actresses, from the dearth of three-dimensional roles to the perpetual daily cuts of casual misogyny and devaluation that happen to women in our society at large but are magnified to an art form in the film industry to, most conspicuously of all in Purgatory, the constant and aggressive sexual harassment and abuse from people in positions of minor or major power.

Relatively speaking, I was lucky in that I, unlike a truly stunning number of my peers during these earliest, most vulnerable years, was sexually harassed but never sexually assaulted.

In 2018, *USA Today* did a survey of eight hundred female entertainment professionals—actresses, directors, producers, screenwriters, camera ops, editors, and publicists, among others—and 94 percent responded that they had been sexually harassed or assaulted while working in Hollywood. That is nearly every single woman in the industry.[1]

These experiences show up in every crack and crevice of our professional lives, frequently at the moment when we have finally convinced ourselves that a situation or person is safe. Over the course of conducting interviews for this book, I discovered that these incidents tend to fall into a pattern of scenarios.

> *The Quid Pro Quo*—the classic casting-couch proposition. A (usually male) person in a position of power—casting director, agent, director, etc.—offers to hire you/represent you/make you a star

in exchange for sexual acts/romantic outings/escort services and/or "lunch."

The Mentor Surprise—a (usually male) person in a position of power who has offered to give advice/career help and has, perhaps, even done so, suddenly turns the relationship into one of sexual or romantic conquest and, almost always, becomes furious if/when rebuffed, shattering both a professional relationship you've invested time in and your sense of worth as an artist and not just a body.

The Audition Surprise—a (usually male) director in an audition room suddenly asks you to take your shirt off so that he can make sure it's all okay for the sex/bikini/nude scene or asks you to perform degrading and humiliating acts in the name of "art," doesn't cast you and, on occasion, even spreads word around town that you are "difficult" or "a prude" if you refuse.

The On-Set Surprise—a (usually male) director with whom you have negotiated ahead of time to a minute level of detail precisely how a nude/shower/sex scene will go down on set suddenly begins demanding in front of the entire cast and crew that you reveal more/get taken doggy-style facing the camera/perform acts you would never have agreed to in advance, screams at and humiliates you if you refuse, and creates the perception that you are simply not a team player if you object.

The Colleague Surprise—a (usually male) sometimes more famous actor you're performing with begins making inappropriate comments during rehearsal, insists on "extracurricular work time" spent together, and even sexually assaults you, leaving you in the no-win situation of having to report him and risk losing your job or continue performing with him night after night, day after day.

I have experienced variations on every scenario described above at a constant low-grade level, have had career-damaging incidents twice, and, again, can count myself lucky in that those incidents never rose to the level of outright sexual assault.

In conducting interviews for this book, I made it a particular goal to see whether I could find an actress who did not have a story along these lines. I was unable to.

In the wake of the Harvey Weinstein scandal, I have had many conversations with men and women outside the film industry in which they lower their voices to say, "Yeah, but for all the women who are coming forward about Weinstein, there must be a lot of women who *did* sleep with him for roles."

And, yes, there most definitely were.

But unless you have lived it, you can only try to imagine the frustration, heartache, and grind of working so hard and so nonlinearly toward a dream that most of us have held since we were kids—and how well the industry trains us to sit down and accept whatever pain we are given from the very moment we enter it. I stand in judgment of no one for taking a ticket forward that was offered to them and had probably been forced on them many, many times before they agreed.

Sexual harassment, assault, and degradation make up the constant, thrumming, crushing backdrop of being an actress.

For those women who this does not drive from the business, who it does not break, these experiences often perfectly shape them into the kind of woman Hollywood adores—one whose voice has been so thoroughly silenced and disconnected from her impulses and emotions that she will smile and giggle and bear all sorts of darkness she should not.

By 2011, after three years in Purgatory, having earned some hard-won stripes, I had my sights set on HBO's *Boardwalk Empire* as my ticket out. The show was both critically acclaimed and had a massive, dedicated audience. Many actresses in New York had begun noticing that whoever was making the casting decisions on that show clearly had a type, because most of the women in the smaller roles had red hair and blue eyes. Well, hey, I thought, *I* have red hair and blue eyes.

One of the major questions all red-haired, blue-eyed actresses were asking themselves and each other at this time was whether they would be willing to appear topless, if necessary, since virtually every woman on the show had to agree to do so. For my part, I'll be honest, I most definitely would have done so if it involved getting a speaking role. I would have found a way to rationalize it for myself. Actresses are exceptionally good at rationalizing.

To boost my chances at getting cast, I paid to take a class—this one was legitimately a class—with Julie Schubert, the casting assistant for *Boardwalk Empire* at the time. Schubert and I seemed to hit it off, so I, naturally, began deluging her with postcards. Six stamps later, Julie called me in for an audition.

I didn't get cast. But she called me in again, and that time, I booked the role.

I was ecstatic. After three years in the trenches, I was on the road out of Purgatory. I was twenty-four-years old and crackling with the promise of a dawning future.

In my scene, it's nighttime. A couple is in bed together. Suddenly, from off-camera, we hear a bloodcurdling scream.

"AAAAAHHHHHHHHHHHH!"

The camera cuts to daytime in an office, close-up of a redheaded woman, her hair in a 1920s 'do, her face contorted in terror.

"AAAAHHHHHHHHHHHHH!"

The camera pans down, following her gaze, in front of her, where Alderman Jim Neary is collapsed, face-down on his desk, head blown gruesomely open by a point-blank gunshot.

"AAAAAHHHHHHHHHHHH!"

End scene.

That was my big moment on *Boardwalk Empire*. My character's name? Screaming Secretary.

Despite the fact that I didn't form any actual words, through some odd technicality in the Screen Actors' Guild contract that must equate "vocal utterance" with "a line of dialogue," the role counted as a "Co-Star" on the show. This distinguished me from an "extra," which is also different from a "featured extra." These title delineations are of serious importance, both from a resume perspective and because they are tied to your level of treatment on set.

If, for instance, you are an "extra" on the show—which means that you are one of the people hired to be in the background and wander around, often pretending to speak but not actually doing so—you are on the basement floor of privilege. This means that during all down time, including meals, you are stuck in a big room with all the other extras and, often, inexplicably limited seating.

If you are a "featured extra"—meaning that you are an extra but in some way become visibly part of the action of the scene, though with no lines—you are also put in this same holding room. But you might, for instance, be assigned your own chair or, if you are very lucky, even two chairs. On a long day of shooting, having an assigned chair can make the difference in whether or not you choose to poke your eye out with a spoon by 5 p.m.

But! If you are a "co-star"—a term covering actors with one or two lines in one or two scenes—you are airlifted away from the plebs and given your own personal "honeywagon," which is a small room about one-fourth the size of a full trailer, typically with a tiny bathroom, chair, mirror, and costume rack. Often, they even put your name, or your character name, on the door. Mine said "Screaming Secretary." In the mind of a struggling actor, this honor feels heart-stoppingly like having "arrived."

I reveled in my honeywagon day on *Boardwalk Empire.* By hour two, I had gotten through hair and makeup. Over the ensuing five hours, as I waited to be called to set, I took many secret photos of myself in there, so I would always remember that day of glory. My grandmother still has one of them on her wall. Finally, around hour seven of the day, a production assistant, or PA, knocked on my door and said, "Ms. McDougall Jones, they're ready for you." He led me out of my honeywagon, and as he did, he intoned on the radio, "Talent is flying to set." This gave me no small thrill.

When I got to the place of production, they assigned me another chair. Half an hour later, they came and got me and told me where to stand in front of the camera. While fifty or so crew members stood around, the show's director said something kind and brief to me, then vanished into the next room where his monitor was. Someone yelled action and I screamed three times in a row. Then they had me do three more takes for good measure.

I was dismissed. As I was leaving set to walk back to holding, an actor who played one of the central characters on the show casually caught up to me and began propositioning me to come back and "see his trailer." I politely declined all the way back to my honeywagon, at which point, I closed the door on him.

I changed back into my clothes and left set with stars in my eyes and music in my heart.

I had had other meatier and more meaningful experiences as an actress down in Purgatory. But the role of Screaming Secretary did begin to change things, even if it could hardly have qualified as a "big break." In the mystical status-ranking game of the industry, I had at last managed to get a chip on the game board. I had one casting director who was aware that I existed, and I had the title of a show that people had actually heard of on my resume. Two points for Naomi.

Once you manage, as I had partly managed, to get a foothold in the System, the rules of the game shift dramatically. Purgatory is filled with actors covering an erratic range of talent and experience levels—everyone from "I woke up last week in Arkansas and decided I'd like to be an actor" to seriously talented and well-trained people who simply haven't yet managed to navigate their way up the ranks. Your primary need in Purgatory is to establish yourself as someone in the latter category rather than the former.

Once you enter the System, though, you become part of a pool with deep benches of talented, interesting, well-trained actors who are not yet famous and are desperately competing for small to mid-size roles. At this stage it becomes of key importance to distinguish and "brand" yourself, such that you are instantly recognizable and memorable to casting directors. Branding oneself can be viewed as a positive, in that, as with marketing any product, it is helpful in the process of selling your product (in this case, yourself) to buyers (in this case, casting directors, agents, and directors) to have a clear, coherent brand to communicate. The darker side of branding, however, is that it very often boils down to what is known as "typing." That is when casting directors and agents sort actors into different buckets of recognizable types of characters, so that when they need to cast a particular type, they can simply dig through a specific bucket of actors, rather than having to look more thoughtfully at the whole field.

Actors, trying to make themselves as appealing as possible for casting directors, become as obsessed with figuring out their type as they are with finding the elusive perfect font for their resumes.

One widely used method for gaining this self-knowledge is a "typing exercise." On the first day of an acting class, for instance—when you can most closely replicate the experience of being judged by a roomful of strangers—each actor, one at a time, will stand in front of the other actors who will respond to such prompts as:

"Name some roles that you could see this actor playing."

"What are the first three words that come to your mind when you look at this person?"

"What professions do you imagine this person would work in?"

Out of all of the answers that are then shouted out by the other actors, some sort of coherent type or themes are meant to emerge, so that you can more clearly understand what "type" strangers will see you as when you walk into an audition room.

In all the typing exercises I have participated in, only three consistent themes ever emerged for me. They were . . .

Secretary.

Dominatrix.

Mentally unstable.

Given that I have never been a dominatrix, that I have worked as a secretary for only two weeks, and that I actually possess an unusual level of mentally stability for an actress, you can see how mind-bending this "typing" business can be.

And although I did not have the perspective to register this at the time, "typing" is another place where our male peers' experiences began to greatly diverge from ours.

In films as they exist right now, when casting directors, agents, directors, and producers go to cast a white man in a film, they really dig around deep for the actor who can bring just the right shading and nuance to meet the exact complexities of the character as he's written. When they're trying to cast anyone else, they generally reach for a "type." For the most part, this is the result of in-the-moment, moving-too-fast, not-enough-time-or-resources decisions of the creators and gatekeepers—who are overwhelmingly white and male—unthinkingly going to the easiest mentally available reference, which, frequently, was planted there by both society and the movies they themselves have spent their lives consuming.

Most actresses sooner or later come to realize that, unlike her white male colleagues, she is not actually getting "typed" by the industry. She is being held up against a set of *stereo*types of women who are allowed to appear in films and on television and are then told whether or not she "makes sense" to the creators and gatekeepers.

If you are black, you'd better be "sassy." If Latina, you must either be the vixen, sexy, bad-tempered, club girl who is angry at her boyfriend or the devastated immigrant mother trying to cross the border and protect her child. Occasionally, you might get to be a cop. According to Michelle Hendley, a trans actress, "There are two options [for my "type"]: 1) They want you to be super-vampy-trans, which is usually what they want if they write 'non-binary' or 2) They write 'passable,' which usually means that you have to appear to be cis in the story until in some huge reveal it turns out that—ta da—you're trans." If you are a visibly disabled woman, you will almost certainly only be allowed to play disabled characters with limited plot lines, though in most instances, you will lose even those roles to able-bodied actresses. White women have more "types" available to them, but hair color is usually taken to be the key determinative factor of your personality. Blondes are hot, flirty, and flighty. Brunettes are smart, serious, probably not much fun. And redheads are a good time, but almost always secretly crazy.

If you do not fit neatly into one of these predetermined types, you are generally given an endless stream of advice on how to fix yourself so that you will.

If you think I'm overstating this, Jennifer Morrison, a now hugely successful actress having starred on *House* and *Once Upon a Time*, told me that early on in her career she ran into the problem that she would always get called in to read for smart, capable characters, which is unsurprising, since Jennifer herself is exceedingly smart and capable. After each audition, her agents would get terrific feedback on her audition, her acting skills, her choices, but would ultimately hear, "Yeah, but she's blonde, so . . . the director just can't really see her in the role."

Finally, in frustration, Jennifer dyed her hair brown—which, according to Hollywood, was the color that matched her personality—and "from that point on, I never stopped working." It wasn't until midway through her multiyear run as a lead character on *House*—once she was a successful, famous, and recognized talent—that she was able to dye her hair back to blonde without the industry becoming completely disoriented.

There's a similar story about Amy Adams, who, spoiler alert, is *not* a natural redhead.

Not every actress's "problem," however, can be solved by hair dye. The utter necessity for women to fit into one of the narrowly defined types preordained by the industry means that most actresses spend the early years of their careers trying desperately to mold themselves, to shave the nuances off their personality and physical appearance such that the industry will recognize them as an appropriate type of woman.

The pressure to alter your physical appearance to meet the industry standard bears down from all sides. These pressures tend to be worse for non-white, non-cis, non-straight women, for whom the stereotypes are even more rigidly defined and limiting. Women of color frequently get asked to take steps to lighten their skin, straighten their hair, and even get facial surgery to make themselves an acceptable (read: "whiter") version of "ethnic." For black women, the texture of their hair is often an issue. Although the natural hair movement and the growing popularity of natural hairstyles is lessening this to a degree, there is still persistent pressure for black actresses to style their hair in some other way than how it grows out of their heads.

An Indian actress I'll call Aastha, whose nose reflects common facial structures of her heritage, was once told by a manager, in a moment of not-so-subtle hint dropping, "Well, sometimes, if you need a nose job, you just get a nose job."

Actress Michelle Hurd, who has naturally less-than-enormous breasts can't recall the number of times a costume designer during a fitting took a look at her breasts and said, "Oh well. You'll get those done at some point." (She still hasn't, decades into her career.)

For actresses with disabilities, the pressure is often to, if at all possible, hide their physical reality. Marilee Talkington, an actress and creator with visual impairment, has been told consistently throughout her career, even by a director she loves and has worked with before, "Do not tell anybody. They will not hire you." Once it was even, "If you can't read that script, you don't belong onstage."

Sometimes the alterations asked of you are not physical but are to reinforce stereotypes in a way that can feel like a fundamental betrayal of yourself and your heritage.

Aastha recalls the many times in an audition room when she has been asked to play heavily into an Indian stereotype. She told me that she usually just takes a deep breath and in her mind apologizes to her grandmother—who, in the 1950s, was a gold medalist in math—"and then I play along because I need the job."

Makia Martin, who is black, has been to auditions when, after her first reading of the sides, the director or casting director will lean over and delicately intone some version of "That was wonderful. Now, this time through, could you try to be a little more . . . black?"

Although in her mind, she'll usually snap back, "Have you seen my skin? I've been black since the late '80s," Makia knows what they mean and, because she wants the job and needs to pay her rent, she'll play along—"rolling my neck and eyes, changing my inflections and tone of voice."

This can get even murkier if you happen to fit really well into your given stereotype, as Makia discovered about herself with some discomfort. "The thing is. I *am* black and I *am* sassy." As a result, she almost always gets cast in a stunningly specific type of role: "a sassy, funny black woman who usually pops into the story to bring a little comic relief and throws shade on the main character to set them straight on some point." Frequently this person is a security guard.

I have to confess, with no small amount of shame, that prior to writing this book, I cast Makia in this exact role in my second feature film, *Bite Me*, although I had written the role in the screenplay with her race unspecified. When I mentioned this during our interview, Makia kindly pointed out that, although that was true, in my film the security guard at least turns out later to be secretly a vampire, making her the most interesting version of that character she's played. But, clearly, it is only too easy, even for those of us aware of all this, to fall prey to propagating these stereotypes, embedded as deeply as they are they in our cultural psyche.

The complicated reality is that playing a stereotypical role has gotten Makia through some pretty amazing doors—she's played it on *Master of None* and in Jemaine Clement's latest film, doors that she hopes and believes will lead to more doors. Sometimes, actors who are able to slot themselves neatly into these predefined stereotypes work substantially more, move more quickly up the chain to bigger and better projects, and are more successful at getting signed by agents and managers. Makia thinks often about the career of Octavia Spencer, who rose up the ladder playing a particular black female stereotype but was able to build on that success to eventually expand the idea of what a black woman is on-screen.

The whole situation is a spiritual double-bind. Either (a) fit into a stereotype that may be personally and/or culturally offensive and which will limit the depth of roles you play but may result in bigger work, or (b) don't fit into a stereotype, in which case you may get to play more interesting roles but probably only in smaller Purgatory-level projects, and you may never make it onto the industry game board at all.

Deciding how to handle this bind can be existentially weighty stuff, particularly in cases when the thing that you are told is keeping you from success is something that you *can* practically change about yourself.

Do you just go ahead and get the boob job? The nose job? Straighten your hair? Whiten your teeth? How much does each of those things really cost you when that one alteration (or two or three) might be the single key to attaining this career that for most actors means not just professional success but the achievement of their lifelong dream and the fulfillment of their soul's deepest wants? That is, of course, assuming you have the financial resources to do these things at all.

A lot of us will go pretty far. Even make harsh financial sacrifices to do so. And sometimes it works. Like Jennifer Morrison with her brown hair—a relatively minor adjustment—sometimes you really do change that one thing and your "type" clicks into place, and suddenly the industry recognizes you and your career jets forward.

It doesn't always work, though. All actors have seen peers turn themselves inside out chasing the advice of those gatekeepers—boob jobs; nose jobs; Botox; braces or veneers for that perfectly straight, perfectly aligned smile; different haircut; different hair color; stricter workout regime; diets galore—and somehow their type never clicks. There is a special kind of devastation that comes with changing so much of yourself—often irreversibly—only to find on the other end that you're still "just not quite right."

I never did figure out my type. Nobody else in the industry could either.

For years I would perform my monologue or scene and look up hopefully only to find the gatekeeper gazing at me in a squinty-eyed, bewildered way.

"Well . . ." the person would say, "You're very talented, but . . ."

". . . if you dye your hair blond, lose ten pounds, and straighten your teeth . . ."

". . . if you could just not lead quite so much with your intelligence . . ."

". . . if you could just do *something* with your hair . . ."

". . . then I could work with you."

The consensus always seemed to be that if I could just find the right hairdresser or use the right product or . . . *something* . . . then I would finally make sense.

One agent looked exasperatedly at me when I was about twenty-three and said, "I don't know what to do with you. You're too smart for the roles written for women your age and you're not quite pretty enough to be the hot one. I don't know. I think you'll work when you're thirty-five."

The agent possibly offered this last beacon of hope because he genuinely hoped that, by the time I was thirty-five—significantly past the time of the juiciest female roles—that I would somehow finally make sense as some "mother type." Perhaps he just figured that this declaration would save him from receiving any more postcards from me for the next twelve years. Or maybe he just was more honest than the rest.

In any event, it didn't sting that much, because by that time it was beginning to dawn on me that there was actually no version of me that the industry was ever going to deem acceptable.

I am not alone in this. The entertainment industry is littered with the ghost careers of women who were told why a real career simply wasn't possible for them.

"You don't act Latina."

"Well, you have an obstacle, because you have a young face and then this Jessica Rabbit body, so Betty Boop characters are all you're good for, and there aren't that many of those."

"You look like you're twenty-three, but you talk like you're twenty-eight."

"I just want to let you know, when I send you for auditions, you send out a va-va voom. People won't understand it if you're funny."

Thanks to the distance I have traveled in my career since this time, I understand now what I was up against, what we have all been up against. At the time, though, I understood none of that.

Like so many women before and after me, I was slowly coming to the painful realization that the industry I had spent my entire life working and aching to be part of simply didn't want me—not because I wasn't talented, but because I was the wrong kind of woman.

CHAPTER 2

DANCE, GIRL, DANCE*

f I was the wrong kind of woman to be allowed on-screen—and if so many of my peers were, as well—then what, precisely, is the *right* type of woman?

As I am no longer twenty-four and doe-eyed, I can actually answer that for you. There's data:

She is in her twenties.

Following is a graph demonstrating the spread of roles at various ages for men versus women.[1]

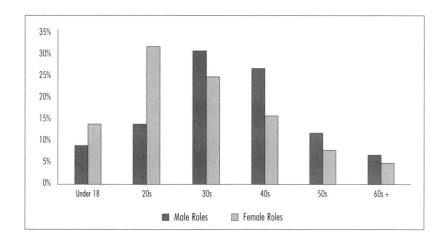

---

* *Dance, Girl, Dance* (1940), dir. Dorothy Arzner.

By far, the majority of female characters are in their twenties, followed by their thirties, unlike male characters who appear most frequently in their thirties and forties. While both genders experience a drop-off after fifty, women experience a dramatic drop-off as soon as they reach age forty.

Michelle Hurd joked, "When I turned forty, it was like someone rang a big bell in the industry. I don't know how they even knew, but it was like one pilot season to the next, suddenly everyone was all, "Now this old lady must always sit behind a desk and must never, ever wear a short skirt.""

She is white, straight, cis, and able-bodied.

Although on-screen representation has improved in the past few years, white women are overrepresented among all women, as a proportion of their presence in the US population.

Following is a chart demonstrating the film character percentages by race and gender out of 1,281 film roles in the top two hundred theatrical films on-screen in 2017 versus their actual presence in the US population.[2]

	White	Black or African American	Latin or Hispanic	Asian	Mixed	Native
Female Percentage of On-Screen Roles	29.1%	2.2%	1.95%	0.93%	2.89%	0%
Female Presence in US Population	31.26%	6.38%	9.08%	2.91%	1.33%	0.66%

Most underrepresented among all female characters are Latinas, Asian, and Indigenous women.

Meanwhile, looking at 2015's one hundred top-grossing films, characters with disabilities made up only 2.4 percent of speaking roles, while making up 25 percent of the population, according to the Centers for Disease Control.[3] A Ruderman Family Foundation white paper found that 95 percent of those few disabled characters on television shows in 2015–2016 were played by able-bodied actors.[4]

Less than 1 percent of speaking characters were LGBTQ+, in contrast to 4.5 percent of the US population identifying as such.[5]*

She is naked or scantily clad.

In the top-grossing films released between 2007 and 2016, 25.9 percent of female characters were scantily clad (compared to 5.7 percent of men), and an additional 25.6 percent of female characters got partially or fully naked (compared to 9.2 percent of men), meaning that roughly 51 percent of the time that you saw a female character on screen, she was in a state of full or partial undress.[6]

Unsettlingly, the percentages are even higher for younger women, with a full 32.5 percent of teenage female characters depicted with some nudity between 2014 and 2016, an *increase* from 2007 and 2012.[7]

She is the victim of physical violence and/or abuse.

Naomi Wolf, in her 1991 bestseller *The Beauty Myth*, noted that one can track the direct correlation between an increase of violence—often sexual violence—against women, with the timing of the 1960s women's movement. Her theory is that the more powerful women became outside the home, the more they were brutalized and degraded on-screen. "Where beautiful women in 1950s culture got married or seduced, in modern culture, the beauty gets raped."[8]

Wolf may well have been onto something, since on-screen violence against women has been on a sharp upward trend over the intervening twenty years, as woman have continued to gain power and rights off-screen. A 2016 article in *The Conversation* on the topic notes, "Violence against women in TV drama has always been high, but in recent years the graphic portrayal of this violence—particularly sexual attacks on and murders of women—is on the increase."[9]

---

* I was not able to find this data separated by gender, but, as with all other categories, representation is almost certainly worse for women.

Indeed, by 2015, 91 percent of movies on TV contained violence. The amount of gun violence in top-grossing PG-13 films has more than tripled since 1985.*[10]

She is either a man's wife or a romantic prospect for a male character.

Female characters are more likely to have their marital status known (53 percent) than are male characters (40 percent).[11]

She may well not work at all, and, if she does, she has a "woman's job."

Male characters are more likely to have an identifiable occupation (76 percent) than are female ones (62 percent).[12] And when they are shown working, female characters are overrepresented in traditionally female-dominated occupations such as teacher, pink-collar worker, and waitress, and underrepresented in high-level occupations such as doctor and engineer.[13]

She is a supporting character (i.e., not the main character).

In 2017, of the one hundred top-grossing domestic films, only 24 percent had female protagonists, which is actually a 5 percent decline from 2016, when 29 percent of films had the same. This number rebounded in 2018 to 31 percent female protagonists, though this may have been a temporary up-trend in response to public pressure related to #MeToo, a phenomenon whose endurance remains heavily in question in terms of representation of women on-screen.[14]

As a reality check, women are 51 percent of the US population.

More likely than not, she does not exist in the movie in the first place.

Research from the Geena Davis Institute on Gender in Media shows that, in films, there are only one-third as many women on-screen as men. For every 2.3 men on-screen in a film, there is 1 woman.[15]

This holds true for leading characters, supporting characters, and, somewhat inexplicably, the nonspeaking background characters in crowd scenes.

---

* Due to the questionable methods of rating films by the Motion Picture Association of America, when it comes to its relative ratings of nudity, swear words, and violence, by 2012, popular PG-13 movies contained significantly more gun violence than R-rated films.

Movies represent an alternate universe in which women are a *minority* population.

What's more, many films don't even reach the average 1 woman for 2.3 men standard mentioned above. In 2017, only 32 percent of the one hundred top-grossing domestic films had ten or more female characters.[16] As a reference point, most films have at least fifty characters in them.

If she exists, she knows that she should be seen and not heard.

The Geena Davis Institute revealed in another study that in 2015 films, male characters received twice the amount of screen time as female characters.[17]

This is consistent with the proportional amount of time female characters get to speak. According to an analysis by the University of Southern California's Viterbi School of Engineering, of a representative sample of 1,000 screenplays of films released in 2017, 4,900 male characters had 37,000 lines of dialogue, while 2,000 female characters had only 15,100 lines of dialogue.[18]

In 82 percent of films, at least two of the three characters with the most dialogue are male.[19]

Out of thirty Disney movies analyzed in 2016, twenty-two of them have majority-male dialogue—including *Mulan*, a movie whose (female) main character's (male) pet dragon, Mushu, has 50 percent more lines of dialogue than Mulan herself.[20]

Even romantic comedies, which are widely considered to be films exclusively for female audiences, have dialogue that is, on average, 58 percent male.[21]

Her story is not Great, Important, or Award-Worthy.

Lest you think these statistics are only true for the biggest box-office fare, it is worth pointing out that of ninety years' worth of Academy Awards, Best Picture has only been given to a film with a female lead character on seventeen occasions.

It Happened One Night (1934)
Gone with the Wind (1939)
Rebecca (1940)
Mrs. Miniver (1943)

All About Eve (1951)
Gigi (1959)
My Fair Lady (1965)
The Sound of Music (1966)
Terms of Endearment (1984)
Out of Africa (1986)
Driving Miss Daisy (1990)
The Silence of the Lambs (1992)
Titanic (1998)
Shakespeare in Love (1999)
Chicago (2003)
Million Dollar Baby (2005)
The Shape of Water (2018)

After 2005, thirteen years passed without a female-led film winning Best Picture, until the trend was finally broken in 2018 with *The Shape of Water*, a film about a woman who is literally incapable of speech. The fact that the first eight of these winners happened in a thirty-two-year span, between 1934 and 1966, and that it took a full fifty-one years to reach the next eight winners suggests that the academy's regard for films with a leading female character has actually decreased as women's power and visibility in society has increased.

The cultural importance of how women are portrayed in movies and in series (both TV and streaming)—arguably the most powerful and far-reaching forms of storytelling available today—is immeasurable. In the US alone, children and adolescents now spend on average seven and a half hours every single day consuming entertainment media—seven and a half hours. Put another way, by the time young people today arrive in their seventies, they will have spent seven to ten *years of their lives* watching TV.[22] The statistics are even more pronounced for US adults who, according to a third-quarter 2018 Nielsen report, spend ten and a half hours each day using or consuming media in some form.[23]

As we all spend more and more time looking at screens and less time interacting with other live humans, characters in the films and TV shows we watch are often the "people" who populate our lives on the most regular basis. For those people living in less diverse, more homogenous areas of the country, the characters on films and TV shows are often their only contact with and reference point to people who look different from them or have backgrounds different from theirs.

Furthermore, film remains one of the single biggest US service exports. Hollywood content is not merely shaping US or even Western culture generally.[24] It is impacting our global society.

For women young and old, both in the US and around the world, who are often still bereft of real-life female role models in the professions they aspire to join, the nature of the content they are watching becomes even more important, as they search on-screen for female examples of the lives and goals they seek for themselves.

In *The Beauty Myth*, Wolf makes the case that the fact that men continue to control the stories, images, and content that shape our world goes a long way to explaining why the second-wave feminist movement—the activist period from roughly the early 1960s to 1980s—couldn't get women in society all the way to full equality and why, since that movement, progress has been so limited and slow.[25]

During and after those fierce, radical women's fight toward progress, male-created media continued to bombard us all with stories that continually push back against more progressive social norms by reinforcing a worldview that almost always centers on and lionizes men while diminishing women's importance, agency, and value beyond that of either a mother or an object of sexual appeal.

If you think I'm overstating the impact of Hollywood on our collective psyches, consider this:

- The year *Jaws* came out, 1975, Americans began telling pollsters that sharks were now among their top-ten major fears, in spite of the fact that sharks had never significantly before appeared on people's lists, and in spite of the fact that who the hell actually gets eaten by a shark, especially in a country where most of the population is landlocked?[26]
- In 1995, BMW paid the James Bond franchise $3 million to have James Bond switch from driving an Aston Martin to a BMW Z3. That one move prompted so many people to buy that same model, that BMW made $240 million in pre-sales alone.[27]

- As the Geena Davis Institute on Gender in Media discovered, in 2012, the year that *Brave* and *The Hunger Games* came out, female participation in archery shot up 105 percent.[28]

Additional studies demonstrate that the movies you watch affect not just your hobbies but your career choices, your emotions, your sense of identity, your relationships, your mental health, even your marital status.[29]

In a study reported on by the *New York Times*, researchers looked at rates of engagement with Disney princesses media (toys, products, and films) in nearly two hundred five- and six-year-olds and found that, for both boys and girls, higher "princess involvement" over a year was associated with higher levels of "female gender stereotypical behavior," such as quiet play, pretending to cook and clean, and avoidance of risks, getting dirty, and trying new things. Because this association was clear even after the researchers controlled for other variables, including a personal inclination to like princesses, they were able to clearly establish that media was driving the association and not the other way around.

The researchers also noted as interesting that while this increase in stereotypically female behaviors in girls was seen as "potentially problematic," the increase in feminine traits in the boys "could have benefits for development throughout their life span, thus suggesting that increasing the amount of female-driven content could actually have even greater benefit for men than women."[30]

Aside from modeling (or not modeling) progressive modes of behavior, the barrage of unrealistic beauty standards and the prevalence of violence against women have, as has been written about extensively, particularly notable real-life consequences.

With respect to violence against women, Ruth Penfold-Mounce observed in her article "How the Rise in TV 'Crime Porn' Normalises Violence Against Women":

Women have traditionally been portrayed as victims . . . largely because they embody the "ideal victim." Otherwise known as being pretty, white, young, and female—making it seem normalised that women are then vulnerable to violence at the hands of men. . . . But by largely focusing on women as victims of violence there is a disconnect between reality and entertainment. Because, although statistically men commit more crimes than women, more than twice as many men are victims of violence.[31]

An article by the WomanStats Project cites studies that demonstrate the ways in which this imagery affects both men and women.

"A portrayal of violence against women tends to increase men's acceptance of interpersonal violence and, especially in the case of sexual violence, may increase their acceptance of rape myths." And that "it has been shown that exposure to violence results in desensitization to that violence."

Conversely, the article notes that "viewing violence against women may increase a woman's feelings of disempowerment."[32]

The volume of on screen violence against women is not only the result of a reigning, older generation of writers who will soon die off. This predilection for creating violent images and scenarios against women seems to be already inculcated in the rising generation of white, male creatives. Jeremy Slater, executive producer of *The Exorcist* reboot TV show, notes, "One of my hard and fast rules when reading spec scripts* was, the second there was a rape that was used for shock value and that didn't have any sort of narrative purpose, I threw that script aside. And I was shocked by the number that had that. I would say out of 200 scripts, there were probably 30 or 40 of them that opened with a rape or had a pretty savage rape at some point."[33]

Images of violence against women are only one way in which Hollywood's on-screen portrayal of women damages the off-screen female population. On the subject of the unrealistic standards of beauty continually propagated by Hollywood and its stars, you may think you've heard all there is to say, except that there's more going on there than you are likely aware of, not just under the knife but also in the editing room.

It has long been widely assumed that that Hollywood's A-, B-, C-, and D-listers use everything from diet pills, Botox, and plastic surgery

---

* A "spec script" is a sample script a writer submits for an existing TV show to demonstrate an ability to write in the "voice" of the series.

to chemical peels, personal trainers, outright starvation, and everything in between to make themselves look like superhuman movie stars. That assumption is quite correct. Puncturing the illusion of perfection can cost an actor millions of dollars in salary and endorsements. For lesser-known actors, looking less perfect than the ideal can mean lost professional opportunities and a longer road to a big break.

However, the truth is even more damaging than creating chronically underfed actresses as, since 2008, there has been a darker, dirtier, and much more successfully guarded little secret: "Beauty work."

While Hollywood's standards of beauty were once limited by what surgeons, trainers, and specialists could achieve on the human body, according to a 2014 *Mashable* article by Josh Dickey, "Everyone Is Altered: The Secret Hollywood Procedure That Has Fooled Us For Years," beauty work has become a "digital procedure of sorts, in which a handful of skilled artists use highly specialized software in the final stages of post-production to slim, de-age, and enhance actors' faces and bodies."[34]

In practice, the software—originally developed for the film *The Curious Case of Benjamin Button*, in which Brad Pitt needed to be convincingly aged forward and backward by decades—allows digital artists to radically retouch every single frame of a finished film. Dickey explains, "Hips narrowed, calves slimmed, turkey-necks tucked, pores tightened, eye bags reduced (often entire hangovers are erased). Hair is thickened, teeth whitened, underarm skin de-jiggled, belly fat obliterated, abs raised." Claus Hansen, a beauty-work pioneer, told Dickey, "We have taken actresses' faces and put them on more muscular bodies for an entire film's length. . . . That happens all the time."

In a particularly nutty example, one A-list actor was unhappy with the way his crow's feet looked in a superhero movie he was starring in, so the beauty specialist eventually copied crow's feet from a younger actor and transplanted them onto this actor's face.

This process is incredibly lengthy—"a three-second medium close-up can take anything from three to six hours of an artist's time"—and almost always involves several layers of people, including studio executives, managers, agents, and, ultimately, the star him- or herself sitting beside the artist to continue tweaking until everybody is happy. "A recent comedy hit featuring a top actress in her 40s required beauty work in every single shot—600 total. With artists working around the clock, seven days a week, the beauty work alone took almost three months."*

As you might imagine, the cost of this process is enormous—"anywhere from $500 to $2,500 *per shot*"†—but studios now routinely include it in their budgets for every film and even on some higher-end TV shows, to keep their stars happy. Hansen explained in the *Mashable* article exactly how prevalent this is.

> Who's the first super-elite, A-list actor or actress who pops into your mind? They've had beauty work, probably a lot of it, and for a few good years now. Garden-variety funnyman in a B-grade comedy? Beauty work. Aging action star? Definitely beauty work. Twenty-something It girl starlet? Hunk-of-the-moment? Swimsuit supermodel just now breaking into the business? Beauty work, beauty work and yes, more beauty work.

Twenty-four years ago, in 1996, Dalma Heyn, an editor of two women's magazines, moaned, "By now readers have no idea what a real woman's 60-year-old face looks like in print because it's made to look 45. Worse, 60-year-old readers look in the mirror and think they look too old, because they're comparing themselves to some retouched face smiling back at them from a magazine."[35]

It is little surprise, then, that after ten-plus years of watching movies with stars who are digitally altered, an international study showed that, as of 2014, "90% of all women want to change at least one aspect of [their] physical appearance. . . . [And] 81% of 10-year-old girls are afraid of being fat. Only 2% of [women] actually think [they] are beautiful."[36]

The further trouble is that, even when you know that beauty work exists, even after you've read this book, that information will not change the impact those images have on you. At least one study has shown that

---

* Dickey, notes wryly, "Nearly everything written about the film remarked on how fit and young the actress looked. No one suspected anything."

† Triangulating that fact with the "recent comedy hit" means that the absolute cheapest it could have been to have "beauty work" on that film was $300,000 and the most expensive would have been $1.5 million. Emphasis mine.

our brains are not set up to exert the required skepticism over images to be able to look at something so real and doubt its reality.[37] We can look at a picture and say out loud to ourselves, "This image is digitally altered. This person does not look like this in real life." And because our brains can't actually grasp that, the image will make us feel terrible about ourselves all the same.

While you could argue, as the creators of this content like to do, that the increase of violence against women or the increasingly-more-impossible-to-achieve beauty standards on-screen are not their fault and, rather, are simply a response to societal trends, I take this as nothing more than a cop-out. For one thing, the "I'm just writing what I see" excuse does not acknowledge the enormous power that storytellers hold in shaping the minds of viewers both individually and as a culture.

But even if we give storytellers the benefit of the doubt and assume that they *are*, in fact, responding to trends in culture and are not driving them—not something I believe—there still persists the question of how and where to shift big cultural trends—such as the prevalence of violence against women or unrealistic standards of beauty—that are so damaging to members of our society. If we imagine culture and filmmakers in a cyclical feedback circuit, there is still some responsibility on the part of the filmmakers to consciously determine whether or not they want to reinforce or disrupt ongoing trends each time the circuit returns to them.

It is neither a surprise nor a coincidence that such images emerge from an industry riddled with serial sexual offenders like Harvey Weinstein and which abuses and devalues women as a matter of routine. The treatment of women within the film industry is transmuted into the representations of women in the content you consume on a daily basis and which demonstrably shapes your brain and behaviors.

Art may reflect life, but it reflects no life so closely as the lives and worldviews of the specific artists themselves. When those artists are so utterly monochromatic, their experiences and perspectives of the world are magnified and are given an unreasonable and unhealthy role in shaping our culture.

What happens to the actresses behind those damaging female characters? Is everything fine if you manage to become one of the mysteriously selected chosen few who then get to appear young, white, naked, and abused on screen?

No. Not really.

Purely on a statistical level, booking jobs is always harder for actresses. Remember, there are 2.3 male speaking roles for every female speaking role.

Compounding that, from a getting-hired perspective, there are also way, *way* more actresses than actors on the scene. This is quite possibly because when girls discover they are storytellers, they are encouraged to become actresses, whereas when boys make the same discovery, they are encouraged to become writers, directors, and geniuses.

Having done some loose and highly unscientific calculations that are, nevertheless, a useful data point, I discovered that, based on the known ratio of male roles to female roles interacting with the roughly 2.8 aspiring actresses for every 1 aspiring actor,* from a purely statistical level, a random actor is precisely 6.44 times more likely than a random actress to be cast in something. SIX POINT FOUR FOUR TIMES!†

This is not something they told us in acting school.

What they also did not tell us is that if you are an actress and you graduate from acting school with the intention of joining the film industry, you are almost certainly already too old to have a career.

There's a well-worn saying that it takes ten years to become an "overnight success." Meaning that, generally, an actor graduates from acting school, slogs away in obscurity for about a decade until suddenly his or her career blows up, and all the trades and glossies talk about how "this guy/gal came out of absolutely nowhere and now s/he's HUGE!"

---

* Based on the number of submissions we received for the male lead role versus the female lead role in the first feature film I wrote.

† I am not a mathematician. My friend Joanna Pickering is both an actress and a mathematician and did this calculation for me. Because she is an excellent mathematician as well as an excellent actress, she would like me to make it extremely clear that this number in no way reflects a real-world scenario. For instance, Leonardo DiCaprio is *not* 6.44 times more likely to be cast in a role than Kate Winslet. For one thing, the statistical calculation does not take into account talent, looks, connections, or any of the other myriad factors that affect real-world casting. So, we're talking about a scenario in which we are comparing a man and woman who, in all other ways, apart from their gender identity, are exactly the same—which is, of course, unrealistic. So, while this scenario is not practically true, it is mathematically true, and it indicates generally what a shit prospect it is to be an actress.

There are shortcuts to success. Being related to an extremely famous actor, director, producer, or otherwise connected industry individual can shave many years off that decade.* If you happen to be one of the genuinely most phenomenally beautiful people the world has absolutely ever seen, that can also sometimes shorten your timeline to the top.† But assuming you're a mere mortal and are starting from square one, there is an oddly specific accuracy to that ten-year runway to a breakout success.

But let's return to that chart of the volume of roles available for men versus women at each age:

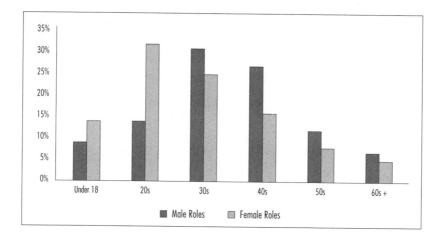

Assuming that an actress did what is recommended virtually everywhere and went to college to train in an acting conservatory, graduating around age twenty-one, by the time she reached the ten-year point in her career—where she would be poised to break out at around age thirty—the number of roles available to her is already beginning to decline. At the very moment she finds herself professionally and personally ready, the door slams promptly in her face.

---

* There's a reason the dynastic lineages in Hollywood are so strong.

† Although Jessica Chastain, who, by any marker, qualifies as one of the rarified beauties of our lifetimes, didn't hit it big until she had rounded thirty, and she'd been at it aggressively for the decade leading up to that. So, if the signifier is "more beautiful than Jessica Chastain," suffice it to say that most of us are out of luck.

The peak-role age tracks closely with awards. Since 2000, the average age of a Best Actress winner is thirty-six, which makes sense only if you hit it big in your twenties, spend a decade having a career, and then receive your award at the peak of your career, which is indeed in the mid-thirties for women.[38] But how can you hit it big in your twenties if it takes a decade to make it and you're just then getting out of school?

The obvious answer to this conundrum, then, is that you must begin your acting career in your childhood or teen years. That way you can spend your decade of career-building/skill-honing during a time when there are fewer roles available but also less competition, since most aspiring actresses are either still in grade school in Kansas or off at a conservatory. Then you can be poised to seize your moment when you are arriving in your twenties, just at the moment that there are suddenly the most roles available to you that there ever will be in your career.

And, in fact, many famous actresses began pursuing professional careers in their teens or earlier: Jennifer Lawrence, Brie Larson, Regina King, Kirsten Dunst, Claire Danes, Angelina Jolie, and Gwyneth Paltrow. Not to say that they're not talented, which they are, but their timelines became viable because of their early career starts.

Yet another downside of this timeline equation is that it pushes actresses who are less mature, less well-trained, and far more vulnerable into the paths of powerful, often lecherous, men, at an age when these girls and young women are more susceptible to psychic trauma from the worst horrors the industry has to offer.

Male actors, on the other hand, experience a substantially less dismal timeline.

There are, relatively speaking, not that many roles for men in their twenties—only 14 percent of all available roles for men. The optimal decade for roles for men is in their thirties (31 percent of roles) and forties (a close 27 percent).[39] So, it is no problem at all for a male actor to finish high school, go to drama school, spend his twenties sorting himself out, growing up a bit, and getting his foothold in the world. He is then perfectly able to stroll on into the newly verdant field of roles available to him as he turns thirty, and then enjoy a solid two decades of substantive work, before the roles start falling off. The average age of a Best Actor winner is forty-four, which does makes sense: you break out in your thirties and have a decade and a half of proving your mettle, before getting your Oscar at your peak.[40]

How lovely for them.

This timeline problem for women, combined with the unrealistic beauty standards and fetishization of youth propagated by our very own industry, drives most actresses to depths of genuine terror over the prospect of visibly aging.

Hollywood is not exactly kind to women and their appearances at any age. There's the story Jennifer Lawrence tells about an experience early on in her career, when a female producer forced her to be photographed almost naked beside a number of other, much skinnier women, and then gifted her the photos so that she might use them "as motivation to lose weight."[41]

The result is a culture for actresses in which, by the estimation of almost everyone I spoke to, somewhere between 80 and 90 percent of actresses are regularly getting injections of Botox and/or filler and/or collagen by the time they are in their mid-to-late twenties.

Amy (whose real name isn't Amy) first got filler on her twenty-sixth birthday and shortly thereafter started getting regular treatments of Botox and filler under her eyes. She says, "I do not regret it. At all. I'm glad I did it. I did feel more confident after doing it. I think I would look like a forty-five-year-old by movie industry standards by now if I hadn't.* But it's a slippery slope. It's so easy to get carried away." If she could afford it, though, Amy says she would "get her whole face lasered."

Actress Michelle Hurd recalled the time she got a recurring role on a big LA TV show and was invited by a female costar to join a crocheting circle† with some other actresses. As Michelle describes it, there they were, sitting around this living room crocheting, when all of a sudden the doorbell rang and a doctor walked in. A "throne" was set up in a corner of the room, and one by one all the women went over to get Botox. Stunned, Michelle looked to her hostess, who said, "Oh, don't worry, honey. This is just what we do."

---

* She's thirty-three.

† I double-checked with Michelle and this was literally a crocheting circle. That's not a euphemism for something else.

Every actress, or nearly every actress, falls prey to some form of anti-aging procedure.

Amy believes this firmly. "Any woman in Hollywood, except maybe Frances McDormand, who says they don't get 'work done' is lying. They're lying. All of them. Maybe it wasn't Botox or filler, but the capabilities of lasers available to tighten, pull, smooth, etc., are something from the fucking future. With the right amount of downtime and money, you can basically have a facelift with never a needle or a scalpel brought to your face. So it's easy for these women to say 'they're above it.' But they're not, and they're still perpetuating a cycle of unrealistic standards. They're all doing it."

Curious if men experience the same pressures, I asked Nate Washburn, who graduated with me from AADA, how he felt about aging. Without hesitation he said, "I'm really looking forward to it. Once I aged into my thirties, I suddenly started getting more work. I'm not a supermodel, so my twenties weren't really my decade, but now I'm getting really interesting roles, and there are fewer guys in the industry to compete with."

When I asked him if he'd ever experienced any pressure to alter his appearance as he's aged, he paused for a long moment, thinking. "I think I remember my first agent telling me that I might try exercising a little bit."

Right.

I'm not saying there's no pressure for men to live up to certain beauty standards. Of course, there is. But there is undoubtedly something women are up against here that men simply are not.

At thirty-two years of age, I have two vertical furrows between my eyebrows—what a dermatologist once called "an eleven." I feel toward those furrows a driving hatred that I bear for almost nothing else in my life. With everything in me, I wanted to get them "fixed" before I appeared in my most recent feature film. It took everything in me not to, but I didn't. When I watch the film now, they are all I can see. I feel a degree of fuck-you pride at not having gotten them altered, but watching them in the film, is, honestly, excruciating.

At this juncture, any reasonable human might be saying to themselves, "*Get out of there, girl!*" and conclude that probably no one should ever again become an actress, because why on earth would you put yourself through all of this.

I know this. I know that what we sign up for is totally and utterly bananas.

But let me explain to you what it is like in those brief, rare, beautiful moments when you actually get to *act*.

You are standing onstage. You have left your own self behind. You have taken off your own body, words, clothes, voice, troubles, neuroses in the dressing room and slipped into someone else's. You expand your soul and heart in the deepest kind of empathy. You lend your corporality and heart to channel another person's existence. You land a punch line at the precise right moment and the audience roars with laughter. You make a speech and the audience begins to cry. You play a character the audience starts off hating and with no more tools than those of your words and body, you turn them, bringing them around to the humanity of your character in a way that no number of political speeches or rhetoric could ever do, and in a way that will transform something in each audience member and stay with them after they have left the theater.

It is an unparalleled kind of sorcery, this storytelling. Even at this point in my life, when I can accept that being an actress is a routinely degrading, humiliating, and compromising profession, there is nothing on earth that I have found to replace the divinity of acting itself.

It is psychotic trying to balance that passion and beauty with the brutal reality of the profession.

A lot of women eventually decide that nothing is worth that kind of sacrifice and leave the business or transition into some other role therein.

For some actresses, survival in the business is about exercising greater control over the types of parts they'll accept. One actress, Nicole Coulon, describes a time recently when she was up for a role "on a really good show." The role was for a white girl who specifically loved threesomes with black men. In addition to a simulated three-way sex scene, one of the character's few lines was, "I love your black cock in my white pussy." She called her agent and declined the audition. "I just can't."

Then there are those of us who can't bring ourselves around to the idea of giving up acting, but who also lack the capacity to compartmentalize or withstand the plight of being an actress. For me, as for a lot of women, faced with this conundrum, there is a slight, bright possibility that starts at some point to twig in our brains: if the roles aren't good enough, what if we just created better roles?

Jacqueline Pereda had been trying to break into the industry for years when she landed one of the coveted slots in a top TV network's Diversity Showcase, a yearly event in which a number of up-and-coming actors of color are given the golden-ticket opportunity to audition for the network. This was truly the break she'd been longing for. Jacqueline had been given sides from a well-known current TV show on the network with which to audition and read them at home with dismay. "It was just such bad writing. I just kept looking at it thinking, 'Women don't *talk* like that!'" Jacqueline, who is usually one of those impossibly uber-prepared people, couldn't bring herself to work on the material in advance.

As a result, when she got up in front of the casting director, she bombed. "I mean, I was stuttering. The casting director had me do it three times to try to get it to be halfway decent, but eventually yelled at me that there was absolutely no way she could send my audition to the network. I knew she was absolutely right." On the verge of tears, Jacqueline busted out of the audition room and, unable to contain her agitation, began pacing the halls of the network building. "I walked around that building precisely three times, torturing myself, saying, 'How could I do this? I am the most committed person, and I absolutely blew my biggest chance.'" As she finished her third lap of the building, she suddenly stopped in her tracks. All at once she realized, "Oh, *I* hate those words. I *hated* those words." In that instant, she made a promise to herself: "Going forward, I am only going to say words I write."

My breaking point was a particularly humiliating pay-to-play audition. The man I had paid $35 to watch me perform my monologue, spent the entirety of it texting, then looked up at me for the first time when I finished speaking, sighed heavily while glancing at my resume and said, "Well, *Boardwalk Empire* is the best credit on *this* resume, but I'd need to see a lot more than that to consider taking you on."

It most definitely wasn't the worst thing someone had said to me. Not by a long shot. But something in me snapped. After only three years, I was tired. I was fed up. I sobbed the entire subway ride home.

As I sat amidst side-glancing subway passengers, all witnessing my uniquely New York public-private moment, two truths slid to the surface alongside my disappointment:

Acting was the only thing that had ever made me feel whole.
There was absolutely no way that I could go on like this.

CHAPTER 3

A GIRL WALKS
HOME ALONE AT NIGHT*

There is an especially panicky stigma—it has lessened a bit in recent years—around actors, most particularly actresses, creating their own work. As I began my own foray into content creation, I could see the judgment drop into others' eyes when I admitted that I had actually *written* something I was also going to *act* in. The term "vanity project" lingered elephantine under each of these conversations. The implication being that, if anyone had to resort to writing their own projects to act in, that person must be so deeply untalented and/or unattractive and/or crazy as to have no other possible options. It did not automatically occur to those people that I might simply want to create projects out of a desire to feel even vaguely connected to the kind of stories I had grown up yearning to tell.

Years earlier, during my initial exploration of content creation, when I proudly told my first agent that I had written and produced a play that I was also going to act in, he scolded me resoundingly, telling me that I would ruin my chances of having any kind of career at all if I tried to be more than one thing. If I wanted to be an actress, he informed me, I had to only be an actress.

Following this talking to, I proceeded to hide from the industry and the agent that, over the first four or so years of my acting career, I had

---

* *A Girl Walks Home Alone at Night* (2014), dir. Ana Lily Amirpour.

quietly begun writing plays, which people then rather amazingly wanted to put on. It got to the point that I had had seven short or full-length plays, which I had written, produced in New York, Colorado, and Florida, including two in the New York International Fringe Festival and yet, nothing about these successes was listed on my website. I never brought it up to industry people, and I never once called myself a "writer" or "producer." I was afraid of clouding the one thing I wanted to make sure everyone knew: I am *an actress*.

By 2011, however, four years and seven plays deep, this in-the-closet-playwright caper had begun to feel silly even to me. As my patience with a straight-up acting career began to fracture, it dawned on me that the female roles *I* was writing in *my plays* were of the meaty, fleshed-out, human variety that I'd been craving to play. What if . . . what if the answer was right there, just waiting for me to grasp?

Although I'd started in theater, it was in film, with its wider potential audience and greater palette of subtlety, that my heart had always lain. So, in a fit of rising excitement, I proposed to a colleague and fellow former AADA student, Caitlin Gold, that we simply make our own feature film. I could write it. I could write two complex, interesting female characters that she and I could play, and surely, the two of us could somehow figure out how to produce it.

The fact that we were both trained only as actresses, that neither of us had been to film school, and that we had no training or experience in making a movie did not seem particularly daunting to us. By that point, we had both acted on enough Purgatory-level film sets to figure that we were at least as organized and intelligent as most of those teams.

Blithely, we started a campaign of cold emailing each and every film producer or production company that we could locate on the internet, asking them to let us take them to coffee and "pick their brains."

Perhaps our inexplicable belief in our own abilities proved persuasive, or, maybe, they were simply amused enough by our cluelessness to humor us with half-hour meetings. But a shocking number, maybe a dozen or so, of them agreed to meet with Caitlin and me, and so we began our regimen of film school by coffee-date.

So broad was our ignorance on the subject of filmmaking that I remember frequently getting to these meetings and not even knowing what questions to ask. In one keenly mortifying example, I had somehow badgered a well-known film producer and producing professor at Columbia University into taking a meeting with me. My audacity level at that time being much stronger via email than in person, I was so nervous going to meet the producer/professor that I was in a cold sweat, on the verge of vomiting, and so obsessively worried that my voice would go high and squeaky when I spoke to him that I kept testing it out on the subway ride.

When I finally arrived in his office, he, looking professional and stern, swiveled in his chair to face me, looked me over and, unimpressed, fixed me with a hard stare. "Well, you've managed to get yourself in here. What do you want to know?" I was paralyzed with nerves. I'm pretty sure I gasped out in a definitely-high-and-squeaky voice, "I just . . . wondered . . . if you could . . . tell me how to make a movie?"

Over the course of the first six months or so, Caitlin and I brought onto the team the incredible Meredith Edwards, a trained actress and first-time film director who had also never been to film school, and Joanna Bowzer, who, in joining as an additional producer, became the sole member of the team who had at least produced one feature film before, which did seem like a useful asset.

Solely, then, through the process of hiring the best people for the jobs, we found ourselves in the position of having an all-female creative team. The script I wrote, *Imagine I'm Beautiful*, told the psychologically twisty story of a friendship between two women. None of this was anything that occurred to us as a radical feminist act.

Over the course of meeting with industry folks, as we were trying to get the film made, this "error" was rapidly and repeatedly brought to our attention.

Comments ranged from the blatant . . .

"Well, you know that you ladies are going to need to bring on a male producer at some point, right? Just so that people will trust you with their money."

. . . to the slightly subtler . . .

"I don't think there's really going to be an audience for this. You should probably think about adding more blood."

And . . .

"I feel like there's a lesbian angle you could explore here . . ."

. . . to the end of an hour-long lecture I received from a male cinematographer we were considering hiring . . .

"I think women have a harder time understanding story structure. I've just observed that in my career. If you want to learn how to write structure, you really ought to go watch Law & Order.*"*

. . . to the constant, never-ending . . .

"Well, people just don't want to see films about women. There just isn't going to be an audience for this movie."

People actually said all of those things. To our faces. In meetings. On multiple occasions.

We were flabbergasted. Here's our privilege as white women showing, but it very honestly had never occurred to us that this level of sexism would surface so frequently in 2011–12, much less that it would be so casually acceptable in a supposedly liberal institution like the motion picture industry as to be stated aloud in meetings.

Furthermore, this continual assertion that audiences didn't want to see films about women didn't make sense on even the level of basic logic. "Women are 51% of the population," I thought. "So the idea here is that women don't want to see stories about . . . *themselves*?! And men *exclusively* want to see stories about *themselves*?"

"But *we* want to see stories about women," we muttered sideways to each other. "We can't be the only ones."

Confident that we could probably figure out how to manage money without a set of testicles and convinced that surely, *surely* there must be an audience somewhere interested in seeing a story about the female half of the population, we forged ahead.

It took three years of peel-yourself-off-the-mat work and rejection, fifty-two drafts of the script, two separate crowdfunding campaigns, and legions of angel people, but we made our movie.* We shot it over eighteen days in New York City with a hard-won $80,000.

We came in under time and under budget.

---

* I still get jelly-knees when I think about the generosity of every person who donated to our crowdfunding campaigns, who signed on to be the cast and crew of that film when the money situation was oh-so-iffy and the work oh-so-underpaid, and, most of all, who eventually invested in the film. I will spend the rest of my career and life trying to be worthy of those people.

More than any other moment from that period, the one I remember most clearly is riding the subway home after the first day on set, absolutely vibrating with excitement.

A theater director friend of mine, Stephen Cedars, has a theory that most people who enter the professional entertainment industry spend their careers chasing the pure, unadulterated joy and creative fulfillment they felt doing community theater growing up. This is an idea I resonate with. Leaving aside the experiences I've had making my own films, when I try to recall the times I have felt happiest, most whole, most alive in my art, the images that most quickly come up are doing musicals with Aspen Community Theater, ages fourteen through eighteen. I'm not joking.

As a professional actress, although I'd gotten a few momentary tastes of that same feeling here and there, what I mostly felt was empty, small, and lost. Then for eighteen days, filming *Imagine I'm Beautiful* in 2013, I found it again. Except it was better. It was my childhood imaginings coming to life, except now I had fifty other adults equally invested in the weaving and building of stories with me.

I fancy that for most women, like me, who eventually find their way to being a woman *behind* the films—and most especially for those of us who have spent any amount of time as actresses—discovering the strength of our own voices and ideas is genuinely intoxicating.

Sarah Wharton describes becoming a producer as well as an actress on a film as "the first time all of the parts of myself came together in the right way. I had to stretch myself to fill that power position, but it felt good to step into something bigger than I was and to have to grow to fill it."

Sonja O'Hara, who made her first feature film *Ovum* during the same period of time I made mine, describes suddenly receiving respect from people "in a way I never had as an actress. It made me start taking myself seriously in a way I never had before."

Other, more famous actresses turned directors have echoed these sentiments after their own directorial debuts. As Jennifer Morrison put it, "I didn't realize everyone had been talking to me like a dumb child my whole life until I became a director."

The bone-aching joy of finding and using our voices to tell stories we cared about, with female characters that reflected the strength, vulnerability, and complexity of the women we actually knew in our lives dialed up our resolve to eleven.

Sonja literally sold her own eggs to get money so that she could make her first feature film. That's how amazing it felt to finally use our voices.

Once *Imagine I'm Beautiful* was finished, my and my teammates' primary goal was the same as most other independent filmmakers': to get a distribution deal. Sure, with the rise of internet streaming platforms, there was the ever more viable option of self-distribution, but that was a path looked on with a similar level of disdain to actors-turned-writers, a tragic last resort reserved for those who were not good enough to be *chosen*. Being *chosen* by an actual distributor, we were told, would mean that more people would eventually watch our film and, in paying to see it, allow our investors to recoup their money. It was clearly communicated to us that getting a distribution deal was the singular major mark of validation, significantly increasing our chances of later busting through industry doors, which might lead to getting hired for jobs and/or getting financing for our next movie. Naturally, a distribution deal became our north star.

On bigger independent films, a sales agent is usually attached to the film, who, much as an agent does for an actor, acts as the conduit to and negotiator with distribution companies. But with a film as small and truly independent as *Imagine I'm Beautiful*, with no recognizable cast or crew, no self-respecting sales agent would take our phone calls, so our one best hope of being noticed was to get into film festivals. Festivals, so we were told, are where industry insiders convene and distributors go to discover the gems of the independent film world.

In 2013–14, when my peers and I entered the film festival word, however, their mythos had become rather disconnected from their present reality.

One female filmmaker I interviewed—we'll call her Tina—who, in the 1980s, was making independent films in downtown New York, alongside Jim Jarmusch (*Stranger than Paradise*), and Amos Poe (*Blank Generation*), recalls how different the industry was then. "Nobody was thinking about the industry. We were not driven by money. There was a freedom in not knowing anything about agents or managers. There was experimentation and risk taking and playfulness."

Some early film festivals, such as Cannes Film Festival's Directors Fortnight, International Film Festival Rotterdam, and Edinburgh Film Festival, seemed interested in these films that took risks, pushed the artistic envelope, and found its roots in punk underground culture, viewing film as another art form in the throes of exciting experimentation, not as a commercial product.

Tina remembers, "As a woman, I never felt I had to define myself. Most of the women making films in the '80s did not think there were barriers; we just did what we wanted to. If you wanted to play in a band, you did. If you wanted to make a film, you did. If you wanted in act in theater or performances, you did. We all felt empowered to do what we wanted."

But with Sundance Film Festival, which had been founded in the 1970s, Tina noticed a shift. "Sundance did not program the edgy films of the '80s by filmmakers who were interested in challenging conventional approaches to cinematic storytelling, but, rather, they promoted straightforward films with subject matter that was personal or original."

As a result, over the ensuing decades, distribution companies began to look to Sundance and other festivals like it as pipelines to find and swoop up indie film projects into their machinery. It turned film festivals—and, indeed independent film—from a hotbed of artistic exploration into a marketplace for commercial products, which began to shift the mind-set of everyone involved.

Tina notes, "It seemed to me that as Sundance gained more and more attention, the celebrated directors coming out of Sundance were mostly male—Steven Soderbergh, Todd Solondz, Ed Burns, to name a few. I began to feel excluded for the first time as a female filmmaker. Before that, in the international community of filmmaking and festivals, I felt respected and celebrated."

By the time my peers and I showed up, in the mid-2010s, the film festival circuit had been through yet another evolution. The more prestigious, well-known film festivals, such as Sundance, the Toronto International Film Festival, Tribeca, Telluride, and Cannes, were indeed places that distributors frequented, but distributors could no longer be said to be discovering the hidden gems of actual independent film.

Starting in 2007, Hollywood studios had begun making far fewer smart, adult films in-house. This created a wider lane for a new variety of "independent" films, that now included films made by, starring, and with the financing of all the same Hollywood players from the studio side of things but which were now considered technically "independent" films, as they were no longer getting made within the studio structure. These new "independent" films, however, had all the hallmarks of a studio's backing—for instance, starring Brad Pitt and possessing deep and wide connections to industry insiders.

As a result of these new types of films suddenly qualifying for festivals on the merit of their being "independent," the top-tier festivals eagerly began packing their time slots with these technically-independent-though-not-at-all-actually-independent films. The top festivals quickly became places where these "independent" films and their Hollywood A-listers show up in snow boots to gather "indie cred" before receiving a mass release by the big distributor they had a deal with before even arriving. The festivals themselves, far-flung from their renegade beginnings, now craving the attention and insider-ness that the celebrities brought with them, had little bandwidth left for true outsiders.

As a result of this shift, and also because having a film festival can be quite fun and mind expanding, an enormous array of mid- to small-tier festivals have sprung up in every nook and cranny of the globe, most with the worthy goal of bringing independent film to their communities.

Today, as I sit here writing this book, I could apply to no fewer than 1,412 film festivals. Those are only the ones with open submissions right now, so there are at least two to three times that number in operation on a yearly basis. From an audience and community perspective, this is wonderful. For filmmakers, festivals provide many wonderful experiences and opportunities to share their work with audiences and with other filmmakers in places they might never otherwise go.

The trouble is that this proliferation has also created problems for filmmakers. For one thing, these festivals vary wildly in terms of size, level of prestige, and quality of experience, because absolutely anybody can start a film festival and begin charging filmmakers money to apply. Like actors clutching headshots and paying for auditions, indie filmmakers are often desperate to be chosen and willing to pay a $65–$110 festival submission fee for the chance to be considered. Deciding where to submit is important but can be bewildering to navigate. And submissions fees add up. Even if you do get into a film festival, the reality is that most distributors only have the time or desire to fish in the very upper echelons of film festivals (the ones playing the Brad Pitt movies). This results in most filmmakers centering their entire release strategy around getting their film into festivals—at significant cost to themselves, between submission fees, travel costs, and marketing—without any clear understanding of or plan for what might happen after that. Almost all indie filmmakers hurl themselves into the festival circuit, chasing the Holy Grail of the Distribution Deal. It was into this madness that my peers and I began submitting our films. Almost immediately, our womanhood again became an issue.

There is almost no transparency around the programming of film festivals, so it is impossible to confirm whether films by and about women are discriminated against in this process, though there is strong evidence to suggest they are. But even for those of us whose films were accepted into festivals, it became clear that there were hurdles yet ahead of us.

Female filmmakers I spoke with, who first experienced the film festival world close to when I did, talked about realizing that every time they attended a festival event—crucial networking opportunities for an emerging filmmaker—people would approach them and ask what film they'd "acted in." "When I went to film festivals with my boyfriend at the time," Jaclyn Gramigna remembers, "people would walk up to him and ask him what film he'd directed. They wouldn't even look at me. They always assumed that I was there as his girlfriend or as an actress." Her boyfriend does not work in the film industry in any capacity whatsoever.

Is this a big deal on its face? Maybe, maybe not. But I can tell you firsthand these kinds of interactions over time eat away at both your confidence and your patience. Worse, you find yourself constantly having to explain that, no, you actually *are* a filmmaker. Being forced to start every networking interaction with a justification puts you instantly in a more difficult position from which to have to sell yourself and your film.

Meanwhile, once again we found ourselves hearing that constant, bewildering refrain—this time from distributors—that, while our films were good, they were sorry, but there was simply no audience for films about women.

"Oh, there was glaring sexism," Leah Meyerhoff says about trying to sell her independent feature *I Believe in Unicorns*, a coming-of-age drama about a teenage girl exploring the complex landscape of troubled young love. "I *knew* that there was an audience of teenage girls out there for this film. I knew that because when I was a teenage girl, I *needed* a movie like this—and I wanted so badly to get it to them. And so many sales agents we spoke to said that audience was too hard to reach and it would be easier with a male lead instead."

Jen McGowan ran into the same wall with her directorial debut, *Kelly & Cal*, about a new and single mother (played by Juliette Lewis) trying to find her own identity through an unlikely friendship with a teenage boy. "Well, there's just no audience for this film," she was told. "What are you talking about?!" Jen wondered. "Not only is there an audience for this movie," she says. "I know where they *are*."

We were all facing down the same conundrum. We had spent years of our lives wrenching these films into existence on the premise that what the industry wasn't seeing about the project when it was just a script, a team, and a dream, would be immediately evident to them once they watched the actual film—that these were new stories, stories that hadn't been told on film before, which would be exciting to audiences of all genders and races—only to be told once again that no audience was going to care, much less watch or pay for, our movies.

So . . . we bootstrapped it. Again. Because what the hell else were we going to do?

Fine, we figured. If the sales agents and distributors didn't believe that there was an audience for our content, we'd just have to prove to them that there was.

Imagine I'm Beautiful eventually played at eleven small film festivals around the country, winning twelve awards, including four Best Picture Awards, three Best Actress Awards, and a Best Screenplay Award for me. My team and I used these festivals and these wins to gather enthusiasm from our core base of supporters through social media and our monthly e-newsletter. At most festivals, filmmakers do the bulk of the promotional work to get audience members to their screenings. So, we guerrilla-marketed ourselves hard in each and every town we played. I, or someone from the team, went to all of them, hustling potential audience members on the streets with flyers and posters. And because our film is a sensitive and nuanced portrayal of borderline personality disorder, we reached out to local mental health organizations in each region we played, asking them to encourage their members to attend our screenings. Very often they did. Using all the ingenuity and tenacity we had learned as actors, we got butts in seats.

As with most US film festivals, we knew that no ticket money from those butts in seats would come back to us.* So, realizing that the only currency we stood to earn was an ongoing connection to our audience members, we hired a local student for each screening to stand outside the theater door and collect the email addresses of people as they left the theater. We added them to our newsletter, invited them to follow us on social media, and asked them to get their friends to do the same. Was it an efficient marketing strategy? No. But did it work? You betcha.

Email address by email address, social media "like" by social media "like," at every small screening, we were finding the audiences that we had been told didn't exist.

My *Imagine I'm Beautiful* team and I were just one group of female filmmakers doing this. For so many of us, speaking to those dreamed-of audience members, seeing their reactions to the work, reminded us why we had begun telling stories. We discovered that we needed the audience as much as they needed us. It was as fulfilling as it was vindicating. Over and over we once again heard a refrain, but this time it was from bewildered filmgoers asking us, "Why don't more films like this get made?"

Why indeed.

Predictably, after we had done all this legwork and audience-building, a number of us female filmmakers did eventually get those sought-after distribution deals from companies that were finally convinced we might be on to something.

My team and I got the head of a start-up distribution company, who had previously passed on distributing *Imagine I'm Beautiful*, to attend our premiere screening of the film at the small but wonderful RxSM Film Festival in Austin, Texas. He came as a favor. We had marketed the

---

* Almost all US film festivals keep all ticket revenue. Occasionally they will fly out and/or give accommodations to a filmmaker, but most typically the filmmaker or film producing team fronts all costs for submitting to, attending, and marketing the film at festivals and receives no compensation for any of this from the film festival.

bejeezus out of the screening and managed to pretty well fill the seats. When the film finished, the audience was invited to ask me questions or comment on the film, and before anything else happened, a man stood up, his face wet from crying. "I just want to tell you," he said, "I have a daughter with borderline personality disorder, and I have *never* seen someone treat that illness with dignity in a story. More than that, though, you helped *me* understand something. Watching your movie today—you just taught me about my daughter."

After the Q&A, the distributor came up to me, full of the emotion we had all felt in the room. "You have to let me distribute this film," he said handing me his card. "When we're both back in New York, I want to talk to you."

I was too afraid to ask the distributor if he remembered that he had already passed on the film before the screening. But when back in New York, we met and, true to his word, he signed us up for a distribution deal with his company. They ran us in theaters for a week in Toronto and a week in LA and did one-night theatrical screenings of the film in eight other cities besides, concurrent to an online digital release on iTunes, Amazon, GooglePlay, and other major platforms.

In the scale of things, this was a small release, but for an $80,000 movie made by unknown filmmakers, with no actors anyone had ever heard of, and centering on two complex female characters, this was a very big deal. It was thrilling beyond all recounting.

Many of my peers won similar victories. Finally, we felt, there is something real, something undeniable, that will make us irrefutable.

CHAPTER 4

BRICK LANE*

When the *Imagine I'm Beautiful* team and I returned to New York following the theatrical and digital release of our film by a real, live distributor, toting our victorious tale of grassroots success, we expected to be taken seriously or, at the very least, to finally be able to get a freaking agent.

It was not to be. Nor were we alone in this.

Victoria Negri recalls how, after her 2017 film *Gold Star* played at festivals, picking up a slew of awards and garnering a distribution deal, "I was really motivated. I thought, 'This is it.'" She sat down and created a big spreadsheet of agents and managers.† She emailed each of them a cover letter and links to her film, sharing her story of triumph against all odds in making this film, how well it had done, how ready and qualified and well-armed she was to take a step into the next phase of her career. She didn't hear back from a single person. I did exactly the same thing after *Imagine I'm Beautiful* with exactly the same results.

It was impossible not to notice that our male peers were receiving offers off their films—jobs, financing, opportunities.

Something was deeply rotten here, and I was not the only one feeling the need for some kind of action in the early 2010s.

---

* *Brick Lane* (2007), dir. Sarah Gavron.
† Spreadsheets are apparently a big feature of a career in the entertainment industry.

Leah Meyerhoff, in 2013, reached out to two female filmmaker heroes: Kimberly Peirce (*Boys Don't Cry*) and Allison Anders (*Gas Food Lodging*), who gave her instrumental advice as she developed her first feature film. Leah found these conversations so valuable and validating that she decided more women needed to be having them. Shortly thereafter, she invited some more female filmmakers she knew over for dinner. By the end of that evening, all the women present had so thoroughly recognized the power of holding the space to share stories, offer advice, and ask each other for help that, as they left, someone said, "Let's do this again next month. I'll host."

Around the same time, longtime directors Maria Giese and Rachel Feldman began together plotting ways that they might break up the good ole boys' club in the Directors Guild of America (DGA). Maria and Rachel started directing earlier than Leah and me, and they had been pushing for decades on their own, but through the power of the internet, they finally had the tools to properly investigate the exclusion of female filmmakers. Maria and Rachel used various internet and in-person groups to try to rally disenfranchised female filmmakers to do something about it.

In 2011, Melissa Silverstein, who had at that time been the lone voice in the blogosphere on these issues, having started the seminal Women & Hollywood site back in 2007, took the project to the next level by cofounding the Athena Film Festival, in partnership with the Athena Center for Leadership Studies at Barnard College, the first festival to focus exclusively on films featuring female characters in lead roles.

During this same period of time, Maylen Calienes, an actress recently turned filmmaker out of frustration over limited roles for Latinas, began looking for a group to join that would help her connect with other members of her community. "I learned about the Blackhouse Foundation at the Sundance Film Festival and what they were doing for black creative voices, but I couldn't find the same thing for Latinos, and it didn't seem like anyone was interested," she says. "So I decided to just go for it and start it myself." This eventually led Calienes to found the Latino Filmmakers Network in 2015, a group now with over four thousand members that promotes the work of Latinx and minority filmmakers and connects them to agents, executives, and other gatekeepers.

In fact, between 2011 and 2013, all over the country, more or less spontaneously, a growing grassroots women in film movement emerged, made up of women like me who were starting to feel that we were up against something much bigger than any one of us. And unlike the generations of women who tried to break into the behind-the-scenes film industry before us, we, thanks to the internet, had the tools and means to take action toward collectively doing something about the rampant gender discrimination on a bigger scale than ever before.

For my part, at that time, I began speaking about the sexism I was experiencing to anyone and everyone who would listen—at Q&As after screenings, at most parties I went to, in conversation with virtually anyone who would sit still long enough. This outspokenness quickly landed me on the rapidly growing panel circuit of industry-hosted discussions about "the women in film problem," as well as getting invitations to give speeches on the topic to the wider public.

That my profile on this subject grew so far so fast was primarily due to the fact that I hadn't yet made it far enough inside the industry to realize the peril I was putting myself in professionally by simply explaining what was happening to women in our industry. I was willing to say things that back then—and even to this day—precious few people were prepared to state plainly in public.

I'm sure that all of us women involved in this movement were emboldened by a new kind of grenade that A-list actresses began throwing into their acceptance speeches around this time. This tradition wasn't new. In 2002 Halle Berry won the Oscar for *Monster's Ball*, becoming the first woman of color to ever win Best Actress* by saying, "[This is] for every nameless, faceless woman of color that now has a chance because this door tonight has been opened."[1†] But in the early 2010s, the tenor of those lines turned from the inspirational—"now this has happened and it's possible"—to, in at least some instances, more openly and aggressively calling the industry out. In 2013 Cate Blanchett accepted her Best Actress Oscar for *Blue Jasmine* by saying, "I'm so very proud that *Blue Jasmine* stayed in the cinemas for as long as it did. . . . And perhaps [to] those of us in the industry who are foolishly clinging to the idea that

---

* Sit with that one for a moment: the FIRST WOMAN OF COLOR TO EVER WIN BEST ACTRESS, in 2002.

† Her optimism, of course, proved not to be quite valid, as #OscarsSoWhite pointed out more than a decade later.

female films with women at the center are niche experiences, they are not. Audiences want to see them and, in fact, they earn money. So . . . the world is round, people!"[2]

Leaping off my couch to cheer her on, I didn't feel as though my peers and I were lonely rebel voices, raging at the system. It felt like we were simply contributing our own stories and experiences to the wider conversation happening within the industry. I was telling my end of things; Cate was telling hers. To me, we were sister soldiers.

It felt exciting. It seemed that, somehow, people must simply not have been aware that this level of sexism was occurring. But now panels on the topic were popping up, and I was talking and Cate was talking and . . . well, surely once we explained to people the ways in which women were being discriminated against and our voices silenced, everyone would be just as incensed as we were.

Not exactly.

When I spoke about this to people outside the film industry, they were horrified.

When I spoke to the people in the lower echelons of the film industry—up-and-coming female filmmakers who hadn't yet had my experiences—the reaction was outrage, and they issued a battle cry to take up arms against such a system of oppression.

Before long, however, I began getting opportunities to speak in front of people higher up in the industry about these problems. At first, I was elated to be able to report to them from the front lines of these injustices, of which they must surely be unaware and would be delighted to know they could be part of solving.

My first real experience of this was when, after the release of *Imagine I'm Beautiful*, I was invited to a tony film festival at an exotic location. I had been invited specifically to give my spiel to filmmakers and festivalgoers about this rampaging sexism I'd witnessed on the ground and, hopefully, inspire other young female filmmakers to do as I had done and go outside the system to make their movies.

I was an anomaly among the VIP speakers at the festival, the other three being elite establishment types: Luke, a hot-and-rising wonder-boy screenwriter who had been nominated twice for an Oscar; Robert, an older male screenwriter who had written almost a dozen of the most beloved and iconic films of the 1980s and '90s; and Cynthia, a bigwig female producer who is practically a legend for having produced twenty years of some of the most critically renowned and award-laden films of our time.*

They were leery of me—me being from the peasant class of Hollywood—but they were kind, until the moment they attended my talk about the situation of women in film. I'm sure I spoke passionately, energetically—as I still do when you get me going on this topic—but I know I didn't speak angrily. I wasn't naming names or calling out specific people or being particularly radical. I was just explaining what was happening and suggesting that perhaps we ought to do something about it.

Following the talk, which had received a generally warm response from the room, Cynthia approached me, now with ice daggers in her eyes, and said coldly, "I don't think it's a good idea to play the woman card." She walked away and refused to either look at me or acknowledge my presence for the remainder of the festival.

The following afternoon, Luke pulled me aside and, in what I'm sure he felt was a kind and helpful piece of career advice, said, "Look, I absolutely agree with everything you're saying. Just be very, very careful where you say it. I've watched women's careers get tanked for saying less than you're saying."

This was in 2015.

I was surprised, but I should not have been. Nothing that I said had been news to anyone. But I dared to say it. And that was my perceived mistake. That I said aloud what everyone knew but quietly accepted.

Maria Giese told me, "When I was elected first-ever DGA Women Directors Category rep in 2013, I walked into a National Board meeting and approached the then DGA president [a man we'll call Dave and who is one of the top five iconic male directors alive today and who is not named Dave] looking to get help. These guys were my heroes. I loved the feminist films they'd made, and I was pretty sure they'd be all over it. . . . I introduced myself and told them I wanted to talk about how to get more women directors working. They leaned back, folded their arms, and rolled their eyes. Dave finally groaned, 'Yeah. Women and everyone else.'"

---

* These are not their real names.

What I realized, as Maria and many other women have realized before and after me, in one vertiginous jolt, was that the entire industry knows exactly what's going on and almost nobody is *genuinely* interested in lifting a finger to do anything about it. How can this be? Surely there are good people in Hollywood who want to do the right thing.

In my opinion, the root of this chronic inaction is that the entire system of Hollywood operates on an intense caste system of Inside and Outside. It works like this:

At any Hollywood gathering whatsoever—be it a premiere, a networking event, somebody's birthday party, a business meeting—there is a clear status delineation between those who are Inside versus those who are Outside. For instance, if you are Outside, you might be invited to the premiere of a film—maybe you played a bit part in it or are friends with the writer—but you will *not* be invited to the after-party. Indeed, you will not be aware that there *is* an after-party until a terribly awkward moment midway through the evening when someone on the Inside says, "Are you going to the after-party?" At which point, you will attempt to recover quickly enough to either mutter vaguely, "Nah, I don't think so," as if you really couldn't care one way or the other. Or better, if you can think quickly enough, "No, I can't. I've got to get to another event across town by eleven."

The question of whether or not you are Inside is amorphous and situation-dependent. An actress who is the star of a relatively successful TV show might be very much Inside at a Screen Actors Guild event filled with less-successful actors—she would be shuttled through the evening surrounded by self-satisfied-looking handlers whose full-time job is to ensure that no "lesser" actor dare approach her. But that same actress would be firmly Outside if she somehow wrangled an invitation to the Oscars. There, it would be she who would spend the evening trying heroically to pretend that it didn't matter that she'd been placed in a seat located only just outside the coatroom.

Inside/Outside has jack squat to do with talent. It also generally has very little to do with personal kindness, integrity, or other human qualities that might be valued in more normal social situations. It has 100 percent to do with *status*—as alchemically defined by how convincingly you give off the aura of someone who doesn't give a shit about anything and doesn't need to + a total absence of expressed need for anything + how many other people in the room are covertly whispering to each other about how big a deal you are or are about to become + (in higher-tier situations) precisely how many Oscar/Emmy/Golden Globe nominations/wins you have had - the number of years since you most recently won one.

It generally takes about five minutes of being in a room to work out whether you are Inside or Outside, primarily because a fantastic amount of energy is spent collectively by the film industry in making those who are Outside understand that they are most definitely *not* Inside.

The Inside/Outside game is addictively seductive for the reason that the game feels horrible until the second you are Inside, at which point it suddenly feels *amaaaazzing* and you yourself become energetically and cultishly engaged with maintaining the walls that now keep you Inside (because you've been Outside and, comparatively, it's *terrible*).

The whole thing is a sillier and more demented version of high school social politics, but the stakes are very, very real. People who are Inside will find themselves getting hired, finding funding for their films, receiving awards, and getting invited to the right parties, where they will meet the right A-list talent to star in their projects and turn their indie film into Oscar bait, while people who are Outside will quite simply not have careers in Hollywood.

As a result, nearly every single person* who has made it Inside, irrespective of their achievements or number of Oscars, is terrified—and I do mean mortally *terrified*—of getting thrown Outside.

That terror sits at the heart of and explains most of the decision-making that goes on in Hollywood, and it most definitely explains, at least part of the collective lack of individual willpower to speak out against or take action to change the status quo. Because everyone knows—and if you don't know, you will be quickly informed, as I was—that Inside people are the type of people who will giggle and waggle their head and gush gratefully about the amazing opportunities they are receiving, and only

---

* With the possible exception of Frances McDormand.

Outside People would talk about dreary, irritating things like systemic oppression.

I asked Denise Di Novi, famed producer of *Heathers* and *Ed Wood*, whether she, embedded deeply in the belly of Hollywood, knew that it was dangerous to speak openly about sexism in the film industry even in the 2010s. "Oh, yes!" she immediately replied. "You were seen as a whiner—complainer—if you spoke out about that. The universal attitude was 'It's just the way it is. Get tough.'"

Once I began to understand this dynamic, it dawned on me that, although by the mid-2010s, we were starting to hear A-list actresses speak out about these issues, it tended to be almost exclusively during award acceptance speeches. You could argue that maybe that is because those are the moments when actresses have the biggest national audiences and when such statements would have the widest impact—which is certainly true. But you can't ignore the fact that those are also the moments when actresses are the least vulnerable to being thrown Outside.

Even Meryl Streep, who has been held up as a real fighter for women, didn't once mention the issue in any of her award acceptance speeches during the 2000s and 2010s. In 2017, post-Weinstein, when it had become far more acceptable to talk about these things, she gave a real barn burner of a speech on the subject in her Golden Globe Lifetime Achievement Award acceptance speech. It was wonderful—it made my skin tingle listening to it—but that's keeping in mind that just five years before, she thanked, "God, Harvey Weinstein," in her 2012 Best Actress acceptance speech at the same award ceremony.[3]

The vast majority of women in the most powerful positions in Hollywood said—and still say—nothing at all.

It's not really fair for me, sitting in my crappy basement apartment in Brooklyn, to say to them, "Where were you?" and, "Why didn't you do more?" From my ever-so-brief peek at the Inside, I can imagine what these A-list actresses have to lose. But if I'm being honest, their silence or declawed protests also felt like absolute horseshit.

Worse, I realized, that if my peers and I continued to speak and act out, the powers that be could squash our burgeoning careers so completely that no one would ever even know we had existed at all.

Throughout the generations, mine included, some indie female filmmakers in the face of all of this, quite understandably, set their dreams aside, leave the business, and find a way to be happy doing something less psychologically damaging.

There has always been a strain of women who have forged ahead, undaunted, into the system and vehemently denied that their womanhood was, indeed, an obstacle at all.*

Some of us find fuel in our anger and indignation to keep going in our careers. Filmmaker Sarah Adina Smith said, "In a funny way, I think I've benefited by not fully succeeding, because it's made me work even harder."

Some of us risk our careers fully by throwing ourselves kamikaze style into activism and rebellion against the industry we dreamed of joining.

I have found that one of the main benefits of discovering that the industry you've spent your life trying to succeed in is foundationally corrupt, broken, and rigged against you, is that I finally understood with clarity that I, like most women in history, would simply have to work twice as hard to get half as far. Okay, fine, I (and so many others) thought. If all it takes is harder work, I will simply work that much harder.

Once you decide as a writer, director, or writer/director that you are ready to try to have a career inside "the system"—say, write or direct for television shows, studio movies, bigger independent films, really do anything that pays you actual money and isn't a <$1 million independent film—your first order of business is probably to try to get an agent. An agent's job when representing filmmakers is to help connect the filmmaker with the people who are hiring for the right projects and to negotiate the best possible deal if the filmmaker is fortunate enough to get hired for those projects.

Almost all agents work for agencies of one size or another. The two biggest agencies in the film world are William Morris Endeavor (WME) and Creative Artists Agency (CAA). They are the Inside of the Inside and rep nearly all the people in the film industry that you've ever heard of.

---

* There has always been a trendy refrain from certain women who refuse to talk about "the women in film problem," saying, "I don't want to be called a female filmmaker. I'm just a filmmaker." While I sympathize wholeheartedly with that comment, it neglects to acknowledge that we are not yet in an industry that in any way treats us as "just filmmakers."

There is then a layer of mid-size agencies that are still big but are smaller and less powerful than WME and CAA. Finally, there are the small "boutique" agencies, which rep far fewer clients and only have a handful of agents.

While the original idea of agents was that they would do the hard work of weeding through the Significant Sea of Talent (i.e., people wishing to be actors, directors, writers, etc.) and pluck out the most talented and promising ones to save those doing the hiring the trouble of doing this weeding, what most agencies have settled into at this juncture is to simply wait and see which creatives drift Inside of their own accord and then represent those clients who have already built careers and are managing to make a lot of money on their own.

This presents a specific problem for women. Because agents are almost always looking for people already working in the system, something which women have not historically had the opportunity to do, women end up in yet another industry catch-22: one can't book jobs or make money in the system until one has an agent, and one can't get an agent or make money until one is booking jobs or making money in the system.

Furthermore, when agents do dip their toes into the Significant Sea of Talent to see if they can "discover" someone new, they are looking for people who have already received highly specific, industry-ordained indicators of success—such as having won an award from a top film school or at a top festival. These, again, are markers that women are demonstrably less likely to receive.

Agents will frequently complain that they'd love to get more female clients but simply can't find any "qualified" ones. This is a complaint called into question by the fact that, frequently, even if a person *has* somehow managed to get those industry accolades or track record but is also a woman, she still can't get an agent.

Rachel Feldman has directed over seventy-five hours of broadcast/network television including the pilot and entire season of *The Baxters*, a new show for MGM, and multiple episodes of *Blue Bloods*, *Criminal Minds*, and *The Rookie* in one season alone. But, as of 2017, even after having decades of experience directing episodic television, including Emmy-nominated series such as *Picket Fences* and several television movies, Rachel was not able to secure representation for ten years, even with introductions made by highly respected executives.

Deborah Kampmeier made, wrote, and directed her first feature film, *Virgin*, which was nominated for two Independent Spirit Awards.[*] She has since written and directed three additional feature films, one of which was nominated for the Sundance Grand Jury Prize. She can't get an agent.

Caytha Jentis, who, at the time of our interview, had directed two feature films, written four produced feature films, created *The Other F Word* web series, which she single-handedly drove to become a top series on Amazon Video Direct *for many months* and drawing *millions* of viewers, cannot get an agent.

Sonja O'Hara wrote, directed, and starred in one indie feature; wrote, directed, and acted in two independently produced TV pilots (produced by her); and had two seven-figure deals on the table from networks that wanted to buy and produce those shows. One agency told her, "We think you're going to be really successful, but we don't know what to do with you." Another agency asked her how many social media followers she had and then declined to rep her. She finally got signed by an agency, but only after a James Bond-ninja level maneuver that required CIA-level backchanneling on the part of her and her manager.[†]

I could go on, but I think you get the idea.

Compounding this problem is that the agents are so supremely powerful in the industry's hiring system that even if you manage to go around them and somehow connect with the person doing the hiring directly, you will still be unable to get hired without an agent.

Caytha, for instance, managed to batter-ram her way into a meeting with a female executive at a studio (i.e., someone in the position to actually hire her—someone you would normally need an agent to get to at all). They had an incredible meeting. The female exec was duly impressed with all that Caytha had accomplished inside and outside of the system and said,

"I like you. You're funny. You're irreverent. What do you want?"

"I want to be in a writer's room," Caytha said.

---

[*] Basically, the Oscars for indie film.

[†] Most actors, directors, and writers have a manager and agent. The general idea is that the former helps you shape your long-term career prospects, while an agent focuses on the short-term work of submitting you for jobs.

The female exec smiled at her forthrightness. "You're exactly the type of writer I'd like to have. Have your agents send me a writing sample."*

Except that Caytha didn't have an agent. Cleverly, she used this positive meeting as an excuse to reach out to agents and say, "Hey, I've got this exec at X major studio who would like to read my materials. Would you submit to them on my behalf, and [even though I've already done the work of cultivating the contact] you can collect your 10 percent commission if the deal goes through."

Response from the agents: "Well, no one will put a woman your age in a writers' room."

Caytha (lapsing into profound existential crisis): "Why the fuck am I even still trying?"

I could sit down and handily write you a list of at least forty women whom I personally know in similar situations. This is not to say that some of us women flinging ourselves at the gates to the kingdom haven't managed to squeeze through. Some do. But a whole hell of a lot of women trying to become writers and directors never make it out of this paradox.

But what of those women lucky enough to get agents? Well, they quickly find themselves banging into a dizzying array of "we can't hire you's." The reasons are remarkably consistent and are probably familiar to women from a wide range of industries: "We tried a woman before. It didn't work out." "If only you had more experience . . ." "If you'd just leap through these seven hoops . . ." And "How are we supposed to do anything fun if there are women around?"

For a woman to ultimately get hired requires a lottery-win-level of luck on top of talent, ingenuity, and tenacity that must be recognized by someone (often several someones) in a position of power willing to stick their own neck out to bring her on board.

Some women, like myself, at this stage, feeling a growing level of despair that we will ever find our way through any door by trying to get an agent, decide to make a second independent feature film. Maybe the first feature just wasn't big enough, didn't have the right names attached, or for whatever other reason didn't quite "hit" in the way it needed to. But if

---

* For legal reasons, most studios won't accept submissions from anyone other than agent, even if you are meeting with an executive who would like to read your material—you still need an agent to submit it to that same executive.

we could just go back and do the thing we definitely know how to do—make movies—benefiting this time from our greater understanding of the system as well as maybe some new connections we've forged Inside, *maybe* someone somewhere might finally sit up and take notice.

Except getting a second feature film made is not easy.

As director Jen McGowan rightly said during our interview, "Every movie, good or bad, is a complete freaking miracle."

This is particularly true for second films—especially if you are a non-white person or a woman. In her article "Why the Second Movie Is the Biggest Hurdle to Becoming a Filmmaker—Especially for Women and Minorities,"* *Los Angeles Times* reporter Rebecca Keegan noted, "First films are often made in a democratic fashion—on low-cost cameras with crowdfunded budgets and crews of college friends. Second movies typically rely more on the machinery of Hollywood—a machinery that has often excluded women and minorities."[4]

In spite of this upward slope, many of us women, throughout time, pulled on our cowgirl boots all the same and—if we were fortunate enough through the right combination of resources, time, willpower, and access to connections—made a second feature, outside the system, not waiting for the say-so of any gatekeepers.

Starting in August of 2013, I set out to make my second feature film, *Bite Me*, a subversive romantic comedy about a real-life vampire and the IRS agent who audits her. Since we'd made *Imagine I'm Beautiful* for $80,000 with no recognizable talent, and since both factors had been given to me as reasons the system couldn't take me all that seriously, I set out bound and determined to make this next film for a budget between $500,000 and $1 million. While we were never going to get Ryan Gosling at that budget level—unless we happened to be best friends with him, which for better or worse, I am not—we were told that it was important to attach actors that at least some people had heard about before.

Through Joanne Zippel, a manager that I had snagged after *Imagine I'm Beautiful* and met through a women in film group, I was able to attach producer Jack Lechner, known for *Blue Valentine*, *The Fog of War*, and, during his studio days, *Good Will Hunting*, *Four Weddings and a*

---

* This, coincidentally, is also the headline you least want to read after gasping across the finish line of your first feature film.

Funeral, and about a dozen other classics. Having Jack on the team felt like validation that I was moving up the ladder. It seemed like a promise that this time my team and I would be noticed. It took us five and a half years to make the film, including three, frankly, brutal years of fundraising. In the scope of filmmaking, that time span is not outrageous—as Jack kept reminding us, *Blue Valentine* had taken nine. But, still. At every turn it seemed like we faced hurdles that didn't need to be there: financiers, actors' agents, and even people we hired not taking us as seriously as they should have.

Some of these hurdles we managed to get around through these ever-growing networks of women in film that were solidifying into networks of connections, resource- and information-sharing channels, and support systems, but those could not together fully balance the scales for us. It was still harder for us to get the film made than it was for our male peers. But we did and that was magic. More on what happened after that later on. But I'll give you a preview: the doors of Hollywood didn't fly open.

Women do not have the corner on indie film being difficult. Making a film, whether it's your first or fourth, almost always seems like an impossible endeavor. There are too many factors that have to converge in too random a pattern to result in a finished movie. By all measures, the process is substantially harder for women, but let's lay that aside for a moment.*

Let's think about those women who have somehow actually managed to make their films and whose films have somehow gone on to play and maybe even won awards at Sundance, Cannes, South by Southwest (SXSW), or Toronto International Film Festival (TIFF), who won Independent Spirit Awards, maybe even Oscars; whose films have made money, maybe a lot of money.

Surely at that point, if a woman has managed to break through that far, into that elite club of filmmakers, the barriers come down. Yes, maybe she had to work harder than a man to get there and put up with a tidal wave of bullshit, harassment, even assault, but if she did the work and got

---

* Don't worry, we'll come back to this next chapter.

it done and proved her skills, there does come a point at which her talent and prowess as a creative is undeniable. Right?

...

Right?

You know where this is going. I'm not even going to write it down.

Let me tell you some stories instead.

Marc Webb's first narrative feature was the indie romantic comedy *500 Days of Summer* ($7.5M), which premiered at Sundance in 2009. For his next feature he was hired by Sony to direct *The Amazing Spider-Man 2*, with a reported budget of $262 million. He was personally paid $6 million to direct.[5]

Colin Trevorrow's feature directing debut was the $750,000 *Safety Not Guaranteed*, which premiered at the 2012 Sundance Film Festival and won the Waldo Salt Screenwriting Award. Steven Spielberg, who has "gone on record saying Trevorrow reminded him of a younger version of himself," vouched for Colin personally, in light of which, Colin was handed the $150 million *Jurassic World* in 2015. Spielberg was on-set "to mentor the upstart director."[6]

Kimberly Peirce's critically acclaimed *Boys Don't Cry* played at TIFF in 1999 and eventually grossed a reported $21 million, more than ten times its modest $2 million budget.[7] It was named one of the best films of the year by the National Board of Review of Motion Pictures, and it won no fewer than forty-seven awards, including a Best Actress Oscar and Golden Globe for star Hilary Swank.[8] It took nine years for Kimberly to gather the resources to make her second feature film, *Stop-Loss*, with a budget of $25 million. In those intervening nine years, her only directing job was one episode of the TV show *The L Word*.[9]

Penelope Spheeris, who had debuted with her features *The Decline of Western Civilization,* parts I, II, and III, directed the $20 million *Wayne's World*, which became a '90s pop-culture phenomenon and grossed $183 million, making it the eighth-highest-grossing film of 1992.[10] Penelope was not invited to direct the sequel, which flopped.[11]

Gina Prince-Bythewood wrote and directed the widely acclaimed *Love & Basketball* ($20M), which premiered at the 2000 Sundance Film Festival and earned her an Independent Spirit Award for Best First Feature. It took eight years for her to make her second feature, *The Secret*

Life of Bees ($11M). In that interim period, she was hired to direct four episodes of television, a made-for-TV movie, and a short film.[12]

Eliza Hittman's feature directing debut, *It Felt Like Love*, premiered at the 2013 Sundance Film Festival. The *LA Times* said of it, "Rarely has the zone between girlhood and womanhood been captured with such urgent honesty." Eliza's phone has rung consistently since then . . . with people asking for her (male) cinematographer's contact information so they can hire him. "It's funny that people responded to the sensibility of that movie enough to hire him," Hittman said, "but nobody would circle back to me in that way."[13]

Lynn Shelton has directed five independent feature films, with budgets ranging from $85,000 to $5 million, that have premiered at all the big festivals—Sundance, Cannes, SXSW—and has not as yet gotten studio directing jobs, all while watching, each festival season, the careers of the male filmmakers whose films screen alongside hers skyrocket.[14]

Ry Russo-Young directed five low-budget indie feature films before she was finally given a studio film to direct.

Ava DuVernay's first narrative feature film, *I Will Follow*, which she made for $50,000, was called by Roger Ebert "one of the best films I've seen about coming to terms with the death of a loved one" and received a distribution deal. But Ava's phone didn't ring, so she decided to make her second narrative feature film, *Middle of Nowhere*, for $200,000, which then won her the US Directing Award at the 2012 Sundance Film Festival.* Still her phone didn't ring. She eventually landed the job directing *Selma* for $20M, but only after the lead actor, David Oyelowo, refused to do the film unless the executives allowed her to direct it.[15]

Lest you think I'm cherry-picking stories here, if Marc and Colin are the outlier success stories here for men, so are Kimberly, Penelope, Gina, Eliza, Lynn, Ry, and Ava for women. They are *the lucky ones*. They got to make their studio film or bigger-budget indie feature.

As Rachel Morrison, the only female to *ever* win a Best Cinematographer Oscar (2018 for *Mudbound*) told the *New York Times*, "Women can reach [the studio level], but they have to shoot two $1 million movies before getting a $5 million assignment and so on. . . . There's never a call

---

* Notably the same year that Colin Trevorrow's film did *not* win him the US Directing Award at the same film festival.

like, 'You did a great job on your $5 million movie, here's a $100 million project.' My experience is that guys get to take a faster route."[16]

None of us women expected to be handed anything. We understand about paying our dues. We understand about work. In fact, we even understand all too well that any one of us may not have what it takes. Indeed, almost every woman I interviewed for this book rushed to assure me that her own career hurdles might be her own fault: "Of course, maybe I'm just not good enough." "I might not be working hard enough." "I might be undercutting myself in x, y, and z ways."

I'll make the same caveat: I may not be that good. In fact, I might be supremely untalented. I don't think anyone who has ever met me can make the argument that I don't work hard enough, but let's say I don't work smart enough. Maybe I don't channel that work in a magically correct direction. Maybe there is some deeply twisted set of personal character flaws and psychic hang-ups that are preventing me personally from getting through the gates of Hollywood to the land of getting-to-make-movies-with-actual-resources-and-paychecks.

Not everyone who wants to make art is good enough to do so at a professional level. It is one of life's particular tragedies, but that is not unique to Hollywood.

But we can't all suck. You can explain the lack of career success of any one woman in a thousand different ways, but to look at what is happening across a gender and say that it is our fault, that it is down to weaknesses in each of us, is to very simply say that women, as a gender, are just less talented, hard working, and psychologically intact. And not a little bit, but so much that we are collectively undeserving of having voices in the industry that creates the stories that shape our culture.

And that, I cannot accept.

CHAPTER 5

MUDBOUND*

Because filmmaking is hard—for *anyone*, even in the best circumstances—I am well aware that there are still skeptics about whether there is discrimination against women in Hollywood at all. Thus far, I've built the case, I hope, for what is happening. But if you work long enough and hard enough at it, you could suggest reasons why discrimination wasn't at the heart of each anecdote and career story I've provided. Let's zoom out, then, to look at the wide shot of what is happening to women and their careers in Hollywood. Let's look at the data.

Women are 51 percent of the US population, as the following chart illustrates.

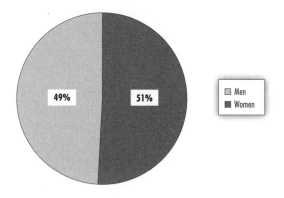

_____

* *Mudbound* (2017), dir. Dee Rees.

In the following chart is the racial breakdown of the US population, according to the 2017 census.[1]

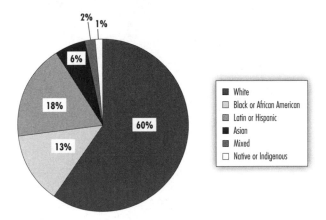

As we look now at the statistics for women behind the camera, I am going to focus primarily on narrative feature films (fictional films, not documentaries) for the reason that they arguably have greater prestige and larger influence over our cultural narrative. Know that, in general, the percentages of women in documentary film are slightly higher than they are in narrative (though still nowhere close to parity), and I would argue that that's because jobs in documentary filmmaking tend to be less well-paying and prestigious and the films less costly to make.

I will also often talk about studies that look at "top-grossing" films in a given period. The reason that stratum of films is so often studied is because of the strong correlation between a film's budget (production and marketing) and the amount it will ultimately gross. Looking at the top-grossing films, then, is an easy way to identify which films have been allocated the greatest amount of resources.

A study by the University of Southern California's Annenberg School for Communication and Journalism looked at the top-grossing narrative features from 2007 to 2016.[2] For those 1,000 films, there were 1,114 directors, since some were co-directed by two people.

Of the 1,114 narrative feature film directors, 1,069 were men and 45 were women, as the following graph indicates.

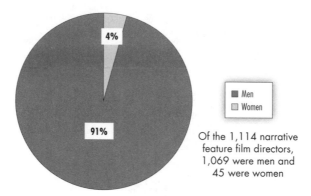

Of the 1,114 narrative
feature film directors,
1,069 were men and
45 were women

Of those directors, 57 were Black or African American, and 34 were Asian or Asian American. There was 1 Latina director. As the following graph indicates, all the rest—1,022—were white.

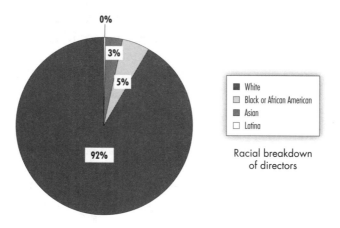

Racial breakdown
of directors

Of those 92 non-white directors, 7 were female (3 were black, 3 Asian, and 1 Latina). As the following graph shows, the rest were men.

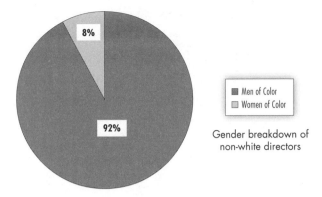

8%

92%

■ Men of Color
□ Women of Color

Gender breakdown of
non-white directors

The following graphs show what that means for the hiring of directors:

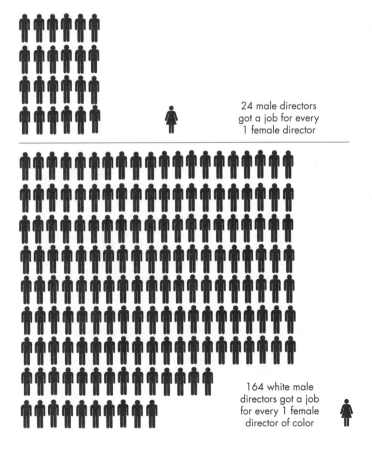

24 male directors
got a job for every
1 female director

164 white male
directors got a job
for every 1 female
director of color

The following chart compares what proportional representation would look like against what is actually happening behind the camera in Hollywood.

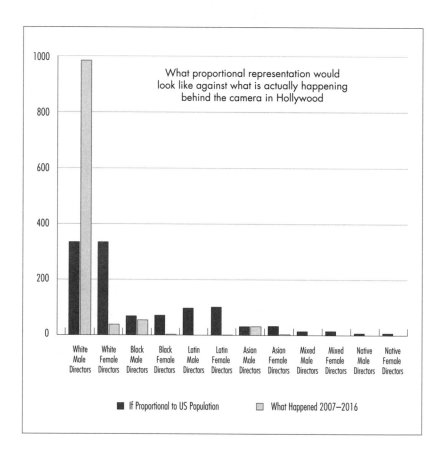

What we see is this:

- White male directors are grossly *over*represented, per their presence in the population.
- All female directors are grossly *under*represented, per their presence in the population.

- Asian men are represented almost at parity.
- Black male directors should have had 14 more directors in their category, but are somewhat approaching parity.
- Latino males and mixed race and Native populations of both genders are not represented at all.
- Directors with visible disabilities and trans directors are not represented at all.

Now let's look at how the percentage of male versus female directors of studio films has fluctuated throughout the history of US cinema.[3] It is virtually impossible to get accurate information on any of this prior to about 2010, both because it was much harder to track these numbers prior to the internet and because researchers weren't studying the issue as they are now, but the following chart is the best picture I can piece together:

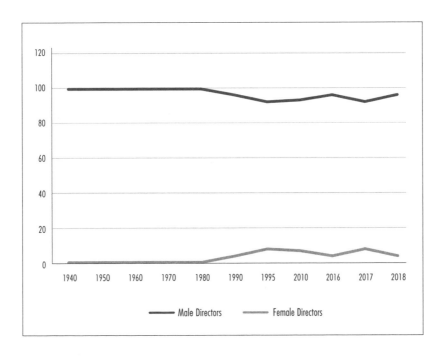

That chart has to represent such an enormously wide gap that it can be hard to read, so here is the percentage of female directors of studio films per decade:*

1940: 0.5%
1950: 0.5%
1960: 0.5%
1970: 0.5%
1980: 0.5%
1990: 4%
1995: 8%
2010: 7%
2016: 4%
2017: 8%
2018: 4%

Ahhh, progress . . .

You may be wondering if it's better for women elsewhere behind the scenes in film. The following charts show the percentages of women in other key creative roles for the one hundred top-grossing films in 2018:[4]

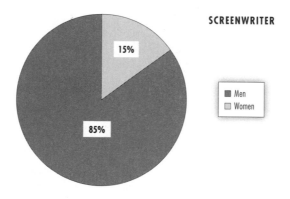

---

* Note that these numbers are additionally imprecise because they refer to different measurements based on what was being studied—sometimes referring to all studio feature films, sometimes referring to just the top-grossing studio feature films, and, in the case of the period 1945–1979, refers to feature films *and* television. The bottom line remains the same, however, which is that the percentages have been virtually immoveable and laughably small.

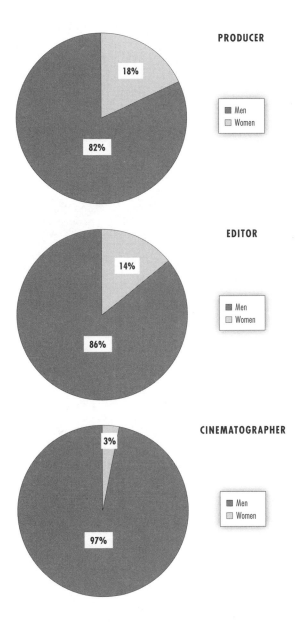

Data from the one thousand top-grossing films between 2007 and 2016 also reveals that for women who do get to direct any films at all, they make fewer over their careers than their male peers.[5] In fact, as the following chart indicates, the highly elite club of women who got to direct a film during those ten years, 80 percent only got to direct one movie.

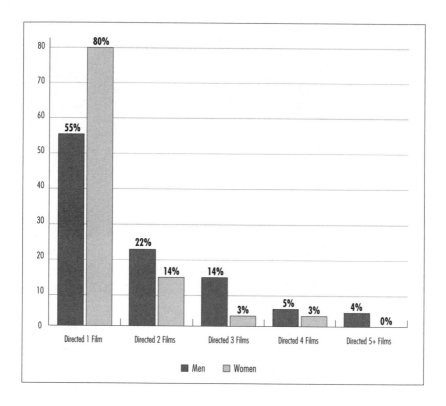

These discrepancies are also reflected come awards season. Only five women have ever been nominated for a Best Director Award in the ninety years the Oscars have existed.[6]

1976: Lina Wertmüller
1994: Jane Campion
2004: Sofia Coppola
2010: Kathryn Bigelow (the only woman to have actually
     won the award)
2018: Greta Gerwig

In addition to noting the paucity of female film directors nominated, it's important to look more deeply at the commonalities between these lucky few, particularly those shared between the three most recent nominees—Sofia, Kathryn, and Greta—since they represent the contemporary film industry.

All are white, able-bodied, and, as far as we know, cis and straight.

The films for which Sofia and Kathryn were nominated center on male protagonists—Bill Murray in *Lost in Translation* and Jeremy Renner in *The Hurt Locker*. That Kathryn became the only woman in the history of the Oscars to win Best Director for a war movie with a male protagonist is conspicuous.

Greta's *Ladybird* centered on a female protagonist, though, notably her nomination for this immediately followed the Weinstein scandals and #MeToo, and it is likely that voters in the Academy of Motion Picture Arts and Sciences were more than usually aware of needing to make a good show of supporting female stories.

But here's the real kicker. Every one of these three most recent female nominees is either the daughter or the current or former life partner of a man who had previously been nominated for or won an Oscar himself.

Sofia Coppola is the daughter of director Francis Ford Coppola, who has won five Oscars for his work.

Kathryn Bigelow was married for two years to director James Cameron prior to winning her Oscar. He has three Oscars.

Greta Gerwig is the longtime life partner of filmmaker Noah Baumbach, who was nominated for Best Screenplay for his 2006 film *The Squid and the Whale*.

Here is what that means in the film industry today: in the last quarter century, if you are a woman, even a devastatingly talented, driven, capable woman, but you are not also white, able-bodied, cis, straight, *and* publicly connected to a male Oscar nominee/winner (preferably a living icon), and ideally making films about men, it has been literally impossible for you to grasp the brass ring of a film directing career.*

As some witty person on Twitter said after Alejandro G. Iñárritu won his second Best Director Award, for *The Revenant*, in 2015,† "Alejandro has now personally won more Best Director Awards than . . . women."

---

* This has not been solely for lack of projects for which to nominate additional women. In my opinion, in 2018 Dee Rees was far more deserving of the nomination for *Mudbound* than Gerwig was for *Ladybird*. Of course, the academy voters could also have gone really crazy and nominated both of them.
† The first one was for *Birdman* (2014).

These results are unsurprising given that the academy voters were, as of 2017, 72 percent male and 84 percent white.[7]

Things are only slightly less dire in the worlds of independent and lower-budget films.

Bruce Nash of The Numbers, one of the key databases tracking the box-office performance of films, conducted an analysis that looked at the gender of directors for all films released between 2011 and 2016, examining those that received any kind of distribution whatsoever, from the tiniest indie that got thrown up on a streaming platform all the way up to the big studio films.[8]

Nash's study revealed the following:

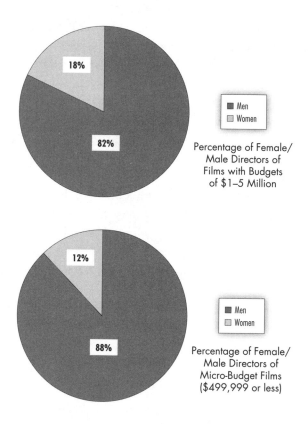

■ Men
□ Women

Percentage of Female/
Male Directors of
Films with Budgets
of $1–5 Million

■ Men
□ Women

Percentage of Female/
Male Directors of
Micro-Budget Films
($499,999 or less)

The percentage of female directors in the independent film industry seems higher only because the percentage of women directing big studio films is so abysmal.

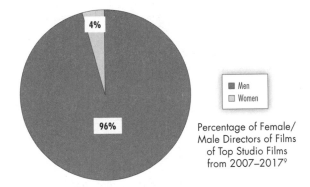

4%

96%

■ Men
☐ Women

Percentage of Female/
Male Directors of Films
of Top Studio Films
from 2007–2017[9]

No matter if it's an independent or studio film, the numbers don't come anywhere close to matching the presence of 51 percent of women in the US population. They also don't track with the number of women *interested* in becoming filmmakers, since close to 50 percent of film school graduates are female.[10]

As Manohla Dargis of the *New York Times* wrote, Hollywood's "sexism isn't in our imaginations. It isn't a female fantasy or a 'hysterical feminist myth.'"[11]

The incredible lack of women in positions behind the camera is, in fact, the result of nearly a century's worth of illegal hiring discrimination against women, as the American Civil Liberties Union of Southern California concluded in 2015.

There is a legal argument, with set precedent, used in the US courts called the "Inexorable Zero." In layman's terms, this says that if, in any given industry, profession, or educational system, there are zero members of a given demographic population (e.g., women), it can be assumed, ipso facto, that systemic discrimination is occurring.[12]

The ACLU of Southern California made use of this precedent when it wrote its report after a 2013–2015 investigation into the hiring practices of female directors in Hollywood. They concluded that the Inexorable Zero argument applies to Hollywood's hiring of directors, since 4 percent of female directors at the studios qualifies as being close to zero.

Melissa Goodman, the ACLU of Southern California's director of advocacy and legal director, wrote at the end of the investigation: "Women directors aren't working on an even playing field and aren't getting a fair opportunity to succeed. . . . Gender discrimination is illegal. And, really,

Hollywood doesn't get this free pass when it comes to civil rights and gender discrimination."[13]

At the end of the investigation, the ACLU recommended that the Equal Employment Opportunity Commission (EEOC) open its own investigation and pursue legal action against the studios for illegal hiring practices. That investigation is ongoing and its present findings are, therefore, confidential.

As those wheels of government and the law turn slowly, however, we women working (or trying to work) in the film industry must continue flinging ourselves against the virtually impenetrable mechanisms of institutionalized and systemic sexism. Every day we persevere with the full knowledge that women, historically and currently, are systematically, and almost totally, being prevented from becoming directors, writers, producers, cinematographers, and almost any other cinematic job we might like to fill in Hollywood.

There is rampant discrimination against women trying to work behind the camera in Hollywood, and the result is and has been our near total exclusion from positions of power within the film industry.

That may be devastating, but it is a fact. It is "inexorable."

The far trickier accompanying question is *"How* is it happening?"

There is something satisfying about imagining a cabal of white men sitting at the top of the power pile cackling maniacally and whispering to each other, "Let's not hire any women. It'll drive them *craaazyyy.*" And while I have no doubt that in certain corner offices that is precisely what's happening, if not in so many words, the more complicated reality is that systems of oppression, particularly in the modern era, work in far subtler formats. In writing this book, I wanted to be able to point cleanly to one or three choke points and say, "Here's where we're losing the women. Here's where they're being kept out." Then, I imagined, we could address those things and move on with our careers.

I'm sorry to report that it isn't that simple.

As I listened to the stories of women's careers—as long or short, as successful or middling as they were—over one hundred hours' worth of interviews, I came to understand that we are losing a war of attrition as much as anything else.

The power structures—patriarchal, racial, cultural, financial, all of which are at play here—are so very, very powerful and so very, very entrenched. We women are trying to succeed in a system that at a cellular level was not built for us. To transform that system away from promoting the elevation of white men to the exclusion of virtually everyone else would require a concerted, sustained, and radical effort to disrupt long-standing mechanisms. It would require visionary leadership to strongly, with courage and an intolerance for excuses, implement a new way forward.

Without that, each woman, on an individual career level, must attempt to struggle up a mountain so slick with mud that there is no step made that is completely forward-moving.

In the rest of this chapter I am going to draw a picture in answer to that question of "How?" What is occurring that is adding up to the systematic flattening of the career trajectories of women in Hollywood?

Throughout the interviews I conducted, as well as calling upon my own experiences and research, I was able to see the patterns emerge.

At each hurdle you may say to yourself, "Well, that's not so bad—she could get around this in several different ways. She just has to keep climbing." And in many cases, you would not be wrong. But as the full picture develops, I hope that you will see, as I have come to see, that the terrible, almost implausibly paltry number of women in film is the result of the sum total of a thousand cuts made to women over the life cycles of their careers. Hollywood is not crushing women so much as bleeding them out.

Although representation of female students at top film schools is now roughly equal in terms of gender parity—women represent 51 percent of graduate students at NYU's School of the Arts and 46 percent at USC's School of Cinematic Arts—that does not mean that women's experience at those schools is the same as their male peers'.[14] From the moment they matriculate, the subtle and less-subtle messaging to women is that they are not destined to be directors and that their perspectives are less valuable.

A female filmmaker was sent a list of one hundred "films-you-must-see" before arriving at a top film school. Almost every single one was directed by a white man. She had seen almost none of them, and as she watched that summer, the films said nothing to her. Throughout her film school career, her male classmates would wax lyrical about the genius of these movies, making her feel like an unsophisticated philistine because she didn't "understand" them.

In a program at a different top film school, an iconic white male director came to guest-teach. By chance on that day, most of the women happened to sit on one side of the room and the men on the other. The visiting director addressed his entire lecture to the men's side. "It was extreme to the point that even the guys noticed," a female student recalled to me. One male student who made a particular connection in the room that day later became that same iconic director's assistant on his next movie and went on to co-write one of his Oscar-winning films.

Male students generally leave film school with their worldviews and dreams validated and reinforced. They are welcomed, heard, understood, and seen. This gives them confidence and a sense of entitlement that allows them to assuredly step out into the industry. Female students, by contrast, generally leave film school deflated, demoralized, and confused; feeling a fundamental dissonance with the work they have been told to venerate; and lacking role models. Director and producer Janet Grillo entered film school "on fire to write and direct my own stories." Three years later, she says, "I felt irrelevant."

While roughly half of film school graduates are female, they make up only 18 percent of directors for micro-budget features (those with budgets of less than $500,000).[15] Shockingly, that indicates that the single biggest drop-off of women from the film industry—more than 64 percent—is happening between the end of film school and the making of a first, small-scale feature film.* Since that 18 percent includes women like me, who did *not* attend film school, we can conclude that even more women are dropping out of the industry immediately post–film school than those percentages suggest.

While a general post–film school sense of demoralization and irrelevance somewhat helps explain those numbers, we must dig deeper still to find out why such a huge number of women are dropping out of the industry before even making their first micro-budget feature film.

There are many statistics and much anecdotal evidence across industries suggesting that a "confidence gap" exists among women, such that they resist putting themselves forward. This argument lays a lot of blame at the feet of women themselves for the chronic lack of progress in the women's advancement in the workplace.

---

* Often a first career step post-school.

Among these studies is a 2014 Hewlett Packard internal report demonstrating that the average woman would only apply to a hypothetical job if she met 90–100 percent of the stated criteria, where the average man would apply if he met 60 percent of the criteria.[16]

Brenda Major, a social psychologist at the University of California at Santa Barbara who studies self-perception, has found that men consistently overestimate their abilities to complete tasks, while women underestimate. She found that the actual performance of tasks did not differ across genders.

This phenomenon is so prevalent that Columbia Business School has coined the term "honest overconfidence" to explain men's blithe and unwarranted self-belief. Their research shows, specifically, that men on average rate their own performance to have been 30 percent better than it actually was.[17]

These studies have been often cited as reasons why this post–film school drop-off rate, as well as an overall lack of women's progress in the course of their film careers, occurs.

The USC Annenberg Inclusion Initiative revealed that, even as of 2018, only 22 percent of the feature films *submitted* to Sundance are directed by women.[18] That could easily be explained away by the fact that it's harder for women to get their films made in the first place, and that there is a huge barrier to entry on getting a film made at all. The problem with this as a sole explanation is that these lower submission rates also seem to apply to screenplays. One interviewee who works on the submissions team of the Nicholls Screenwriting Awards told me that their submission rates show similar gender breakdowns—with women only submitting around one-quarter of all scripts. This discrepancy has a less clear barrier-to-entry justification, given that to enter the Nicholls competition, you only need a screenplay and a $45 submission fee.

Indeed, learning that the largest drop-off point for female filmmakers is prior to entering even the micro-budget film space gave even me pause. Because while, yes, there are certain barriers to making a micro-budget feature, the largely democratic nature of financing by crowdfunding does suggest that women themselves are opting out of taking this first career step and/or are getting stalled in making short films for too many years and never make it to feature-land.

Annie Doona, chair of Screen Ireland, formerly the Irish Film Board, conducted an exit survey of graduates of IADT National Film School in Ireland to try to figure out why a similar phenomenon was happening there. The council asked graduating seniors what their plans were after graduation. "Almost universally, the boys said, 'I have a production company, and I'm going to make movies.' We'd ask them what that meant, and it eventually emerged that their 'production company' was a laptop in their mother's basement. The girls almost all said, 'Well, I'm going to try and do X.' I wanted to shout at them, 'No! You have a production company!'"

This confidence-gap theory—as widespread as it has been—has certainly led to a lot of women blaming themselves for their lack of career success.

Forty-four percent of women in the *New Female Tribes* survey—a five-year survey of over eight thousand women across nineteen countries on subjects ranging from their religious beliefs to their careers and identities—cited themselves as a barrier to their own achievements, with 27 percent pointing specifically to their insecurities as a barrier.[19]

Almost every woman I spoke with has dedicated considerable energy to divining some internal fault—often citing a lack of confidence—as the reason for her lack of professional progress.

I will admit that I have wavered myself throughout the course of this research and writing process over to what extent our unquestionably invaded brains and societally programmed self-doubt cause us to hold ourselves back.

After all is said and done, however, I have come to the conclusion that, while I do think that a certain amount of "opting out" occurs, the amount of weight put on that argument is a particularly sophisticated form of gaslighting, which neatly takes the onus of change off the people who sit atop the system and hold the actual power and puts it instead onto the victims of that system. There is also the significant reality that white men probably arrive at the conclusion that they can try something they are only moderately knowledgeable about and good at and will be met with support and success *because that has been their experience.* Women, by contrast, have learned through hard knocks that they *will not* get the job/financing/opportunity unless they are three times better prepared than their white, male counterparts. Their ensuing reticence to put themselves up for jobs and opportunities unless they are almost ridiculously well prepared is an entirely rational response to what is most likely to occur.

Setting that argument aside, then, let's look at the external factors impacting the careers of women behind the camera.

Discriminatory hiring practices don't start in the upper echelons of the industry; they exist at every level. Though I have not been able to find adequate research on this subject, anecdotal evidence suggests that female film school graduates have a far harder time than their male peers acquiring even the lowest-level entry jobs in the industry, meaning that from day one, they have less access, build fewer connections, and have a less stable income, resulting in less time and space to work on their own artistic endeavors.

A lack of access to financing for those artistic endeavors hit women seeking to make films especially hard since the financial threshold for making a film is so high compared to making, say, a painting, which can be produced for the cost of a canvas, a brush, paints, and your time.

Studies indicate that no matter the amount, no matter the industry, women are less likely to be given money, either as an investment or a donation.[20] So raising even modest amounts for a first micro-budget feature film is a more difficult task for women than it is for men.

As women move on to their second, slightly-bigger-budget films or if they aim high out of the gate (say, $500,000 or more), getting a big-name actor attached to their project becomes a crucial step. This is extremely difficult for any filmmaker who isn't already Inside (this is one reason familial industry connections give early career filmmakers a major leg up). Unless you happen to be friends with a famous actor, you are almost entirely reliant on the actor's agent to pass along the project. Agents, who make a living off the 10 percent commissions they take from their clients' fees, are structurally disinclined to fill up their clients' schedules with projects that don't pay well—even if those actors would actually *love* to be sinking their teeth into meatier, indie-leaning roles— and they frequently decide not to even pass along the offer of a project to the actor if the project is deemed too small or unworthy. Agents would much rather keep their client's schedule open in case Marvel calls than take a chance on an unknown director. A filmmaker's career can quickly be made, however, when an agent—hearing that some rising wunderkind director is going to be the next Spielberg—does decide to take precisely that chance.

Because these actor-attachment deals happen behind closed doors, there has been no hard research done on them, but I did a lot of digging and, anecdotally at least, it seems clear that agents are far less likely to attach their high-profile clients to projects with female directors.

In just one example, Rachel Feldman, an accomplished director with a long list of credits in one-hour drama television episodes, as well as made-for-television movies, wrote a powerful, Athena List–winning, Oscar bait-y script, but she has repeatedly received "passes" on the project from A-list actresses (and/or their agents) because they considered her a "TV director" or worse, a "first-time director." Conversely, I can cite dozens of examples of A-list actors who signed on to star in a male director's first feature film—a director who had maybe directed a short but not, notably, tens of hours of television—because the industry had decided that he was a rising male genius. The poster boy for this is Justin Zackham, who in 2013 received the opportunity to make his feature film directorial debut, *The Big Wedding*, which starred no less than Robert De Niro, Diane Keaton, Susan Sarandon, Robin Williams, Katherine Heigl, Topher Grace, and Amanda Seyfried.[21]

Of course, some women, like me, manage to overcome these hurdles to make our micro-budget and/or larger-than-micro-budget indie films. We battle through smaller budgets. By hook or by crook we sometimes even attach name actors. But as discussed, once we turn to film festivals, the key conduit to the "system" of the industry, we run into the reality that US festivals screened nearly twice as many documentary films with male directors as female in 2017–2018, and high-profile US festivals screened three times as many narrative (fiction) feature films directed by men as women in the same period.[22]

As several examples in the last chapter demonstrated, à la Ava Du-Vernay, even if you do manage to get into one of the top film festivals and win a major award, that's no guarantee that your phone will start ringing. For those seeking to be hired by Hollywood, then, whatever your festival success may or not may be, you are still left trying to get an agent.

There is no single guilty party for the systematic exclusion of women from film, but no matter what route my research took, all roads led eventually to talent agencies. For better or worse, fair or unfair, as the uber-powerful gatekeepers of Hollywood, a great deal of responsibility for the hiring disparity lies at their feet. I see four primary mechanisms by which they are contributing to the problem.

#1) AGENCIES ARE INSTITUTIONS MADE UP OF WHITE MEN. Of the partners running the dominant talent agencies, 96.7 percent are white, as are 90.8 percent of the agents brokering deals. Of the partners running the dominant talent agencies, 71.4 percent of partners were male and 68.1 percent of agents are male.[23]

These agents' biases—unconscious or otherwise—become especially pronounced when they are evaluating something as subjective as the relative commercial and artistic value of a story.

Jessica Hinds, creator of the Meditative Writing method, has studied the science behind how humans respond to art and stories. She explains that while it is possible to objectively assess to some degree how talented an artist is, what we respond to when we watch or read something is far more than talent, or even technique, but is how deeply it resonates with our own personal unconscious "themes," created by "the emotional wounds" of our lives. For instance, let's say an agent has a particularly complicated relationship with his successful father and has spent much of his life feeling inadequate in comparison. When this agent reads a script that specifically plumbs the depths of a central character wrestling with a painful father-son relationship, the experience of reading that script is going to hit an emotional theme for him. If the script is truly terribly written, the agent may not like it, even if it does hit on one of his "themes." But if the script is reasonably good, the agent is likely to think it's fantastic, because it brought on such a depth of feeling in him.

Now imagine that same agent reading a script about a woman's psychological experience of being pregnant and having to emotionally wrestle with the deeply complicated identity issues associated with motherhood. Let's imagine that this agent is not married, perhaps, has spent no substantial time at all with pregnant women, and has no emotional wounds tied to issues of identity around parenthood. That script is not going to tap into his thematic inner life. He is going to evaluate that script far more critically from a craft perspective. And even if it is really, really well written, there is still a possibility that the agent will get to the end of it and think, *Well, it's well-written, but it just doesn't feel like it's going to have much emotional resonance for people.**

I am not suggesting that men only resonate with stories that are written by men and women only resonate with those written by women. But I am saying that if you have walked through the world as a white man for however many decades, you are far more likely to have emotional resonance or share themes with stories written by other white men and to discount as less universally resonant stories by people whose experience of the world are totally different from your own.

#2) THE AGENCIES ARE ALL POWERFUL. Agencies, as discussed, help determine which well-known talent signs on to which film, which in turn informs which films at all levels get financed and distributed. They are also the control valve by which all "above-the-line" creatives—directors, writers, actors, and producers—are plucked from the masses and put up for jobs.

#3) THE AGENCIES HAVE A CLOSED (AND HIGHLY UNUSUAL) HIRING PROCESS. The process by which studios look for writers, directors, and producers to hire is closed, based heavily on the Inside/Outside game, and relies on an intel-gathering, gossip-ridden set of relationships, rather than on any sort of normal, transparent hiring process that might give openings to as-yet-undiscovered talent.

#4) THE AGENCIES COULD "FIND THE WOMEN" BUT ARE NOT DOING THE WORK TO DO SO. There is a favorite new excuse that has emerged now that there is some awareness that perhaps Hollywood should be representing/hiring more women, which is that they would love to but simply can't "find any." To those of us women screaming to be found, this excuse is as maddening as it is nonsensical. Agents are theoretically the people *specifically designed* to "find" new talent of all kinds. I managed to get one to speak to me off the record about the process of how an agent/agency decides to sign a new client. I asked the agent to describe a typical set of circumstances under which a new client would be signed.

---

* This is a reason women are *constantly* given as to why their script can't be bought/movie can't be made.

AGENT: Well, definitely if the person gets hired for a studio job, every agent in town will be trying to snatch them up.*

ME: Okay . . . what else?

AGENT: We attend film festivals and scout for talent there.

ME: Oh, great! Okay, so I'm assuming you don't mean *all* film festivals.

AGENT: No, no. Just the big ones.

ME: Right, okay. So what would you consider the "big ones"? Toronto International Film Festival, obviously.

AGENT: Yep.

ME: Sundance?

AGENT: Yes.

ME: Telluride?

AGENT: Yep.

ME: Tribeca?

AGENT: Yep.

ME: SXSW, obviously.

AGENT: Well . . . one of my colleagues was complaining the other day about whether or not we really need to bother covering SXSW.

ME: . . .

The undisputed top five "most prestigious" film festivals in North America are TIFF, Telluride, Sundance, Tribeca, and SXSW. Getting into one of these festivals—particularly if your movie does not star Brad Pitt and you are not somehow already Inside—is roughly akin to your chances of swiping left and having Ryan Gosling pop up on your dating app. Once again, the chances of getting into one of these if you are a woman is even worse than for the average male filmmaker.

ME: Okay, so you have to get your film into one of the top *four* film festivals?

AGENT: Yeah, but realistically, most of my colleagues don't give a shit about those festivals either. They really want clients who are already working for the studios.

---

* How anyone would get a studio job without an agent or somehow being Inside already (generally via familial connections) is mystifying and improbable.

ME: (my limbs start to feel numb and very heavy) Right. Okay. So,
   are there any other ways you can get the attention of an agency?
AGENT: Well, if multiple people* are calling us about you,
   that's good.
ME: Uh-huh . . .
AGENT: Basically, you need a certain tipping-point amount of buzz.
ME: (perking up slightly) Oh, okay! What constitutes buzz?

We explore this question for a while and eventually work out that, practically speaking, "buzz" means some combination of the following:

1. Awards (from a top film festival, or from one of the top film schools or studio programs)
2. Having your film play at a major film festival
3. Selling something to a studio

All of these are substantially less likely to happen if you are a woman.

AGENT: The truth is, though, that very few agents want to take on developmental clients anyway. It's really only young agents looking to build up their rosters who do that.
ME: What's considered to be a developmental client?
AGENT: Well, I'll give you an example of one. There's a [male] filmmaker that we discovered out of SXSW. One of the biggest studios is developing his third feature. He's up for a ton of studio writing jobs. He's developmental.
ME: (has minor stroke) At what point will a writer be considered not developmental?
AGENT: When he's consistently booking writing jobs with the studios.

Hearing this firsthand confirmed my experience and the experience of nearly every woman I interviewed for this book.

---

* The agent doesn't, of course, mean "people" in the traditional sense of the word but rather means Inside People, who, again, are outstandingly hard to get the notice of unless you are related to them or are already Inside. This is particularly the case if you are a woman.

Worse, from those who have spoken to me off the record, it's clear that, even when women are represented by agencies, they are rarely put on the hiring lists. One television series centering on female characters with a female showrunner received a short list of potential directors from the agencies, only to find that there was not a single woman on the list. The showrunner had to go back to the agencies and demand that they come back with at least some female names.

#5) THE AGENCIES HAVE A MULTI-HYPHENATE PROBLEM. Stymied, as so many women are, in their efforts to achieve a fruitful career, many of us have evolved in our approach and our dream to take on more than one film-related job. I wanted to be an actress, but nobody was casting me in roles I was interested in, so I started writing. A person outside the industry might consider this plucky, even smart. The catch, however, is that, being a multi-hyphenate can make it substantively harder to get signed by an agency.

Within agencies, there are different agents for each type of representation that a creative who is a multi-hyphenate might need. One department handles actors, another handles TV writers, another handles screenwriters (for film), another handles producers, and so on. These are completely separate departments. There is generally one "point agent," but there is also a team covering the full range of the client's work. All representation is generally within the same agency.

Tina Fey, to use an example, has one agent who reps her as an actress, one as a screenwriter, one as a TV writer, one as a voice actress, one as a producer, one for acting in commercials, and one for speaking engagements. Because she's Tina Fey, her team of agents is at William Morris Endeavor.

If you are trying to get signed by an agency as someone who is only, say, a director, you need to win the buy-in of one agent who reps directors at the agency. Depending on how the agency functions, you might need to convince all the agents within the directing department of your worthiness. But what the agents in *other* departments within the agency think about you is immaterial to whether or not you will be signed.

But if you're a multi-hyphenate, you need buy-in from multiple departments before you can be signed. A directing agent might love your work and want to rep you. But if you're a director *and* a screenwriter, then a screenwriters' agent at the same agency has to love your scripts and also want to rep you. The more hyphenates you have, the more agents at the same agency you need to convince. And with each additional department, your chances of getting signed overall by the agency decrease.

Furthermore, if you are a multi-hyphenate, it is likely that your career trajectory has moved forward on all fronts, but on no one front very quickly.

For instance, take me and my career. Looking at the whole picture of me as an artist, there are quantifiable signs of success. But if you consider me only as an actress or only as a screenwriter, my career appears much less impressive, because I have been splitting my time across disciplines. My overall success means little to an agency, because each department wants to see big strides forward in its particular field. A great, great many women are similarly hamstrung by career choices that were initially necessary to get out of the gate.

Okay, but let's say you win the lottery: you are a woman, and you've somehow managed to get an agent, *and* that agent is actually putting you up to be considered for jobs. What happens then?

Well, then, a whole magical mystery tour of conscious and unconscious biases slam you in the face.

Studio hiring biases were a central theme in the ACLU's report on hiring discrimination in Hollywood, in which it was noted:

> Propelling this paucity [of female directors] is an industry-wide boys' network in which gender discrimination is often on overt display. The organization collected stories from 50 female directors who had reported being told by executives that a show was not "woman friendly"; learning that producers had repeatedly told agents "not to send women" for prospective jobs; or being informed at a meeting for a television job that "we already hired a woman this season."[24]

The characteristics that people in the film industry are used to seeing as authoritative and commanding play a subtle but powerful role in creating these hiring biases. As noted in a study by the Annenberg Inclusion Initiative, in which film industry leaders were asked to describe the attributes of a successful director, they consistently invoked "masculine-leaning language."[25] This is a classic example of a phenomenon known as "availability bias." That's the human tendency to think that examples of things that come readily to mind are more frequently occurring than is actually the case. For example, when researchers asked people whether there are more words in the English language that begin with the letter "k" or have the letter "k" as the third letter, participants universally said the former (since it's easier to think of those words), even though the latter is resoundingly the truth.[26] In the film world, availability bias provides a crippling barrier for young, aspiring female directors and filmmakers. Studio executives—usually men—take a longer, more forgiving look at filmmakers who remind them of successful filmmakers they can easily think of. This can be true no matter the level of preparation or experience. For example, a first-time male director may benefit from coming into a meeting with a studio executive dressed in a baseball cap, hoodie, and jeans precisely because that is what the executive is used to seeing in a director. (*My god, he reminds me exactly of Steven Spielberg when he was that age. I bet he's a genius.*)

But there aren't nearly as many positive frames of reference for studio executives to attach to female candidates. If a woman filmmaker comes in dressed like a young Spielberg, the reaction is not the same. (*God, what a slob. She couldn't even put in the effort to get dressed up for this big meeting.*) Or maybe she looks great, wearing a nice skirt and blouse, and having gone to a lot of trouble to make herself look professional and attractive. That's no good either because, on a conscious or unconscious level, the executive can't remember ever meeting anyone who looked like her who then went on to be successful. (*She's trying sooo hard to impress me. She must not be that talented. Geniuses never dress up.*)

These kinds of scenarios play out routinely. There have been so few successful female filmmakers in positions of power, that there is hardly anybody high up Inside available to see themselves in us or to recognize us "as young versions of."

These biases hit women of color and trans women even harder, since they are even further from the usual frame of reference. An industry analysis conducted by ReFrame concluded, "Interviewers often select candidates similar to themselves in background, education, race, and gender."[27]

Visibly disabled women are perhaps at the greatest disadvantage here. Jenni Gold, who is the *only visibly disabled female director in the*

Directors Guild of America (there is also one visibly disabled male director), says that producers and executives consistently assume she won't
be able to keep up, given that she is in a wheelchair. Jenni says, "They
tell me, 'Set is fast-paced. You're going to get tired.' I say, 'Tired?! I'm not
even standing up!'" Jenni may joke, but the hurdles these biases create
are both real and serious.

We know that women are likely to come to these interviews with
fewer industry-recognized credentials on their resume due to further-
down-the-ladder hiring biases. When you combine that with a body
of evidence across industries that male candidates are judged based on
potential where female candidates are judged based on experience, the
result is that even those women lucky enough to get into an interview
room at all enter it at an extreme disadvantage.[28]

These biases persist even in the face of substantial evidence that hiring women into creative roles produces higher financial returns, something we'll dive properly into in later chapters.

As Stephan Paternot, co-founder and CEO of Slated, an online film
finance marketplace, says, "That's the institutional bias, that you've somehow been taught as you've risen through the ranks in the studio that it's
a safer bet to go with a man. That's the trust gap. The women have given
you better financial results, yet your gut's still telling you to give them
less money to work with."[29]

Until we get a critical mass of successful and powerful women in the
upper ranks or train executives to break this bias, we will be left with an
industry chock-full of white men that continually replicates itself.

One hurdle in overcoming these conscious and unconscious biases
is that the gatekeepers—even those who say they genuinely support
and believe in the idea of hiring more women—tend to get panicky, feel
threatened, and/or become affronted at the suggestion that discrimination exists at all, much less that they themselves might be contributing
to the problem.

The specter of past discrimination can threaten male creatives who
have benefited from and succeeded within the current system, because
it calls into question their hitherto unimpeachable status as unequivocal
geniuses.

As William Friedkin, the (old, white, male) director of *The Exorcist*,
recently raged, "I've been in Hollywood for 50 years and I have never met

an executive of a TV or movie company, or a talent agency, that was prejudiced against people of different colors or against women. I've never met anyone. . . . I know it's an open playing field. . . . Wherever women can compete, they get jobs."*[30]

People who make it in Hollywood have generally worked themselves mercilessly to get where they are. That does not mean it is not harder (indeed, nearly impossible) for a woman to achieve the career that a white man has.

For studio executives, the request to spend time and energy dismantling biases or finding/hiring women candidates only adds to the fear and panic they generally feel.

As legendary screenwriter William Goldman (*Butch Cassidy and the Sundance Kid, All the President's Men*) once famously wrote, like absolutely everyone in Hollywood, studio executives wake up every morning utterly terrified of losing their jobs.[31] Film producer Jack Lechner, a former studio executive himself, explained this to me:

> The Pit of Fear has always been there. . . . Being a studio executive has always been an insanely great job and one that is very easy to lose. The *only* way you lose it is by saying "yes" to something that flops. Perversely, no one ever loses their job by saying no to something that *succeeds*. But the fear has gotten worse over time, as studios become more corporatized and as the studio film industry becomes more and more geared towards giant tentpoles and nothing else.

So, like agents, studio executives are highly disincentivized to try anything new—or at least to try anything that isn't generally agreed upon in their fear-based, risk-averse studio culture to be the smart way of doing things. If you go rogue and do something weird like hire a female director, and she fails, you are likely to get thrown Outside. It is a culture that specifically breeds "institutional knowledge" and leaves out voices and whole communities that would enrich it.

. . . .

---

* I would like to use this opportunity to get a personal "Go fuck yourself" to William Friedkin down in print.

As pressure has mounted on the studios to address their "women is-sues," executives have become increasingly spooked about how to hire women if they have to. The most comfortable move for them under the circumstances is often to hire women who have already made it Inside via some other Hollywood job and ask them if *they* would like to become a director. Because the executives already know these women, have had good experiences with them as fellow humans, and don't have to worry about getting tainted by anyone from Outside, this apparently seems like the least horrible version of being pressured into hiring female directors. The result is that the executives frequently hire actresses or producers for the biggest and most high-profile directing jobs. *Look, we finally hired a woman to direct this blockbuster.*

Meanwhile, legions of actually trained female directors, who have been to film school and made independent films, can't so much as get an interview for the same studio film directing jobs.

The studio executives then subsequently complain privately about women's lack of training and craft as directors. This is the equivalent of hiring a roofer to fix your sink and then blaming the plumbers that your drain is still clogged.

The studios'/networks' other big move to try to get people to stop yelling at them about their lack of hiring women and people of color are "diversity programs." These most often take the shape of some kind of "training program," which is supposed to be a feeder pipeline for women and other historically underrepresented voices to then get actual paying jobs. In reality, these almost always end up being time-killing dead ends for directors wanting careers, as there are notoriously few directors who are hired out of these programs.

The most expeditious way out of the haven't-had-experience-therefore-can't-get-hired-to-gain-experience catch-22 for any film-maker is to have a powerful mentor or advocate vouch for you, as Spielberg did to get Colin Trevorrow a job directing the $150 million *Jurassic World* in 2015, though Trevorrow had only previously directed the $750,000 indie feature *Safety Not Guaranteed*.[32]

The problem here, once again, is that there are simply not enough women who have made it into powerful enough positions of the film industry to recognize themselves in us lower-level women and advocate for us in this way.

For the few women who have made it into these positions, they are inundated with requests for advocacy and mentorship by the desperate sea of women below them. They are asked to give huge amounts of their time and resources to help other women, which can take focus, time, and resources away from their own careers, or they are lambasted if they are perceived as not doing an adequate job of lifting women up the ladder behind them.

There is a frequent feeling that women in power are, in fact, working against other women. An oft-cited data point shows that female studio executives have, on average, a worse track record of hiring female directors than male executives.[33] Indeed, there was no shortage of stories that cropped up during my interviews of young women who got stepped on, thrown under the bus, or outright sabotaged by women above them on the ladder.

It must be acknowledged that a real culture of scarcity for women within the industry has resulted in some less-than-stellar behavior, particularly within the generations preceding the Millennials. *There is only one seat for a woman at this table, so if you get it, I do not.* But it is important to note that alongside such stories of women hurting women is the fact that almost every key creative decision an executive makes must be then signed off on by layers of other executives, studio heads, and chairpeople of the board. Those roles are very rarely held by women—only two of the chairs of major executive film teams in 2019 were women.[34] As a result, even if a female executive wants to hire a female director, her decision must be approved by those above her, who are likely white men and who may be more likely to shoot down *her* proposal of a female director than if a male executive had suggested the same. *Oh boy, Wanda's getting all radical and feminist again.* Women in power face enormous expectations and are disproportionately tasked with helping other women, all the while protecting and navigating the professional politics of their own ascension.

For female directors fortunate enough to be working, they can expect the average production budget for their film to be smaller than those of their male peers. Film budgets shrink by 20 percent when a woman has the starring role due to untrue but enduring industry "common knowledge" that "no one wants to see films about women."[35] Since female directors are more likely to either choose or be given films with female leading characters, they disproportionately suffer from these smaller budgets that are assigned to such films.

Not only is it harder to carry out your creative vision as a director when you have fewer resources, but these smaller budgets have led to a couple of key misperceptions. The first is that that women are only equipped to direct dramas and maybe comedy and so are rarely hired for lucrative genres, such as action films or thrillers. "Males, in contrast, work across all genres."[36] The reality is that there is no substantiating evidence that there is any difference in the proportion of women versus men who choose to direct drama versus other genres at the indie film level. The majority of all indie films are dramas, because that's the genre you can most easily make work when you're dealing with tiny budgets.

The second misperception is that women only like to direct small, intimate films. Again, this is circumstance-driven more than anything else—if you have a limited budget, the only real option available to you is to make small, intimate films. You can't make *Star Wars* on a million bucks.

Female directors are then constantly handed the extra baggage of having to go out of their way to disprove these entrenched misperceptions in their work. Jenni Gold, who feels the weight of having to bust stereotypes of women and of women in wheelchairs, chose to direct an action film for her first feature. "I wanted to prove that anywhere a dolly can go, I can go. I blew stuff up. I loved blowing stuff up!"

Of course, because she's a woman and a woman in a wheelchair, she had to blow stuff up with far less money. "I just once want a real budget," Jenni told me. "It's like being told, okay, you and this guy are going to have to each make a chair. And he's going to have cushions and plywood and steel, and you're going to have a toothpick. Then those chairs get judged against one another."

When women are hired into positions of leadership on set or on a production, they often have to fight to command the respect from typically majority-male crews.

Director Jaclyn Gramigna showed up on the set of a film and a production assistant walked up to her and said, "Oh, good. I'm glad you're here. I'm going to get the director a coffee. Can you watch the van?" Except that Jaclyn, in spite of being a woman, was the director of the film, not, as he assumed, another production assistant.

One rising star female film producer—we'll call her Bee—was working with a special effects professional on a film, and the objects he was creating were consistently of lesser quality than she'd requested. Bee called him up and asked, "Why are you sending us objects that are subpar?"

"Excuse me, but how many films have you made?" he shot back.

"Five films. All of them have been nominated for Independent Spirit Awards and one of them won one of the top film festivals in the world."

The props came back better after that.

These scenarios are so prevalent that an entire Tumblr account has been dedicated to it. If you ever want to spend a couple of hours on something that is equally hysterical and soul-crushing, visit shitpeople-saytowomendirectors.tumblr.com.

Ava DuVernay, famously, when she (finally) got her first studio job directing *Selma*, anticipated this problem—which is compounded for a woman of color. She took each one of her crew members out for coffee prior to the shoot and let them know who was boss.[37] She didn't have any problems, such as lack of respect or being mistaken for a PA, but has said she is 100 percent sure she would have had she not taken that extra step.

The work of filmmaking is difficult and strenuous enough without the added obstacle of having to constantly prove your authority and worth on your own set. Or not getting credit for work you've done, as also frequently happens to women in film, as in other industries. Or getting fewer resources than a man would.

Fueling all of this discrimination is the film industry's fetishization of the male "genius" auteur filmmaker. A prime example of this mythic status is George Lucas, without question one of Hollywood's Boy Wonder geniuses.[38] In 1977, however, before he was *George Lucas*, he invited some friends over to watch a rough cut of the first *Star Wars* film. Brian de Palma, one of the friends and fellow filmmakers present, according to Steven Spielberg, who was also present, reportedly called the film "nonsense" and said it didn't make any sense. Hearing the criticism,

Lucas hired de Palma and screenwriter Jay Cox to rewrite the entire opening crawl, asking them to please help him make sense of the story. Even more crucially, Lucas's then-wife Marcia Lucas, Richard Chew, and Paul Hirsch—all of whom were editors for the film—heavily reworked the film in post-production to the extent of cutting most of the first half, inserting basic plot points,* and reordering dialogue within scenes to create completely different meanings. That iconic male classic, *Star Wars*, was saved in the edit, primarily by a woman most people have never heard of. None of this is a secret. Lucas's entire original cut of the film is available on YouTube, along with some great commentaries and mash-ups showing the differences between the original and eventually released versions.

Hollywood also knows this—and has acknowledged it. In a sly nod, the Academy of Motion Picture Arts and Sciences gave Marcia and Paul the Best Editing Oscar for the film, while snubbing Lucas for Best Director. Yet Lucas is the one who gets the lone male genius auteur label.[†]

None of Lucas's work has ever been done alone. No filmmaker does it alone. And those considered to be the best filmmakers in the world are so, in part, because they surround themselves with the best teams of people. Every film is the sum total of a collaboration, many times the collaboration of a hundred artists or more,[‡] and it is virtually impossible to know, when watching the end product, which of those artists was responsible for what. As the lead voice for how a film comes together and as the person in charge on set, a director's role is absolutely crucial. But the final product of their work is not based on solitary effort. Neither is their success or failure.

Where this becomes particularly problematic is that women do not benefit from the genius myth. When a woman's film succeeds, it's because of the team effort, and a female director is frequently replaced on the sequels since her work isn't seen as all that crucial. When her film fails, however, the failure is hers alone.

---

* In the original script and cut of the film, the Death Star does not *ever* threaten to destroy the rebel base and there are, therefore, no stakes whatsoever for the climax of the film.
† I am not going after Lucas specifically on this. He is only one in an industry riddled with examples of "genius male auteurs."
‡ Far more than that on studio films.

There's a common sort-of joke about the existence of a "director jail," the consequence of a "one strike and yer out" policy that is applied only to women. In the film world, this means that if you make one bad, non-money-making, or even just, for whatever reason, discredited film, you never get hired again, no matter how many fantastic and financially successful films you've made in the past. In television, this means having, by some vague metric, a "bad" time on an episode and then never getting hired back for that show (or, sometimes, any show).

Elaine May (after *Ishtar*, 1987), Penelope Spheeris (after *Wayne's World*, 1992, in spite of enormous commercial success), Amy Heckerling (after *Clueless*, 1995, in spite of enormous commercial success), Mimi Leder (after *Pay It Forward*, 2000), Sharon Maguire (after *Bridget Jones's Diary*, 2001, in spite of enormous commercial success), Betty Thomas (after *I Spy*, 2002), Karyn Kusama (after *Aeon Flux*, 2005), Catherine Hardwicke (after *Twilight*, 2008, in spite of enormous commercial success), Lexi Alexander (after *Punisher: War Zone*, 2008), and Sam Taylor-Johnson (after *50 Shades of Grey*, 2015, in spite of enormous commercial success) are just a few examples of women who have been sent to director jail.

The excuse for sending women to director jail, to not rehiring them, to firing them off movies in the first place, is almost always that she is "crazy," "difficult," or "impossible to work with." This is not so far flung from the days of sending women to their beds for being perceived as hysterical and it is no less powerful. As with the archetypal Cassandra, with that one word "crazy," we remove her ability to tell the truth to the world.

Catherine Hardwicke describes running into this wall after directing the massively successful (and financially lucrative) *Twilight*. "My agent had sent me some neat scripts that I loved," she remembers. "One of them was a very intense family drama kind of thing, very gritty. Of course, that's not like *Twilight*, but it is like *Thirteen*, which went all the way to the Academy Awards. But they wouldn't even let me have an interview. They would not even meet me. They just flat-out said, No, we think a guy is going to direct this movie. So the reality hits you pretty hard, pretty fast. At the time I didn't understand when people were dinging me for being, whatever, emotional or difficult," Hardwicke says, referencing a *Deadline Hollywood* report that quoted sources who called her "irrational" and unfit to direct the franchise's second film, *New Moon*. "Yet they're praising all the male directors I've worked for being passionate and visionary and sticking to their guns, fighting for what they want. But a woman is emotional, difficult, bitchy, whatever. I didn't know those code words and I didn't know they were used pervasively, and so I just took them personally."[39]

Indeed, given the reverentially thrilled nature with which most filmmakers talk about the abuse director Stanley Kubrick put Shelley Duvall through during the making of *The Shining*[40] to elicit a great performance; the fact that Quentin Tarantino almost smothered and maimed/killed Uma Thurman while filming *Kill Bill*[41] and still directs a movie a year or more; that Roman Polanski and Woody Allen, both of whom face credible allegations of sexual predation, are still getting not only financing for their movies but also Oscar nominations, while Hardwicke and countless other female directors are labeled "difficult" or "crazy" for fighting for their creative visions while not assaulting, maiming, or psychologically brutalizing anyone does indeed suggest that the scales may somewhat be weighted.

In an industry where, as Bat-Sheva Guez says, "half the time hiring decisions come down to likeability, and the people making those hiring decisions are almost always men," this double-standard view of behavior means that women have to consciously and precisely hone their personalities and behavior to a razor-thin and generally unwinnable standard. This can be particularly challenging for black women. Filmmaker Gabrielle Hawkins told me that she has to constantly remain vigilant about her tone and way of speaking while on set, because of being a woman, being African American, and looking younger than she is. "I know that if I am speaking too passionately that I will be viewed as emotional and ignored. There have been many times when I worked very well on set but maybe didn't check myself in terms of speech, and I wasn't hired back."

We all understand that the stakes are high. Especially at the studio level, executives, producers, and financiers hand over millions of dollars (now often hundreds of millions of dollars) to a team, helmed by the director, and have to trust, frequently through a frighteningly messy process, that something watchable and saleable will emerge on the other side. In many ways, subscribing to the male genius theory allows executives to sleep at night. Except that it's men who benefit from this trust time and time again. And the men who are considered geniuses get this trust even when their movies are falling apart. For every James Cameron, whose *Titanic* went on to phenomenal success after running colossally over budget,* there are films like *Waterworld, The 13th Warrior, The Adventures of Pluto Nash, R.I.P.D., I'll Do Anything, Elizabethtown*—all films directed by men—that went way over budget and flopped, and yet those directors continued to work. Directors like Max Landis, Guy Ritchie, Ron Howard, David Fincher, David O. Russell, Josh Trank, and Michael Bay continue to get films funded in spite of a lack of consistent financial returns.

The power of the "genius" label is so strong that even major, expensive, public failures are excused. Those filmmakers get second, third, and fourth chances. This is not a bad thing. It's a good thing. Great films are made by daring greatly, and if a filmmaker dares greatly with consistency, inevitably, sometimes those big swings will be big misses. It is wonderful that studios and financiers understand this. It is enormously problematic that they reserve this understanding for white men only.

The deification and elevation of male geniuses over everyone else hurts women at every turn: in raising financing, convincing agents to attach their high-profile talent to our projects, support and resources, before, during, and after production, and, as we're about to see, even after the film has finally been made.

One of the most depressing barriers is that even if and when women do finally, somehow, get their movies made, they are far less likely to receive distribution compared with their male counterparts and, when

---

* Peter Chernin, who was the chair of 20th Century Fox when it made *Titanic*, talks about the experience of making that film: "On my own gut level, the movie was fantastic. I remember saying to [James Cameron, the director] that first afternoon, 'The great thing about this movie is we have absolutely no idea if it's going to work. . . . And we're not going to know until we make it. I love it! Let's do it! So we green-lit what I believe at the time was the most expensive movie ever made. . . . The film was green-lit at a hundred ten million dollars. It went a hundred and fifteen million over budget. . . . I was considered the stupidest person in the history of Hollywood . . . Three months before we started principal photography, I was told that someone spiked the soup with LSD. That's not a normal call to get as head of a studio. . . . Everything that could go wrong went wrong, and yet I kept coming back to 'I love this movie.'" No executive has ever put that kind of blind faith behind a female director (Lynda Obst, *Sleepless in Hollywood: Tales from the New Abnormal in the Movie Business* [New York: Simon & Schuster, 2013].)

they do, it is likely to be on a smaller scale. Slated, the "leading online film finance marketplace," by its own description, analyzed nearly 1,600 feature films that were released on at least one screen theatrically in the US between 2010 and 2015. It concluded that there is an undeniable "trust gap" in how films by women versus men are treated in distribution.[42]

Deb Verhoeven, the associate dean of Engagement and Innovation at the University of Technology in Sydney, has extensively studied issues surrounding women in film. She looked at all feature films that were distributed in any fashion worldwide in 2016 and discovered that, although 16 percent of all those films were directed by women (which is, on its own, atrocious), of all the films that received a theatrical release, a mere 2 percent were directed by women.

Stephen Paternot at Slated found a similar trend in the US. Here, low-budget films (which he defines as under $25 million, though that's not really low-budget) by female directors were released on one-third as many screens as male directors' films were.[43]

USC Annenberg studied a thousand films released from 2007 to 2016 and, of all the distribution companies studied, not a single one consistently released even one film per year by a female director during that ten-year period.[44]

Even for those films that are released, anecdotal evidence heavily suggests that films by women do not receive adequate prints and advertising, or P&A, money. As filmmaker Jen McGowan says, "Marketing is where women's films get screwed all the time—we just get dumped."

Chances are that this is partly due to a biased perception on the part of the industry (and most of society) that stories by/about men are Big, Universal, and Important, while stories by and about women are small, personal, and irrelevant. But it is also due to the industry's use of outdated market testing of films.[45] Executives, who have already decided that these films have no audience, put no effort or give misdirected effort into determining who should be in a film's test audience. The film then tests poorly with audiences because the film's correct audience is not in the theater, at which point the executives' conclusion that the film has no audience is confirmed by the "data," and so they "dump" the film, releasing it on few if any screens and making the "smart" decision not to put any real advertising money behind it, since who wants to throw good money after bad?

Paternot wryly explains this quadruple bind for female filmmakers after his study of the numbers:

> Women are being given fewer films, and not only is that true, but they're having to make their movies with less money, so they're doing it with one arm tied behind their back. That effectively puts less production value up on the screen, meaning movies with a little narrower scope. And once the product is made, assuming it's as good despite having less money, it's then handicapped by being shown on two-thirds fewer screens. Those movies just don't get seen.[46]

The very, very lucky women whose films are released frequently have their content and stories routinely diminished, brushed off, and/or viciously attacked by critics, the media, and the industry alike.

Often an industry-wide dismissal begins with bad reviews by critics whose opinions hold outsized sway in determining the life of a film. Here again we run into the problem of an elite group of gatekeepers speaking from only the white, male perspective. A 2018 Annenberg Inclusion Initiative study determined that out of 19,559 reviews written in 2017 of Hollywood's one hundred highest-grossing movies, 77.8 percent were written by men and 82 percent were written by white critics. The study recommended that, in order for the critic pool to reflect the US population, outlets should strive for 30 percent white men, 30 percent white women, 20 percent men of color, and 20 percent women of color.[47] Currently, media outlets are not even in the ballpark of those figures. Recalling Jessica Hinds's science-based theory of unconscious "themes," is it any surprise that films by and about white men receive better, more positive reviews? Reviews, which then, in turn, elevate the cultural cachet and financial success of those movies? It is not.

Sometimes, women's films that are dismissed by critics and the industry do eventually find their audiences and make money, but they are still hung around their (female) director's neck as an albatross of failure. Karyn Kusama's 2009 film *Jennifer's Body* is a prime example of this. As Karyn recalls, "That film was hard for the studios to understand how to market." This was presumably because it was, as Karyn says, "specifically, adamantly, a movie for girls, about girls, by girls." Naturally, then, the studio executives decided to market it to teenage boys. "Some of the first trailers for that movie that were released in theaters didn't even tell you that Amanda Seyfried was in the movie. And she's the main character." Instead, the trailers focused on a secondary character, played by Megan Fox—who they decided was teenage-boy bait. The studios, hot on their beloved-teenage-boy-marketing-plan, set hopeful expectations for the film—projecting a $10 million opening weekend box office for a film made for $16 million. When it made $7 million on opening weekend—a take that, given that the film had been marketed to completely the wrong demographic, seems astonishingly high—the industry concluded that the film was a bomb. Over the next ten years, *Jennifer's Body*, rather amazingly, found its intended audience of teenage girls and has since become a cult classic, eventually grossing at least $40 million—a decent return on its budget.[48] But the episode still hurt Karyn's career. "It was pretty viciously taken down and defined as a 'failure.' I have often thought about what it would have meant to be a man in that situation. How would the story have been spun or recontextualized to protect me?"

It is essential to note that, while the factors I am outlining affect women poorly as a whole, if you are a woman of color, a trans woman, a disabled woman, a woman who is a member of the LGBTQ+ community, everything is disproportionately more difficult. As I've noted in the statistics throughout this book, both on and off screen, these women, even more so than white, cis, straight, able-bodied women, are getting hired at fractional rates compared to their presence in the US population.

This is not just happening by chance. This is the result of cultural and institutional biases and systems of oppression that exclude all women, but excludes those who stand at any additional intersection most of all, making every hurdle higher and tougher to clear. When we talk about women in film, it is dangerous to assume that, as things improve for women that they will improve in equal measure for all women. Historically and, it seems in this current, unsettling political moment, the opposite has been the case. What meager progress has been made for women overall has tended to disproportionately benefit white, cis, straight, and able-bodied women.

It would take another whole book to adequately investigate the nuances of issues facing each sub-demographic of women, but let us be clear here that, while there are issues that affect women as a whole, the harm and the effect is not equally distributed and is based sometimes solely—sometimes purely—on the intersection she's at.

If you are a rare and particularly stalwart woman and all of this has not forced you to leave the business altogether, it is likely that sooner or later something else will finally do it for you.

Every single woman over the age of fifty that I interviewed, like so many women in so many industries, had lost years or decades of her career to a life event of some kind, be it having children, a divorce, having to take care of an aging parent, a personal or family health crisis, or some combination thereof. Although my methodology was wholly unscientific, I did notice that in a striking number of interviews I did with female filmmakers of color, these absences from their careers were specifically the result of an incident of physical violence or injury, after which they were out of commission for a significant period of recovery. These incidents seemed to occur far more often than in the lives of their white, female counterparts. Whatever the reason for their absence, when the women returned, it was to find that the narrow opening they'd managed to create for themselves was closing or had closed permanently, sending them reeling back down the slope of career progression.

The lack of access to those not-totally-desirable but paying entry-level directing jobs squeezes out women over time, as do the lower wages when women do get work, and the substantially longer gaps of time between being able to get films financed. The combination often creates such financial hardship in female filmmakers' personal lives that a great many of us must eventually make the heartbreaking decision to leave the industry altogether in favor of a reasonable and regular paycheck. The creeping exhaustion of poverty doesn't exclusively knock women out of filmmaking careers, but it does hit women harder.

And if you make it through all that, if you are still, somehow, miraculously clinging to the side of the mountain through it all, you will, sooner than you might think, age out of your window of opportunity altogether. Because as much as Hollywood is sexist, it is also ageist to a strong degree. With everyone racing to find the newest Wonder Boy or Hot Young It Actress, Los Angeles is a young person's town. Although this ageism affects everyone, it is worse for women whose trajectories have already been stymied earlier on. Following is a table from USC Annenberg showing the age spread of directors in their sample size of a thousand of Hollywood's top films from 2007 to 2016:

Age spread of directors in 1,000 film sample size of Hollywood's top films from 2007–2016[49]

Age →	20s	30s	40s	50s	60s	70s	80s
Female	0	7	22	8	7	0	0
Male	8	257	467	230	69	21	6

Aside from the shocking disparity in general, it's notable that men get a substantial head start in their thirties (when their female colleagues are often taking time off to have children), which they can then build on in their forties and fifties and even sixties. Women on the other hand, get no real foothold until their forties and then get knocked out almost completely again come their fifties. A decade is not a long enough time to have a real career.

The reality, though, is that there is no magic age at which Hollywood considers you to be the right kind of woman to be a director. As Deborah Kampmeier says, "I was banging my head against the gender door for thirty years. Now that it's finally starting to open, the ageism door is slammed in my face. When exactly was my window?"

When I first learned the woeful statistics for women in film, I was shocked to find out that there were so few women behind the camera. After writing this book, I have come to feel that the truly astonishing thing is that there are any at all. The fact that there are is a tribute to the sheer tenacity, bravery, stubbornness, hard work, and hard-won luck of those women who have commando-crawled their way up the mountain.

But let's be clear, there is not a single woman in the film industry today or ever who has achieved the kind of career she would have had if she were a man. Not a single one of us.

CHAPTER 6

SONGS MY BROTHERS TAUGHT ME*

A persistent and damaging question, particularly now that the industry is slowly coming around to the idea that it may be important to put more women *in front* of the camera, is whether or not getting more women *behind* the camera, allowing them to tell stories themselves, actually matters at all.

The 2016 *Ghostbusters* reboot is a perfect example of this lukewarm gesture toward change. Hollywood decided it would throw us women a bone and remake a story conceived, written, directed, and made by men about men—but put women into it. Not a perfect antidote to sexism in cinema, but a step in the right direction. The reboot was then co-written by one man and one woman, produced by four women and eight men (a two-thirds majority of men), and directed by a man.

Wonder Woman, released in 2017, was widely heralded as the harbinger of real change for women in Hollywood because it starred a woman and was directed by Patty Jenkins. This *is* progress. But *Wonder Woman* was also written by four men and produced by eleven men and only two women.

The 2018 *Oceans 8* reboot with a leading female cast—again, based on a concept and series by and for men—was co-written by a man and a woman and produced by three women and six men (again, a two-thirds

---

* *Songs My Brothers Taught Me* (2015), dir. Chloé Zhao.

majority); it, too, had a male director. When it comes to roles on the producing and writing sides—where crucial decisions get made and new perspectives can emerge or be quashed—women are barely being let in the room.

As discussed in the previous chapter, the matter of who authors films is neither straightforward nor singular. Even when women are given directing opportunities, it's important to assess the larger context in which the voice and perspective of the film are being shaped. A director, particularly at the studio level, often has limited control over script decisions, casting, editing, or the final version of the film.

Making a woman the co-writer on a film seems to be an increasingly more common solution to the barrage of criticism about a lack of women in film for two reasons. The first is that the studio has the good PR look of having a woman's perspective on the team, but there's a man present to troubleshoot in case she gets too radical about "woman" things. The second is that because the film is then at the script stage, there's nothing a woman writer can do that won't have to get passed through several layers of studio executives (usually white men) before it ever arrives on set. How much damage could she do?

Don't get me wrong. We should take advancement where there is advancement. Let's just not be too doe-eyed about what's happening. There hasn't exactly been an unleashing of the female perspective in Hollywood, despite the occasional PR blitz about how great it is that things are finally changing. Women are still struggling to tell their own stories. The impact is consequential: for the artists themselves, for the films they never get to work on, and for movie audiences around the world.

The Artists

Does the gender of the director/writer/producer matter to the other artists participating in the process of making a movie?

This was a question that I posed to nearly everyone I interviewed for this book. The overwhelming answer was "Yes!"

On sets dominated by male authority with a majority-male crew surrounding one sole female director, that female director often has to go above and beyond in asserting herself to gain and maintain respect and control of her set. But when we look at instances where women are *actually* in charge and are *actually* allowed to construct the set, crew, and power structures to their own liking, the actors and crew are downright effervescent about the results.

Michelle Hurd recently had the experience of acting on a majority-female and non-white film set. "I have never felt more embraced as an artist in my life," she said. "You didn't have to walk in and prove yourself every time." She says there was a different baseline of respect and care for every artist participating in the process. She had that experience again on the set of the *Cagney & Lacy* reboot she starred in.* The show had two female showrunners, two female leads, and a 70 percent female crew. "Everyone said it was one of the most nurturing sets they'd ever been on," Hurd said.

Indian actress "Aastha" agrees and said, "My favorite experiences have been on sets where there has been a large female creative team and crew. I'm really not trying to be sexist here, but the women I've worked with thus far have made [filmmaking] a very inclusive experience. Your thoughts are welcome. You are a valued collaborator. There is a feeling that everyone is welcome at the table and valued. There is a basic trust that now that they've assembled the group they want, they will allow them a freedom to bring their best work."

Angela Lansbury, who finally worked with her first female director at the age of ninety-two, on PBS' *Little Women*, spoke glowingly of the experience working with director Vanessa Caswill. "[She] was quite wonderful in her ability to come to us actors—not in a loud way, from a distance she would come and whisper in our ears. And in that way, she was able to impart very subtle things that otherwise perhaps as a woman she might not have wanted to, for everybody to hear. But for the actor to hear it was delightful and I loved working that way with her." Lansbury draws a sharp contrast between that experience and her previous experiences. "I've worked with some of the loudest, shouty directors, believe me."[1]

As anyone who has worked in film knows, that loving, open, considerate, collaborative atmosphere on set is very, *very* far from the norm. Indeed, even those who have only read about the film industry from afar are likely to be familiar with the outrageously toxic atmosphere that normally reigns supreme—once again excused by the understanding that we

---

* The major network ultimately decided not to pick up the show after shooting the pilot, preferring to pick up the male-led, male-centric *Magnum P.I.* reboot instead.

are all to sacrifice our experience (and sometimes safety) in service of the Great Male Genius's Vision.

Don't get me wrong. There are women directors who cut their teeth, so to speak, on sets where belligerence, insensitivity, and borderline abuse are the standard. Some female directors bring that same energy to their own sets. It's what they know. It's what they believe conveys competence and power. And there are male directors who are every bit the warm, open collaborators that Michelle Hurd, Aastha, and Angela Lansbury experienced. What I'm saying is that productions and sets led by women and filled with women are, at the very least, not *worse* than those led by and filled with men. Perhaps, even, women have something to contribute to an expanded exploration of how sets can be run.

There are several factors that support the notion that women can, in fact, be incredibly effective leaders of sets and improve the overall experience for all connected artists.

For one thing, there is a lot of evidence that female directors, when given the power to do so, are far more likely to hire other women and people of color in their crews and casts, thus creating an environment with a sea of diverse and inclusive perspectives, rather than the almost universally white and male sets usually selected by white male directors.[2] Evidence also exists showing that, as a general rule, diverse groups of people make stronger decisions with better outcomes than do homogenous groups.[3]

Further, brain science can explain actors' experiences that many majority-female sets engender a more supportive and collaborative creative experience than the everyone-bow-down-to-my-genius vibe of many male sets. Testosterone—more present in most male brains—has been linked to an inability to see other people's points of view, as well as encouraging a focus on demonstrating power.[4]

That idea pretty closely matches my own experience of being on majority-male sets. I'm sure that I have, at some point, been on a set where the male director didn't get into a massive multiday (if not for the entire shoot) penis war with the (male) cinematographer, one of the (male) producers, or some other (male) department head, inevitably resulting in the loss of many hours (if not days) of valuable set time to shouting matches, storming-off-with-hurt-feelings, and/or actively working to undermine each other—but I'm having trouble recalling one at this present moment.

Estrogen, on the other hand—which tends to be more present in female brains—encourages bonding and connection, supports social skills and observation, and drives women to avoid conflict.[5] Now, there are times when a producer or studio might be interested in having someone with a singular vision hell-bent on executing it at all costs, in spite of the damage doing so may inflict on anyone else involved in the making of a film. But if we expand the definition of leadership, there is *also* an argument in favor of having a director who is actively invested in collaborating with the other artists on set, who places value on each person's feelings of inclusion in the process of filmmaking, and who works to resolve conflict rather than create it. As screenwriter and director Lisa Tierney-Keogh noted, "A set doesn't have to be a toxic place. Creativity gets better in the face of kindness and compassion."

In other words, if everyone on the set doesn't feel constantly in danger of being yelled at and fired, or made to feel that they are simply there as props in someone else's master plan, but instead they feel safe, encouraged, and respected, it is just possible that, aside from having a better experience on set, the creative life of the set will flourish and result in a better end product.

Unfortunately, the experience that almost all of us who are not white men have had on most film sets is of being on someone else's playground, where we are not entirely welcome and, in some unfortunate cases, are physically unsafe. Those experiences result in women having to consider things they shouldn't have to waste time and energy considering.

> JACLYN GRAMIGNA: "How do I need to dress to be taken seriously and avoid the men on set from hitting on me?"
>
> RACHEL WATANABE-BATTON: "Oftentimes, just to get through my career, I've had to operate in 'mommy mode,' because otherwise it gets complicated. If you're their mother, at least they won't hit on you."
>
> FILMMAKER ARIEL MAHLER: "Is it okay that I'm dressed this way/ speaking like this? Am I being too trans/not trans enough? Am I making other people feel uncomfortable?"
>
> EVERY WOMAN EVER ON A SET: "How do I avoid getting constantly sexually harassed and/or assaulted?"

We often don't even realize how much energy these kinds of questions take up until we have an alternate experience.

Ariel told me about a revelatory experience working on a majority-trans set. "It was one of the most foundational, inspirational weeks I've ever had creatively, artistically, personally. It was so exciting and so safe. I was just able to get the work done without worrying if I was making anyone uncomfortable. Some of the older trans actors on set were even more amazed. This was the first time they had ever, *ever* been in a space where they had felt safe that way."

Having now worked on majority-female sets where I felt unfettered freedom and safety to just do the work, I understand white men wanting to hold on to that same kind of space for themselves. There is a certain freedom and comfort in being on a playground where everyone looks and thinks like you and where you don't have to worry about other people with different perspectives getting offended or put off by yours.

The problem is that the white, male version of what a film set is has such a stranglehold on everyone's minds. It's as if anything different must be wrong or, worse, radical.

I am not, ultimately, advocating for siloed and monochromatic sets—female-only spaces where women can feel safe, trans-only spaces where trans folks can feel safe, black-only sets where black folks feel safe. That is a lateral move and will ultimately result in only more of the same. I believe that as the film industry moves forward, we need an abundance of people who are not white, cis, straight, able-bodied men to be the people in charge. Leaders who have had a variety of life experiences would reinvigorate and challenge the industry in a way that is sorely, sorely needed. If and when that happens, ultimately, everyone—including white men themselves—will be better off, both with the on-set experience and with the work itself. Making work from more inclusive sets would force all of us out of our comfort zones and into a richer perspective.

The Film

"Does it really matter whether a man or a woman directs a film?"

"It's all just about the story."

"Are you saying that a man can't direct a film about a strong woman?"

To say that the gender of the director/writer/producer of a given film doesn't affect the finished film is to misunderstand entirely the role of an artist. The role of an artist is not simply to select the subject matter of their art—although certainly that is part of their role—but rather to place over that subject matter their own frame, filter, and viewpoint, which, inevitably, is a direct result of their life experiences, which will naturally have been shaped by their gender, race, economic background, sexual identity, parental relationships, social relationships, geographic locale, the historical moment, and everything in between.

What made Vincent van Gogh a great artist was not that he decided to paint a vase of sunflowers. There was nothing intrinsically remarkable about that particular collection of flora. Rather, it was that his eyes, brain, and life experiences (including his mental illness) fused together and were able to transmit themselves into his art. Part of van Gogh's talent was the way he made the rest of us feel as though, before seeing his painting, we had never *really* admired the simple majestic beauty of sunflowers. Van Gogh took his personal perception and understanding and rendered it in his artwork. Sunflowers may not mean to us what they meant to him. But his feeling about them and his rendering of that feeling can change how *we* feel. That is the power of all art. Movies are no different.

A great film is not great because of the decision to tell a story about a subject, but rather in the millions of micro-decisions that are made about *how* to tell that story, what *deeper meaning* about the human experience that story can be used to reveal.

Let's take, for instance, the basic plot of *E.T. the Extra-Terrestrial*: an alien comes to Earth and meets a little boy and his sister, then the alien becomes ill, which eventually results in a government intervention.

There are an infinite number of films that could be constructed out of those plot points. One of the first decisions that has to be made, for instance, is who the protagonist of the story will be—i.e., whose viewpoint we are watching this movie through. Here are merely three possibilities:

1. A little boy is going about his life when he discovers an alien who becomes his friend, but then becomes ill, and later the evil government comes and takes him away and very nearly ruins everything until, luckily, the little boy is able to save the day.
2. A lovely fellow, E.T., from a lovely planet disastrously falls to an alien planet called Earth, where the people look weird and have

delicious little chocolate/peanut-buttery pebbles but are generally kind of upsetting. Later, much larger Earthlings than the ones he first met come and brutalize E.T. In the nick of time, the smaller humans come back and help E.T. get off this terrible planet, whence he wishes never to return again.

3. Extremely competent, cool, and attractive government officials work hard every day to keep planet Earth safe. They spot an alien landing, but, frustratingly, the alien somehow vanishes before they can reach him. This is code-red disastrous, because what if this alien is belligerent and has come here to blow up Earth? This governmental agency enters into an intense, all-hands-on-deck hunt to save the planet, which involves a lot of men getting to broodily gnaw on toothpicks while staring at walls covered in computer monitors. They eventually discover that the alien has been hiding, aided and abetted by some pre-adolescent, hoodie-wearing twerp, who has managed to make the alien deathly ill by feeding him too much chocolate.

Those are three completely different movies, and that's only a result of the first decision that has to be made—where do you focus the story and from whose perspective do you tell it?—which comes ahead of the several million other decisions that will be made in the course of making the movie.

To say that the gender, race, economic, and general background of the director or writer or producer or cinematographer or anyone else involved in the production are irrelevant is to say that there is some definitive version of each movie that the director only has to steer everyone to reach. It's saying that *E.T. the Extra-Terrestrial* would have been the same whether or not Steven Spielberg directed it.

I think most people will agree that such a statement is patently ludicrous. *Of course* the identity and life experience of the director matters. And the writer. And producers. And everyone else involved with the making of the film. Their collective life experiences, beliefs, and perspectives reverberate out and into every layer of the finished piece of art.

White men have created 95 percent of the cinematic images we've ever seen in American mainstream films, have made all the micro-decisions related to the shots, the framing, the lighting, the sound design of movie images *that we have ever seen.* So powerful is the impact of film and so ubiquitous white men's perspective in shaping it that their worldview has been normalized to the point of being considered the one true, accurate, and all-inclusive reflection of reality. It is not. It is one narrow prism through which we are all being forced to look.

So completely has the male perspective controlled cinema that, at this point, until someone clearly points it out to us, it often simply doesn't occur to us that there could be any other perspective.

I would argue that this perspective is the least damaging when it is the most obvious. For instance, if a male director chooses to make a western about a bunch of gun-slinging, eye-squinting, he-men cowboys, and there is only one woman in the movie and she's playing the local prostitute, it's quickly understood that this is a movie by men for men and is probably not doing a great deal to advance feminist causes. Although images in that film that sexualize or marginalize women can still be damaging, we are more likely to consciously process the fact that they are so.

But it is in the subtler choices, in the harder-to-put-your-finger-on-it design of the visual language of film, that I believe affect the impact these images have on us and our culture to a far greater degree specifically because we largely *don't* notice that it is happening. These images slide unstudied directly into the slipstream of our subconscious.

As veteran filmmaker Nina Menkes says in her lecture "Sex and Power: The Visual Language of Oppression," now being turned into a feature documentary entitled *Brainwashed*, "We are trapped in a massive web of visual language, which has permeated our consciousness on multiple levels and from which it is extremely difficult to escape."[6]

That massive web of visual language, which has been so loud as to drown out virtually everything else since the creation of film, is created by men.

"The male gaze" is a term coined by film critic Laura Mulvey in 1975 to describe the way in which, in movies, women have almost always been looked *at*, while men do the *looking*. Often the woman is looked at by other male characters on-screen, often by the male director and/or cinematographer, and always by the audience.[7]

The critical thing, though, is that, if we remember lessons from grammar school, the woman is almost always the "object" rather than the "subject" of an activity. She is not the doer (subject); she is the object that is being done upon.

Menkes, in her lecture, dissects how shot design is gendered, outlining five specific ways in which the male gaze occurs in cinema and how "women are photographically coded as objects."

The cinematic tropes of the male gaze are ubiquitous and quite easy to spot once you know what to look for. Here is your guide to forever ruining movies for yourself, but also to watching them with your eyes fully open.*

#1) WHAT IS THE POV? This one is pretty straightforward: who is doing the looking and who is being looked at?

Sometimes within a single frame (shot) one character is looking at another. Notice how often it is a man doing the looking.

Sometimes the point of view is implied. A man looks off-camera—cut to the woman he is looking at. Notice how often it is a man who is looking and a woman who is being looked at.

Sometimes, it's incredibly subtle. Menkes points out a famous scene from *Raging Bull*† at a swimming pool in which Robert De Niro looks at a woman, played by seventeen-year-old Cathy Moriarty, who is off in the distance. She is lounging around, looking impossibly beautiful. As he looks at her, we see that her lips are moving because she is talking. But in the sound design, we don't hear the words or any sounds coming out of her. We *do* hear De Niro talking to his friend *about her*, which reiterates that the viewer is to see the scene through his perspective. Astonishingly, there is another table of men who are further away from the camera than the woman (and should, therefore, logically, be less audible than her words), who are *also* talking *about* the woman, and we *do* hear what

---

* Ideas and examples courtesy of Nina Menkes's cinematic talk "Sex and Power: The Visual Language of Oppression."
† The cinematic "classics" are positively dripping with the male gaze. It is further insulting that incoming female film students are excoriated for not "understanding" or loving those classic films as their male classmates do, given that those films are designed to alienate and objectify female characters.

they are saying. Both sets of men are talking about this woman, yet her voice has been literally removed from the audio of the scene.

#2) IS THIS WOMAN'S BODY PART CONNECTED TO HER HEAD? This is one I am embarrassed to say that I never noticed before hearing Menkes's lecture and have since not been able to watch almost anything without jumping up onto my couch in distress and rage at its ubiquity.

When a woman's body part is in a shot, simply ask yourself, "Is her head also in this shot?"

You will be astounded by how often the answer is no.

A woman's hand toys playfully with her drink.

A girl swishes her shapely legs through water.

A woman's leg—emerging from under a high-cut dress—steps out of a car onto a sidewalk.

A woman's breast is in the foreground, while a man ogles it from the background.

Frequently, these shots include a camera panning across a scene. The camera begins on the shoulder blades of a woman's back and pans down, eventually, reaching her shapely buttocks. We've all seen these images.

In *Do the Right Thing* (1989), Spike Lee, the film's writer, director and star, has a sex scene with Rosie Perez, who plays his girlfriend. In one scene, she stands on the bed so that all we see are her legs and lower torso, while he remains lying on the bed and in full frame. Later on, he goes and gets ice cubes and, in the most erotic part of the scene, rubs the ice cubes all over her body. We see close ups of her various body parts, we barely see him at all, and we almost never see her face or head.

Men's bodies are almost never segmented visually this way. If we see a portion of a man's body as separate from the rest of himself, it is most likely to be his head/face, indicating that the important part of the man is his face, eyes, humanity, and experience; while the most important part of a woman is her body, which can be looked at, ogled, and panned across.

These shots further dehumanize women since they are now not only the object of the gaze, but their body parts—as disconnected from their head/face/personal identity—are themselves objects, completely separated from a person.

#3) HOW IS THIS HUMAN LIT? Male characters tend to be lit in ways that allow us to see their wrinkles and the contours of their face, giving us a sense of depth and personal identity. They tend to be shot in realistic, three-dimensional spaces to show that he is a real person in a real space having real experiences.

Female characters are almost always front-lit with soft, flat lighting to the point that no lines or specific personal attributes are visible on their faces at all. Even more subtle (and *super* weird once you start paying attention) is that their close-ups tend to be against 2-D spaces that are not located in a specific place (i.e., a wall or a flat surface that could be anywhere, anytime, anyplace), and in being so, subtly cue us that the woman herself is not real; these close-ups code her as a timeless fantasy object.

Men are lit and shot to look like humans. The visibility of their unique facial characteristics invites us to relate to and identify with them as humans and, therefore, key into their experiences and emotions. Women look like perfectly flat and unlined fantasy creatures that we may desire but do not relate to.*

Menkes points out that Dennis Villeneuve's 2017 film *Blade Runner 2049* takes the woman-as-object trope to "dizzying new heights." The main female character in the film is literally not a human but is rather a product of technology who appears only when Ryan Gosling's character wants her to—and then appears in exactly the form (maid, '50s housewife, etc.) that he wants her to. One of the other "main" characters in the film is a giant, naked, female-depicted hologram that struts around the city and has no eyeballs. In one particularly enraging scene, Ryan's character sits in his car looking super broody and having a lot of *really important feelings* with a toothpick in his mouth, while this giant, naked female/object hologram leans over and peers into the window at him with her no-eyes and giant fantasy breasts.

I have often been given the argument that I'm misunderstanding the point of such films, that a movie like that is itself a *commentary* on the

---

* Two additional thoughts here: (1) After watching Menkes's lecture, I now feel like the appearance of my two brow furrows in my latest feature film is a genuinely important feminist act, and I feel much fiercer about that decision now. (2) If you want a counterexample of what it's like to see women actually look like humans, go watch almost any English TV show. It is startling (and relieving) to see the extent to which the women's foreheads move.

sexual objectification of women's bodies in movies, so let me address that here. How about we just collectively decide that the sexual objectification of women is no longer something that needs to be commented upon in this fashion? We are all now extremely clear that women's bodies have been objectified throughout cinema and history. This no longer needs to be pointed out. How about we just try *not* objectifying women's bodies for a while and see how that goes?

#4) WAIT A MINUTE, WHY IS THIS WOMAN BEING SEXUALIZED RIGHT NOW? Watching sexy characters in sexual situations on-screen can be great and fun and really enjoyable. Trust me, I am not advocating for a removal of human sexuality from cinema. But watch for the timing of it. A key indicator of whether or not a woman's body is being objectified is the presence of a sexual/nude situation that has nothing to do with the actual plot of the movie.

You will notice that in the rare instances when a man is naked and/or in a sexual situation, it almost always has to do very specifically with the story of what is happening (i.e., the characters are about to have sex and must get naked to do so).

Each time you notice a woman's body being eroticized on camera now (whether in a full-on sex scene or a quick little pan over her breast or buttock) ask yourself, is this in any way connected to or advancing the plot of the story we're supposed to be paying attention to? Or is this for the sole purpose of titillation?

It is important to note that while white women have suffered from being the objects of the male gaze, women of color often have a different struggle. They are frequently left out of the narrative altogether. When they do appear, they are either desexualized (as service workers or asexual matriarchal figures) or they are hypersexualized, with the male gaze directed upon them at steroid levels. Their humanity is generally gutted even more fully than white female characters', and they are more radically turned into living props in white men's stories.

The male gaze in cinema does not necessarily have to be created by men. Menkes makes the keen point that the opening sequence—indeed the first three shots—of *Lost in Translation* (2003), directed by Sofia Coppola, is itself a glaring example of the male gaze.

- Shot #1: We open on Scarlett Johansson's butt, isolated from any other part of her body, visible through the sheer panties she is wearing. We don't know it's her butt yet, of course, because literally all we see is a woman's butt, looking cute, shapely, and inviting.
- Shot #2: Bill Murray is asleep. He is snoring—a human thing to do. His face is wrinkled—something we can clearly see because of how he is lit. He does not look particularly cute, shapely, or inviting. His is the first human face we see. He wakes up.
- Shot #3: The camera pulls out, and now that Bill Murray is awake, we see that he is in the world. We watch him process and experience the world around him.

That a female director shoots characters in a way that propagates the male gaze might feel surprising, but it shouldn't be. Of all films in the history of cinema, 95 percent have been directed by men—mostly white men. They have shaped *everybody's* cinematic visual language. They have chosen which tropes to multiply and reinforce. Most importantly, they have determined which characters get centralized as protagonists and subjects of the stories (mostly white men), whose experiences get marginalized (mostly everyone else's), and who to turn into the object of the actions, desires, and gaze of those subjects (mostly women—mainly white women).

The fact that Sofia Coppola, a talented and female director, could make work that reinforces the male gaze only shows the extent to which that gaze has monopolized not only our cinematic imagery but our own experiences of the world.

As Menkes points out, "The saddest part is that this [male perspective] gets internalized, and we [women] often perceive ourselves [as objects rather than subjects] as well, something that could be described as the opposite of entitlement."

As we look to transition to a world in which women are allowed to tell stories, we are going to have to actively battle against our own internalized objectification and marginalization and work to break free, instead, to portray our own lived experiences, rather than continuing to perpetuate the world as created by film.

Although not all female directors will succeed in achieving an unfettered female voice in their work—especially not right away—I know for certain that we will not progress to the point of rightly diluting that white, male perspective into its proportional place as only one side of the rich, variegated experiences and stories available in the world, without increasing the percentage of female directors to something at least approaching 51 percent as quickly as possible.

The Audience

When it comes right down to it, telling stories is a fairly bizarre activity for a species to spend time on. Particularly in times past, when such an enormous amount of energy and hours had to be exerted in the tasks of survival—gathering or killing food, building shelter, running away from tigers, etc.—why on earth would our species sit around a campfire at night making things up and telling them to each other?

And yet, we always have. There has never been a civilization that didn't include storytelling centrally in their culture—whether it be in the form of religion, myths, fables, or just good old-fashioned fiction. In contemporary life, we have movies.

The fact that people love movies as popcorn-gobbling entertainment can obscure the fact that movies also fulfill a majorly primal need within each of us to use stories as a framework to understand ourselves, other people, the world, and our place in it.

Stories entertain us, yes, but they also teach us, shape how we think and what we think about; they connect generations, instruct us on who is good or bad, trustworthy or shady, whose stories matter and whose do not.

The power of stories is enormous.

Understanding that film and TV are the most-consumed modern form of storytelling, an impressive stack of studies have shown that the movies we watch affect our hobbies, our career choices, our sense of identity, our judgments of other people, our relationships, our mental health, and even, quite literally, our brain chemistry.[8]

The impact is broad, dynamic, and substantial.

There is a well-documented problem now experienced by trial lawyers as a result of the widespread consumption of shows like *Law & Order*.

Jurors of late too often turn in innocent verdicts when they should not because, unlike what happens on TV, the prosecutors in real life usually fail to produce some final piece of shocking, incontrovertible evidence in a dramatic eleventh hour reveal.[9]

So widespread are problems like these that now virtually every branch of law enforcement—the FBI, the CIA, police precincts, the US Army—all have designated liaisons available to members of the Writers Guild of America to help ensure that screenwriters more accurately portray the procedures of criminal investigation and prosecution. When we get it wrong, it adversely affects their real-life interactions with the public.

Wendy Stock, author of the essay "Toward a Feminist Praxis of Sexuality," discovered that exposure to rape imagery has increased women's sexual arousal to rape and increased their rape fantasies.[10]

A 2016 study found that half of a sample of medical students and residents believe that blacks feel less pain, which has been linked to the lack of humanity attached to physical assault in media.[11]

The New Female Tribes compiles the results of a recent survey of eight thousand women worldwide in which 82 percent said that the sexualized representation of women and girls teaches us that if we're not pretty then we don't matter,*and 58 percent said that seeing a strong female role model on-screen directly inspired them to be either more ambitious or assertive.[12]

Consider that if you have watched primarily mainstream US-made movies during your lifetime, as certainly can be said of a great many humans living around the world, almost all the films that you have ever seen were directed by men, the overwhelming majority of them white. Between 80 and 90 percent of all the lead characters you have ever seen were men, the overwhelming majority of them white. And 55 percent of the time that a female character appeared on-screen, she was naked or scantily clad.[13]

The effect of all that is more staggering and profound than we can imagine.

---

* A fairly logical conclusion to draw given that, in US movies especially, the number of not conventionally beautiful women on-screen is fractional.

The stories we tell, hear, and internalize through film influence the entire mental framework by which we organize the world around us. And it's been constructed *almost exclusively* by white men.

I want to be really clear here—I am not saying that their experiences and worldview are invalid or unimportant. They are not. But it is deeply damaging to have our society constructed around the perspective and value system of one group of people that demographically makes up only a small percentage of the global population.

The rest of us have internalized their assessments of us to the point that even I—a successful woman, who spends at least 50 percent of every day working to bring about change for women and wrestling with feminist ideas—look at my face at the end of the day and hate it for having wrinkles, and still check every mirror I walk by trying to figure out whether my thighs are out of proportion with the rest of my body.

If no female filmmaker's career has ever made it through unscathed from the biases of system, then none of us audience members have escaped the stories produced by that same system. The white male gaze has invaded and taken up residence in the hidden nooks and crannies all over the brains of even the most woke among us.

Does it matter who directs, writes, and produces the film we watch?

The difference between white men (finally) telling more stories about women and people of color and all other historically underrepresented voices versus giving us a chance to tell our stories ourselves is the difference between giving a person who is dying of cancer a lollipop versus doing actual surgery to remove the fatal tumor.

It is no hyperbole to say that the white male patriarchy will never be toppled, in any corner of society, until women, people of color, and all historically underrepresented voices are able to contribute their experiences, perspectives, and voices to our collective cultural framework.

Until that happens, we will never be able to see each other, our world, or even ourselves through anything but a white man's eyes.

CHAPTER 7

ONE WAY OR ANOTHER*

It may surprise you to learn that before 1925, during the silent film era, almost half of all films were written by women.[1] In fact, a great many women were behind the camera in those days—producing and directing films and running studios. Proportionally, there were more women in positions of creative and structural power than at any other time in film history.

When writer and satirist Dorothy Parker and her writer husband, Alan Campbell, moved to Hollywood and signed contracts with Paramount, she was paid almost four times as much as he was.[2]

Frances Marion, who would go on to found the Writers Guild of America, was the highest-paid screenwriter in the 1920s and '30s, with more than a hundred of her scripts being made into films.[3] In 1930, she became the first woman to win an Oscar.

Lois Weber, a prolific screenwriter and director, was the first woman to establish and run her own film studio, and by 1916, her wage as a director was higher than any other at the time.[4]

Rosa Cianelli became the first female cinematographer in the world when she shot *Uma Transformista Original* in 1915.[5]

Predictably, most of these women were white, as people of color were largely kept out of even this nascent art form. There were fewer than ten black women known to be part of the film industry during this period,

---

* *One Way or Another* (1977), dir. Sara Gómez.

including producers Eloyce King Patrick Gist and Alice B. Russell and directors Tressie Souders and Maria P. Williams. Others earned power and influence managing their husband's careers, like Eslanda Goode Robeson, the wife of actor Paul Robeson.[6]

The early period of cinema was rich with opportunity for what we would now call independent film. Opportunities at the grassroots level and on the fringes provided fertile ground for different types of voices to emerge. The Chinese American artist Marion Wong acted in, produced, and directed her own films during this era. Her first feature film, *The Curse of Quon Gwon: When the Far East Mingles with the West*, which she made when she was barely out of her teens, in 1916, is considered to be the first film to authentically document the Chinese American experience. As her grandson later marveled, "How did this twenty-year-old woman get this idea? She wrote the script, directed the film, played the villainess and she was the producer. She raised the money!"[7]

In fact, as the medium of film was first being imagined, developed, and explored, and before behind-the-camera roles were as firmly defined as they are today, there was a strong tradition of actor-producers.[8] Many actresses who were dissatisfied with the roles being written for them by men became writers and directors themselves, and began production companies to make their own films.*

The greater abundance of female creators and power players during this time made sense since, in pre-1930s America, women made up 75–83 percent of the moviegoing audience, higher even than the 52 percent of moviegoers today.[9] African American newspapers understood the power of film to change and shape culture and, seeing that audience marketplace demand could drive the kinds of content being made, exerted significant effort and influence between 1918 and 1929 by publicly "applauding the efforts of companies that produced films appealing to black audiences."[10]

Not only were women hugely present in that earliest era of film, but they also pioneered much of the technology that still exists today. Lotte Reiniger, a German-born director, invented and first utilized silhouette

---

* Sound familiar?

animation and made the first feature-length animated film, *The Adventures of Prince Achmed*, in 1926, a full ten years before Walt Disney's first feature.[11]

So, what in the hell happened?

During the silent era, nobody took films all that seriously. Cinema was viewed as a fringe medium, an eccentric hobby, not something meant to last or make any real money. In such a context and, given that a lot of men were away fighting in World War I during this period, women had the space and freedom to express themselves through this new art form.

Within a decade after the end of the war, however, "talkies" were coming about—in part, through the technology of the "boom microphone," which was invented by a woman, by the way.[12] Wall Street caught the whiff of money and began investing, with the caveat that the menfolk had better get in there and take the industry out of the hands of the women, who were likely to make god knows what business decisions each month when their Aunt Flo came to town.[13]

At this point, the danger of women in the film industry was not just that they were seen as ignorant about how to run a business but also that they were creating radical, feminist films that "question[ed] and expand[ed] cultural understandings of gender."[14]

The films, particularly by women from this period, "were much more permissive and liberal than we might imagine. There were films that explored sexual orientation, cross dressing, birth control, abortion, and even nudity."[15] In 1915 Lois Weber produced, wrote, and directed the film *Hypocrites,* which "brazenly" presented "female nudity on celluloid." The film "sparked riots in New York and was banned in some parts of the United States."

That these films were being seen by increasingly large numbers of the public was making the men in charge jumpy.

There were a number of references made in contemporaneous documents to the "tyranny of the woman writer" in Hollywood studios in the 1930s and the widespread concern that these radically feminist films would begin to infect the broader culture and increasingly fuel popular demand for more of the same subject matter.[16]

Thus began a systematic elimination of women from positions of influence within the very film industry that they had helped to birth, all in the name of capitalism, progress, and keeping the broader female population from getting wild ideas in their heads. As the avant-garde days of the silent film era turned into male-dominated, vertically integrated studios that controlled films' development, production, and distribution, many women were squeezed out or left behind by an industrialized system that did not mesh with their maverick approach to filmmaking. As talkies engendered a growth spurt of ever-more-innovative technologies, women were further pushed out as these innovations came to require the kind of specialized training unavailable to women back then.[17]

So efficient and complete was the extraction of women from film that between 1945 and 1979, women directed less than one half of one percent (0.5 percent) of all studio films and television episodes.[18]

Not only were the silent-era women removed in real time from the industry, but their legacies were written out of the medium's history and, in many cases, falsely credited to men.* Only recent scholarship is bringing their innovations back into the light.

Little is known about coordinated attempts to reopen the gates of the film industry to female creatives en masse between 1945 and the 1960s, although I have to assume that they occurred.

In the 1960s, there was a rather tepid move toward rectifying the situation when the Equal Employment Opportunity Commission (EEOC) held hearings about hiring discrimination in Hollywood (for the first time) and asked the US Justice Department to intervene. The Justice Department found evidence of employment discrimination, but it reached a settlement with the Alliance of Motion Picture and Television Producers and several other unions. The oversight was ineffective, and women's employment percentages did not move.[19]

Finally, in 1979, a half-dozen female directors, now known as "the Original Six," formed the Directors Guild of America's Women's Committee. The group began when Susan Bay, Nell Cox, Joelle Dobrow, Dolores Ferraro, Victoria Hochberg, and Lynne Littman—all DGA members—were sitting together at an industry event. As Victoria recalls, "We were all experienced directors who had won awards—one of us an

---

* Some things, apparently, never change.

Oscar for a documentary, another a prime-time Emmy nominee music video maker and Fulbright Scholar, another a Peabody award winner, another a graduate of Yale Drama School, another had already made a two-hour dramatic film for PBS. . . . At one point, we looked at each other and asked, 'Are you working?' 'No.' 'Are you working?' 'No.' None of us could get hired by any Hollywood studio or production company to direct episodic narrative TV, which is the entry-level position for all industry work."[20]

In those pre-internet, pre-IMDb (Internet Media Database) days, no one had clear numbers on how many women were or weren't working in the industry. The Original Six decided that they should see if they could put together that data and learn whether this discrimination they felt was, in fact, real. They spent a solid year analyzing copies of all the DGA deal memos they secretly took from the DGA ("a carton of print-outs about a hundred pages long"), researching motion picture statistics at the library of the Academy of Motion Picture Arts and Sciences (the Academy Awards organization), sending forms to production companies, and asking them to self-report hiring numbers.[21] It was these women's hard work that uncovered the shocking reality that, as of 1979, just 0.5 percent of studio projects had been directed by women since 1945.

Once they had that data, the six realized they were right. As Victoria says, "This was not just us. This was the whole industry. And a clear pattern of sex discrimination."

The Original Six courageously put their own careers at risk and set out to sue the studios for being in violation of equal employment laws and, with much difficulty, persuaded the DGA to help them do so. Although the suits—one against Warner Bros. and one against Columbia Pictures—were eventually thrown out on a technicality,* the threat of legal action finally goosed the studios into taking some real action to address their discriminatory hiring practices.

---

* Judge Pamela Rymer, a President Reagan appointee, eventually threw out the suits because of the DGA's involvement, stating that the DGA "is not a proper representative of the 'class' because the Guild itself discriminates against its women and minority members." While this judgment was correct—the DGA was not the appropriate body to carry out the lawsuit for the reasons stated—it is crushing to think that this was the reason the suit was thrown out, given that the underlying case of hiring discrimination on the part of the studios was so clear.

Over the course of the decade following that lawsuit, between 1985 and 1995, the number of women directing film and television jumped from 0.5 percent to 8 percent.[22] As filmmaker Maria Giese notes, this was largely because, as a result of the suits, "the DGA and the studios did get together in subsequent Collective Bargaining negotiations to set up diversity agreements and programs in compliance of Title VII, which prohibits employment discrimination based on race, color, religion, sex and national origin. These programs included TV directing fellowships, mentoring projects, networking programs, panels on various diversity issues, and events to glorify the success of women directors."[23]

Jan Eliasberg recalls the extent to which she owes her directing career to the work done at this time. "At the time of my first job, the Original Six lawsuit was making its way through the system, and people [at the studios] were scared [of being sued]. There were a couple of women—only a few, but including me—who were suddenly in demand, and I started working a lot. I became the first female director on *Miami Vice*, which was the biggest show of the decade. I directed *LA Law*, *Crime Story*. I was off to the races. I didn't realize how much that lawsuit had impacted my ability to be hired. I'm very grateful to those women."

I was not able to locate sufficient data or scholarship to adequately parse out whether these temporary gains elevated one group of women more than another. In general, such moments have elevated white, straight, cis, able-bodied women above others, though in this instance, I cannot state definitively whether or not that was the case. According to Victoria Hochberg, the Original Six and DGA delayed their original lawsuits for one year "so that the Minority Committees could conduct parallel research and be part of the class action suit with the Women's Committee." It is clear that there were at least some women of color who benefited in the short term from this hiring surge, including Neema Barnette, Debbie Allen, Janice Cooke, and Darnell Martin. I am unsure, but doubtful whether trans or disabled women substantially benefited.

In any case, it was a moment of great hope and movement in hiring numbers, and there seemed to be no reason to suspect that the upward-leaping trend wouldn't continue. In the course of time, one could believe that it would result in inclusive hiring across marginalized groups.

Except, of course, it didn't. After the upswing from 1985 to 1995, the numbers of women being hired leveled off and slowly began to dip.

The reasons for this, Victoria writes, are complex: "The culture changed. Feminism, the women's movement, and most political activism had come to seem passé. Because the percentage of working women directors had greatly increased, it appeared there was no longer a 'problem.' If 8% of film jobs and 16% of TV jobs were going to women, many women hoped they could be one of the 8 or 16%. Why rock the boat? The problem was that the same 20 or so women were getting all the work. And they were not inclined to help other women."

Maria Giese, who graduated from film school in 1994 at the top of her class and felt sure that an unstoppable directing career awaited her, laments this stagnation. "No one did anything on this issue for twenty years, and I guess I'm referring mostly to myself, because perhaps a certain measure of complacency on the part of my generation of American women figured into it. I believe in my heart that this must be true, because twenty years ago, when I entered the profession, I didn't see any community of women filmmakers to join, and I didn't try to create one. My generation did not seem to carry forth the torch of women's liberation and equal rights as exemplified by the Original Six." Maria felt the blow of this in her own career, graduating the very year the backslide in female directing percentages began. She directed her first feature, *When Saturday Comes*, in 1995 in the UK with major stars, but despite getting an international theatrical release for the film, she could not get directing jobs for the next fifteen years.

By the late 1990s, the percentage of women directing studio feature films had plummeted to 5 percent, where it has basically stagnated—wiggling only slightly year to year—ever since.

In January 2015, April Reign, a full-time attorney working in Washington, DC, was getting dressed for work while listening to Chris Hemsworth announce the 2015 Oscar nominations. April, a film enthusiast, regards the Oscars as her Super Bowl. "I'd watch the red carpet and everything." Struck suddenly by the total lack of people of color among the nominees, April tweeted, "#OscarsSoWhite they asked to touch my hair," then went about her day.[24] When she looked at her phone again hours later, her tweet had gone viral, and her hashtag was trending internationally. The hashtag was even more popular the following year when, once again, people of color were locked out of every single category of acting nominations.

Two years later, in October 2017, the *New York Times* investigative reporters Jodi Kantor and Megan Twohey revealed sexual assault allegations against Harvey Weinstein dating back to the 1990s. The Me Too movement, originally started by activist Tarana Burke in 2006, became internet wildfire as #MeToo kicked off national public discussion about sexual harassment and assault against women in America. In the aftermath of the Weinstein allegations, the movement had special resonance.

There was an outbreak of grand sentiments about sweeping and everlasting change in the wake of all this.

While that has not proven to be the case, the biggest benefit to the #OscarsSoWhite/Weinstein/#MeToo trifecta is that a new level of awareness around issues related to women in film does seem to have penetrated Hollywood's inner sanctum, at least somewhat.

The areas that have seen the most significant increases are in on-screen roles for women, people of color, and other non–white-cis-straight-male characters. Heidi Miami Marshall, a former casting director and longtime acting teacher and coach, says, "Five years ago there was a directive for diversity, but it would appear in the smallest roles. Now it's the leads. There's a sense now that if you don't have a diverse cast, your show is not going to fly."[25]

Actress Makia Martin agrees. "Before #OscarsSoWhite, I would always get called in for the small sassy-black-lady role and I'd be auditioning alongside the same group of sassy-black actresses. I noticed during pilot season 2018 that so many of the roles I was going in for were different. Now there are auditions I go to where no one else looks like me. To me that means that the director isn't just looking for someone to fill their exact—usually stereotyped—idea. They're open-minded. That's happening more now. I'm also noticing that a lot of the roles I've been auditioning for have changed, because there are more women of color in the writers rooms."[26]

This more inclusive approach to casting is giving actors the opportunity to challenge stereotypes in all directions. Heidi recalled a recent session in which she was coaching an actress for an audition for the role of an FBI agent that was written in the script as male. "A year ago, this would have gone to a man, but now this actress and I are getting to explore the question of what a woman's strength is. We uncovered layers of vulnerability and compassion in this role that, as written, would have normally been a stereotypically strong white man."

Michelle Hendley notes that she's seen a real uptick in roles specifically written for trans actors, though she's looking forward to a time when trans women are considered for roles not specifically written for them as well. "My dream role would be playing an action heroine that kicks a lot of ass." She laughs and says, "We haven't made it *that* far yet."

Casting directors, too, agree that questions of representation have become a conversation in a way that they never were before. Ally Beans, who has helped to cast for *Homeland* and other film, TV, and theater projects, says she feels more responsibility post-#OscarsSoWhite and #MeToo to call out a lack of inclusion when she sees it. "Part of my job is to challenge the gender and race of all roles. If a team of white guys come to me with a script and all five principals are white, I will ask them why. 'Is there any reason in the script that they have to be white men?' About 50 percent of the teams are totally receptive to that and are very grateful to have been given the wake-up call, since most of the time they hadn't even noticed that that was the case in their material. The other 50 percent get pretty defensive and protective of their original ideas of the characters. I push where I can."[27]

These anecdotal experiences do seem to be borne out in the on-screen data: The year 2017 was the first since the 1950s that the top-three highest-grossing US films (*Rogue One: A Star Wars Story, Beauty and the Beast, Wonder Woman*) had female protagonists.[28]

In 2018, the first year that movies made after #MeToo/Weinstein began to be released, of the one hundred top-grossing films, forty featured a female lead or co-lead, which is an increase of 8 percent from 2017 and a 20 percent increase from 2007. Twenty-eight films featured an underrepresented lead or co-lead character, a gain of 7 percent from 2017 and 15 percent from 2007. Eleven of those leads or co-leads were underrepresented women, almost three times as many as in 2017 and an enormous leap from 2007, when only one top-grossing film featured an underrepresented female lead or co-lead.[29]

This is all extremely good news. It is particularly encouraging that at least on-screen, unlike in past moments of progress, there appear to be short-term proportional gains for women of color and other historically underrepresented groups, though these percentages still do not match their presence in the population.

Whether this trend will hold if and when the public conversation around these issues dies down is unclear, but the largest reason for pause in celebration of this moment is that films with increasingly inclusive casts are still largely written, directed, and produced by white men. To me this suggests that, though the white men are beginning to get the idea that they can't just tell stories about themselves forever, they have not yet managed to make the mental leap to understanding that other people can tell stories too.

The lack of an actual shift in numbers does not mean that there isn't a new consciousness. As Jill Soloway, creator of the hit Amazon series *Transparent* and *I Love Dick*, has said, "At least [now] you should be aware that you should be ashamed of yourself if your show is 90 percent written by male writers."[30]

For those men and women who fall into the category of honest actors who genuinely hadn't previously noticed the degree to which women and people of color have been kept out of the system, this awareness has sometimes been enough on its own to lead to real change in their actions.

Deb Verhoeven, of the University of Technology in Sydney and a major women in film activist in Australia, told me of an instance in which her colleague, a woman named Courtney, approached a leading distributor about hosting a women in film initiative, an idea to which he enthusiastically and immediately agreed, noting that he had always been a firm supporter of women. When Courtney encouraged this distributor to check his own company's track record on distributing films made by women, however, he came back to her dumbfounded. "I did check," he said, "and we have never green-lit a project with a female director." He seemed to genuinely not have realized. The revelation was enough to cause the distributor to become an enthusiastic leader of and participant in Deb and Courtney's women in film initiative in Australia.

For one junior talent agent, "Stacia," the movement has made her feel bolder and more empowered to act and speak up within her agency. "I was in a recent situation where we had both a male and female director of color who were in pretty comparable career places. I made a point of telling my colleagues, every time you put him up for a job, put her up for a job too." When I asked Stacia if she thought her (and others') efforts were leading to change within the agency, she sighed. "I mean, our numbers have to be moving," she says. "Everyone I've personally signed in the last year is a woman."

Watching (some of) our male colleagues grapple, often for the first time, with their past behaviors and unpack ways in which they may have been complicit or even participated in a culture that allowed Weinstein and his compatriots to run unchecked for so long has felt hopeful.

A veteran female TV writer recalls that shortly after the Weinstein story broke, "I went to a birthday party at a fancy showrunner's house, walked into the kitchen, and six white dudes—showrunners, actors, and agents—were standing in a circle having a come-to-Jesus about sexual harassment like, 'I looked down into my soul to ask myself, 'Have I done anything wrong?'"[31] She'd never seen anything like it before.

In the wake of this soul-searching, there have been some banner moments, certainly for women directors of studio films, that are cause for celebration.

The summer of 2017 had the historical distinction of having for the first time five films directed by women released in more than a thousand theaters: *Wonder Woman* (Patty Jenkins); *Everything, Everything* (Stella Meghie); *Rough Night* (Lucia Aniello); *Detroit* (Kathryn Bigelow); and *Megan Leavey* (Gabriela Cowperthwaite).[32]

Cathy Yan became the first Asian American female director to direct a super-hero movie with the Harley Quinn film *Birds of Prey*. It is worth noting that as well as "Yan's presentation for *Birds of Prey* [being] exceptional," Margot Robbie, the film's lead and backed by the weight of her production company being a producer on the film, lobbied hard and held firm in her desire for the film to be directed by a woman.[33] Major props should be given to Robbie for putting her neck on the line to fight for this outcome. Although she is certainly an A-list actress, few other A-list actresses, even those who purport to care about getting more women behind the camera, have gone to the mat to use their influence to make that happen.

Before 2017, only twice in Hollywood history have live-action feature films with budgets of $100 million or more been directed by women: *K:19—The Widowmaker*, by Kathryn Bigelow, in 2002, and *Jupiter As-*

cending, by Lana and Lilly Wachowski, in 2016. But since 2017, that club has expanded to include Ava DuVernay (*Wrinkle in Time*), Patty Jenkins (*Wonder Woman*), Niki Caro (*Mulan*), and Anna Boden (*Captain Marvel*, which she co-directed).[34]

Full authorship of these bigger films, in the sense of getting to truly create, write, and direct with support behind their visions, has not yet been extended to women. But the fact that such authorship was given to Ryan Coogler, a black male director, on *Black Panther*, a film that "probably couldn't have gotten made just five years ago," seems like a positive harbinger of possible change to come for everybody.[35]

Except that I know too much now about the patterns of this industry not to maintain a healthy skepticism about the future trends of all of this, and I am not the only one. Martha Lauzen, executive director of the Center for the Study of Women in Television and Film, cautions, "It is very easy to be misled by a few high-profile cases. We see Ava DuVernay or the success of Patty Jenkins . . . and we assume that everything must be okay and that women have achieved some kind of parity. The truth couldn't be further from that." As an *LA Times* article written the summer after Weinstein notes, the slate of films for the summer of 2018 included only two widely released films (*The Spy Who Dumped Me* and *The Darkest Minds*) out of the fifty that were directed by women. To make matters worse, those films both came out on the same date, meaning the audiences likely cannibalized each other.[36]

Meanwhile, the Academy of Motion Picture Arts and Sciences does appear to be taking steps in the right direction. After the 2016 #OscarsSoWhite hashtag went viral and levied fierce, pointed criticism at the academy's overwhelming whiteness, the academy invited more people of color to join its voting ranks. The current 16 percent representation of people of color among academy voters, while still far below adequate representation, is double the percentage in 2016. In 2018, following #MeToo/Weinstein, the academy added 928 new members, of which 49 percent were female.[37] This trend continued this past year, with 50 percent of their 2019 class of new members being women. It is indicative of how egregiously their membership was formerly slanted that these two strong years still only bring their overall female membership to 32 percent.[38] We will hope that their progress continues, and swiftly.

We may be seeing early results of the demographic changes in voting ranks reflected in the Academy Awards.[39] In 2017, *Moonlight* became the first film with an all-black cast and the first LGBTQ+-themed film to win Best Picture.*[40] The same year, Viola Davis became the first black actress to win a Tony, an Emmy, and the Oscar for Best Supporting Actress for *Fences*.[41] Following #OscarsSoWhite, in 2018, Jordan Peele became the first black man to ever win Best Original Screenplay, for *Get Out*, in spite of the fact that many academy voters refused to even watch the film saying that it was "not an Oscar movie." The same year, in the wake of #MeToo/Weinstein, Greta Gerwig became the first woman nominated for Best Director for her solo directing debut and also the first woman in twenty-eight years to have been nominated in that category for a film with a female protagonist.[42] The same evening, *The Shape of Water* became the first film with a female protagonist to win Best Picture in thirteen years.

Supporting my skepticism on the staying power of these trends, the 2019 Oscar nominations brought mixed results, as public heat over inclusion began to die down. There were a slew of historic firsts, particularly for people of color, even for some women of color, but women as a whole were locked out of every major category apart from Best Actress and Best Supporting Actress (where women literally *must* be nominated). The only exceptions were that a woman was nominated for both Best Adapted Screenplay and Best Original Screenplay, though each of them shared writing credit with a man.

Overall, the ceremony that night felt like a perfect metaphor for Hollywood's response to its inclusion problem in general: make some moves that will result in good PR stories (a handful of historic "firsts," give a win to the documentary short about women's periods, give Spike Lee his first Best Director nomination after outrageously overlooking him his entire career, and so on), grab lots of people of color and put them onstage in various roles so that the photos will look super diverse, and then, at the

---

* It also became the lowest-budgeted film to win that award by a mile, with a shockingly low $1M budget.

end of the night, give all of your most important and prestigious awards to the same old white dudes.*

Progress has been faster in television. The 2018 pilot season[†] marked a real breakthrough, when fourteen of the forty-two broadcast drama pilots (the most prestigious category) had female directors.[43] That's an improvement from previous years. In 2015, only four broadcast drama pilots were directed by women; in 2016, there were two; in 2017, there was just one.

Even more hopeful is the fact that eight of those fourteen female-helmed 2018 pilots (57 percent) were picked up to go to series, while only 46 percent of male-helmed pilots did.[44] This suggests that not only did the networks take real swings on female directors, but when they did, the results were terrific.

Television is more inclusive right now than film for three clear reasons.

REASON #1: COMMITTED CHANGE-MAKERS ARE IN POWER POSITIONS. The most exciting story to come out of this recent movement is that of the FX network. In 2015, it was publicly called out for having the least diverse roster of directors of any network. Of their series, 88 percent were directed by white men. FX's CEO, John Landgraf (a white man himself), took the criticism seriously. "We wanted to accept the shame that has been heaped upon us, and prove that it wasn't a given," Landgraf said.[45]

Whereas previously FX had strongly leaned toward directors who already had extensive episodic television experience—which disproportionately excluded women and people of color—the network began considering directors who had previously directed short films, music

---

* White dudes, who made a film that would have been about an incredibly fascinating black man and instead centered the narrative on a far-less-interesting white man's feelings and journey, resulting in a film that is as offensive as it is soothing to the feelings of white people. We see you, *Green Book*.

† The time of year when networks make and test out first episodes of TV shows that they're considering putting on the air, before committing to a full season.

videos, and independent films, projects that are not usually considered to be qualifying directing experience for television. That simple shift in hiring practices, Landgraf says, "unlocked a huge amount of talent and potential that was simply being overlooked." He pointed to Hiro Murai, who had never directed narrative television before being hired to direct the FX show *Atlanta* and then went on to garner an Emmy nomination for his work on the show.

By 2018, FX's stable of 88 percent of white male directors dropped to 51 percent. Landgraf has said that there is still work to be done, both on the director front and to address the fact that, even after this overhaul, only a third of its senior writers and executive producers that season were women or people of color.[46]

A number of other networks and high-powered showrunners have made similar commitments with similar success. Ryan Murphy's initiative at Fox, in which he aimed to fill 50 percent of all director slots on his shows with women, people of color, and LGBTQ+ folks, launched in 2016, exceeded its goal, reaching 60 percent in the first year alone.[47]

The Lifetime network's Broad Focus initiative, a partnership with the American Film Institute's Director Workshop for Women, is yet another training program for female directors, except that this one *guarantees* that each of its ten graduates receive an actual paid directing slot on a TV show. This program has resulted in 55 percent of all its shows across platforms now being directed by women.[48]

These stories should be held up as crucial case studies to demonstrate that when the people in charge actually commit to change, take a serious look at why their hiring practices are biased, and then correct those biases, change can happen, not in decades but in a matter of years.

These examples more than anything make me call bullshit on the film studios that claim helplessness when asked to figure out a way to change their percentages. Change requires work and a willingness to shift your mind-set, not, in fact, a PhD.

REASON #2: THEY HAVE THE DATA. Netflix and Amazon have unquestionably led the way on content by and about women and other historically underrepresented voices. In 2018, Netflix released more films (five) directed by women in four months alone than the six major Hollywood studios released during that entire year *combined*, which totaled four films.[49]

Shows like *Master of None, Transparent, Dear White People, On My Block, One Day at a Time, Chewing Gum, Orange Is the New Black*, and a great many others have opened a window for audiences to see characters, worlds, and perspectives they've never seen before, which is, arguably, another factor driving the speed with which competing TV networks are scrambling to get on the inclusion train.

Notably, Netflix and Amazon have access to a more granular level of audiences' behavioral data than has ever existed in the history of any medium. They not only know what people watch but also how long they watch it, how long their cursor hovers over a title before choosing (or not choosing) to watch it, and what people are rewatching. Netflix and Amazon know in astonishing detail what their viewing audiences like. And although they won't release that data, which is a giant problem for independent creators who cannot effectively market their films without that information, what we do know is what they are choosing to make *based on that data*. And what they are choosing to make is content that, more than any other studios or networks, is by women and people of color.

REASON #3: DIRECTING TELEVISION IS LESS PRESTIGIOUS AND LESS OF A FINANCIAL RISK. It's less of risk to take a chance on giving someone an episode of a show to direct where the cast and crew work as a well-oiled machine versus handing them many millions of dollars for a stand-alone film that will be far more reliant on the director's abilities. This isn't a *good* reason for denying women directing opportunities, because it represents a paternalistic "trust gap." Yet it is *a* reason, and at this point, we'll take change over motivation.

This progressiveness has brought ample rewards to the networks and streaming platforms, including rooms full of awards and an unprecedented shift of prestige and cultural cachet away from film and toward television, which, until recently, had always been viewed as Hollywood's slightly embarrassing cousin. Indeed we are living through what is widely being heralded as a Golden Age of Television.

Programming on some networks and streaming platforms has also given audiences a thrilling taste of what it's like to watch stories that represent the multitudes of the world, and the progress in television has given our industry some prime examples of what happens when women are given positions of real power over storytelling and hiring.

Research from these recent examples shows that female directors tell stories with more female characters, more characters from underrepresented racial/ethnic groups, more women over age forty, and that they hire more women in key behind-the-camera positions.[50] Further, films with at least one female director or writer feature an average of 45 percent female protagonists versus 20 percent in films by men.[51]

A slew of female showrunners have earned critical acclaim, awards, and monster ratings, even as they are bringing their unique perspectives to the small screen and are committed to hiring at parity. For Shonda Rhimes (*Grey's Anatomy, How to Get Away with Murder*, and *Scandal*), Jenji Kohan (*Orange Is the New Black*), Melissa Rosenberg (*Jessica Jones*), Tig Notaro and Diablo Cody (*One Mississippi*), and Ava DuVernay (*Queen Sugar*), the shows they created have become part of our cultural zeitgeist. Their work *seems* fresh because it *is* fresh. These women make entertaining, must-watch TV that gets discussed at the proverbial watercoolers the next day. Yet their work also demonstrates the possibility of exploring, for example, the experience and trauma of sexual assault in sensitive and creative ways that, amazingly, manages not to sexually objectify women during filming or on-screen, nor make men the center of the story.[52]

Along the way, these women have become TV titans.

Rhimes has insisted that she and her teams "make TV look like the world looks."[53] With her first hit show, *Grey's Anatomy*, which debuted in 2005, Rhimes landed a direct hit in driving the small-screen landscape toward more diverse casts. By not specifying the race of any characters at the script stage, and determined to have a cast that looked as colorful as the world she knew and recognized, Rhimes created a show that quickly started to make other shows on television look very, *very* white. In 2012, Rhimes's network hit *Scandal* made history by featuring the first female black lead seen on TV in forty years. Not only have Rhimes's shows inspired her peers to create ever more diverse content, but she has built an empire that has won her real clout, clout that she recently used to get her agency, ICM, to agree to commit to fifty-fifty gender parity among its department heads, partners, and board members.[54]

Jill Soloway (*Transparent, I Love Dick*) hired only female or non-cis male directors on *Transparent* in season three and hired the only scripted-series writers' room at the time with an all-female staff for her show *I Love Dick*.[55]

Ava DuVernay committed to hiring only female directors for her series *Queen Sugar*. To do so, as John Landraf did at FX, Ava looked to first-time TV directors who had previously directed indie films. In doing so, Ava opened a door that had been locked shut to these women for decades. Tina Mabry, one of these directors, says of the enormity of this move, "We just never had the opportunity. And that is something that Ava provided all of us with. That opportunity to actually showcase the skill that she knew we had already had but had not gotten the chance to due to our industry, which struggles with inclusiveness."[56] Even better, once Ava took a chance on them, those directors all went on to book additional directing work on shows including *American Crime, The Vampire Diaries, Dear White People, Gypsy*, and *The Good Fight*.[57]

On top of everything, these shows are succeeding with audiences. Rena Ronson, a sales agent at United Talent Agency (UTA), said recently, "Sales agents have said they're looking for female-driven stories because they're working. There's definite awareness, and more and more in the international space as well."[58]

A. O. Scott, a respected film critic at the *New York Times*, agrees. "The demand for other stories and experiences will persist and other companies will try to turn that desire into profit." he says.[59]

This is creating more opportunity for women than ever.

Rachel Feldman, who has endured many gaps in work throughout her three-decade career, now has "the phone ringing all the time." She adds, "My career has changed since Weinstein. Yes. Definitely. Finally, people are *looking* for women with experience."

The work of author Karin Slaughter, who has sold over thirty-five million books worldwide over her career, was ignored by Hollywood for seventeen years for adaptation because it was considered "too female-centric," an idea that contradicted Slaughter's clear and naturally built-in audience. But in the wake of #MeToo, Slaughter's books, which dealt with domestic violence and sexual harassment long before it was trendy to do so, are now flying into development deals—with two films and one TV series in production.[60]

Sonja O'Hara, ever the hustler in chief, managed to get onto a panel at SXSW a few months after the Weinstein scandal broke. She had with her a spreadsheet with contact information for all the industry members in attendance at the festival. Seizing the cultural impact of the moment,

Sonja cold-emailed every person on the list, sharing her story of grass-roots content making, audience building, and success, and letting recipients know that she was an experienced and available writer/director/actress ready and available for work. She received twenty-five responses; landed meetings with the seven biggest agencies, most of the studios, and many indie film companies; and eventually got herself a deal at WME, no doubt launching a real career in Hollywood. This, after ten years of silence.

It is critical to remember at this celebratory juncture, however, that this is not the first time our industry has been through this, not the first time there has been a fight for change. After women were pushed out of the film industry in the 1930s and 1940s, there was an effort in the 1960s to get women back into studio filmmaking, but that failed to move the needle. It took the Original Six's formation in 1979, and the threat of legal action, to force Hollywood to correct itself. Only then did the percentage of women in Hollywood improve even a little, and it took less than a decade for those numbers to slide back to even-more-paltry levels.

Four decades later, it's taken #OscarsSoWhite, Harvey Weinstein's penis, and the ensuing #MeToo movement to spur another corrective moment. But we find ourselves now at a critical danger point. Only as the public conversation around sexual harassment and gender discrimination in the film industry fades away will we find out for sure whether all of this inclusion was yet again a short-term change resulting from Hollywood wanting to stop the bleeding of some bad press, or whether Hollywood is finally committed to the far harder, longer, and less sexy work of cleaning and healing the actual wound.

As film critic Manohla Dargis of the *New York Times* wrote in 2018, "It's instructive that we haven't heard about many (any?) concrete institutional actions that the industry is taking to correct its wrongs from the inside. . . . The problem is that industry talk is cheap and its apologies feel the same."[61]

And realistically, particularly now that we're a few years out from the point of impact, a whole lot still feels the same.

PERFORMATIVE DIFFERENCES

In the wake of the Weinstein scandal, when the Academy Award–winning film producer Cathy Schulman walks into a man's office and tries to close the door for business meetings, he objects.[62] The industry-wide implication is that it's not enough for men to not assault women; they need to *perform* it. Meanwhile, the sexual degradation of women in Hollywood is as persistent as ever.

I heard no shortage of abuse and harassment stories, post-Weinstein, in the course of doing interviews for this book—many of which happened in professional settings, in front of other people who could have stepped in to help and didn't. Even in the #MeToo era, the career costs of speaking out against powerful abusers is still too high for many victims and witnesses alike.

One actress I interviewed, after getting cast in a popular and high-caliber television series that has been decorated with at least one Golden Globe and airs on a top-three prestige television network, was blacklisted by the show's showrunner, director, and casting director for refusing to perform a series of sexually objectifying and degrading acts on camera—acts to which neither she nor her agents had agreed in advance, but which were demanded of her on set in front of cast and crew. She fired her agents when they refused to step in and help her on set. This happened in 2018.

In May of 2018, a twenty-three-year-old actress was invited to a dinner party by one of the top five most powerful men in Hollywood—an agent—under the auspices that he wanted to help her out with her career. At that dinner party, in earshot of a who's who of Hollywood's A-list, this fifty-plus-year-old man persistently and aggressively badgered this young woman to "date him." Not one person, male or female, at that dinner party stepped in to help the young actress or rebuke the agent for his wildly inappropriate behavior. Instead there was a lot of, "Oh my god! He's so fun!" Later on, after the agent had watched some of her short films and when the actress refused to go to bed with him, he told her, "Well, you're a crap film director, but you look good on-screen, so if I can't date you, I'll at least help you." After an ensuing weeks' worth of pestering, petulant, and eventually apoplectic text messages from the agent, the actress's "no" finally got through to him. She has not heard from him again and will now likely never get a meeting at his agency, one of the two most powerful in town. This happened seven months after the Weinstein story broke.

Hollywood is not even close to excising even the most blatant and public examples of sexual harassment and abuse. Let us be extremely clear about that.

"DIVERSITY" AND "TRAINING" PROGRAMS

One of the big moves from the studios and networks after this outcry— as it was in the Original Six era—has been to implement various "diversity" or "training" programs for women, people of color, and other historically underrepresented voices. Some of these programs can be effective, like Lifetime's, which, like NBC's Universal TIPS, is one of the few that actually guarantees participants a job at the end of the program. More typically, though, these programs are used as good PR stories that take some short-term heat off the studio or network, without requiring it to do any real work to change. Ultimately, these programs rarely result in movement in hiring percentages.

In one of the more brain-melting examples of a PR-based program, in the wake of Weinstein and in response to a public outcry about a lack of female directors, 20th Century Fox proudly announced a program that would allow female graduates of the American Film Institute (AFI) directing program to apply to get a film made.[63] The headline for the article announcing this program—"Film Studio Fox Seeks Female Blockbuster Directors"—sounded quite promising. Except that from the applicants, Fox was going to select just *one* woman and give her financing for *a short film* that she would be allowed to direct. Most people didn't read the full article, of course, nor understand the program's limitations. Instead, Fox was widely applauded for making moves, then happily carried on hiring male directors for their feature films.

These "diversity" and "training" programs continue to be largely dead ends. As veteran director Jan Eliasberg says, "I've had friends who directed Academy Award–winning shorts and then done a number of diversity programs and still can't get a job."

These programs have the added benefit for the studios and networks of keeping women busy, as they go through the extensive process of applying for the programs and undergoing the training if they are selected.

This gives women less bandwidth to complain about not getting hired for *actual paying jobs*.* Fundamentally, these programs also reinforce the insulting notion that the failure to succeed in the industry is with the women themselves ("if you just got a little more training . . ."), rather than with the hiring practices of the studios that demonstrably choose less-qualified men over more-qualified women.

There are real and actionable steps to address this problem, such as the ones FX took, that all networks and studios could be taking to correct their hiring practices. But they are not taking them. Current DGA president Thomas Schlamme claims that he has long been pushing the studios to adopt the "Rooney rule," which, borrowed from the National Football League, would require that the studios at least *interview* equal numbers of men and women for each job before making a hiring decision. Schlamme says the studios refuse to seriously consider that practical measure.[64]

THE REAL AND LESS-REAL PIPELINE PROBLEMS

Everyone is now hungry to discover the next Issa Rae or Shonda Rhimes. Dailyn Rodriguez was told by an executive that she was a "unicorn," a Latina woman who had risen through the traditional television ranks and was, therefore, considered hirable. The executive told her, "We're scrambling because there's like five of you, and they're all working."[65] According to an agent I spoke with, one African American, lesbian director with a produced credit is considered "gold" by her agency, because she ticks diversity boxes six ways to Sunday *and* has the industry stamp of approval and, hence, is safe to hire. Great. Except that there are *plenty* of women who are talented, experienced, and desperate to be discovered and hired, if only the industry could slightly expand its vision of what being qualified means (or cared to do the work to do so).

As Christy Haubegger, a former agent at CAA at the time I spoke to her and also a strong activist for change, said, "Diversity doesn't happen by accident. You have to do things differently than the way you were doing it before."[66]

---

* A win-win from the studios' perspective.

Another agent I interviewed notes that, although male colleagues talk a good game about needing to get more female clients, "they don't really have the passion to go out and find them. Some people at the agencies say they want to rep more women, but then everyone they bring up is a white dude."

The agent went on: "I think we're definitely not looking hard enough, taking enough risks. There need to be agents at a higher level taking risks on women and people of color who have the talent and experience, but maybe not the exact credit that would make them 'qualified.'"

It's not hard to figure out that these intractable agents, studio executives, and other gatekeepers are neither as dumb nor as incapable of figuring out solutions as they are pretending to be.

As FX demonstrated, if you simply widen your scope of thought and vision slightly, you can fix your hiring numbers. There are a number of agents and lower-level studio employees—particularly those under forty and female—who, emboldened, empowered, and awakened by recent events, are indeed beginning to look outside the traditional places, acknowledging that decades of institutionalized sexism and racism simply mean that women and people of color are not going to have made it into the standard pipelines—e.g., top film schools, top film festivals, particular film industry awards. The studios and networks whose numbers are truly moving are most often those with renegade insiders. We have not yet—by a long shot—hit a critical mass of gatekeepers willing to take concrete actions to address the real and less-real pipeline issues.

BEHIND THE CAMERA, THE NUMBERS AREN'T MOVING IN FILM

There is no clearer demonstration of the fact that these diversity hiring programs are bunk than the fact that the numbers of women behind the camera have remained static.

A particularly deflating tweet from USC Annenberg on October 5, 2018, said, "Where are we at a year after October 5, 2017 [the day the *New York Times* broke the first Weinstein story]? The industry is still reluctant to hire female directors in major motion pictures. 2018 will not look different than 2017 or 2007."[67]

As it turned out, 2018 *did* look different than 2017. Whereas 2017 saw the percentage of female directors of top studio films spike briefly at 8 percent, 2018 saw it fall back down to 4 percent.[68]

When the DGA released its 2018 numbers of directors on all films released that year with budgets over $250,000 (so, everything above the micro-budget), it revealed that of the 175 films released that year, twenty-two were directed by women and fourteen were directed by people of color (down from twenty-one in 2017).[69] That means women directed 12 percent of all films above the micro-budget space, which is *precisely* where they have been since at least 2016.

Even over in TV-land, which has seen some serious upward movement for female directors recently, there has been an overall *decline* in the number of female creators over the last half decade. It is important to note that, although the director is considered the primary creative driver on a film, in TV, the show creator/showrunner is the primary creative driver, not the director. So, although female TV directors—a less powerful role than it is in film—are on the rise in TV, there have been lurching upswings and then downswings among the showrunners over the past several years, as the following chart indicates.[70]

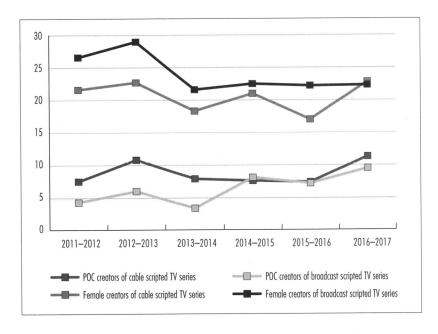

The only sustained progress has been among creators of color for broadcast scripted TV series. Every other category has been overall in decline, with occasional brief upticks of "progress."

The continuing dominance of white, straight, cis, able-bodied men in the role of storytellers, even as the on-screen stories have begun to shift at least somewhat toward greater inclusion, has led to a lot of good news/bad news scenarios. Marilee Talkington, after twenty-two years of playing sighted characters, was, in 2018, authentically cast for the first time as a blind/low-vision character on four different television shows (good news). Except that the shows were all written by sighted, non-disabled writers, so Marilee "had to carry the mantle of both artist and advocate onto every single set. Which is a huge amount of emotional labor on top of the actual work." When she would offer insights or feedback on how her blind/low-vision characters were portrayed, she said, "some [writers] were 'willing to listen,' just so they appeared 'willing,' but were still very much pushing their own agenda. Some others were authentically desiring to 'get it right.'"

THE GATEKEEPERS ARE STILL WHITE MEN

Whatever wiggles of movement we're seeing further down the food chain, what has decidedly not happened is a shift in the demographics of the leadership/power players within the industry, and that suggests that any other movement is likely to be short-lived and cosmetic.

Each year the *Hollywood Reporter* releases its report of "the 25 players who can get an indie movie made." Their May 2018 report included thirty-two people (some of the "players" were teams of two or more people).[71] Of those thirty-two people, twenty-seven were men (two were Asian, one of whom was in a producing team with a white man; one was black; the rest were white). Five of those thirty-two people were women (two were black, and three were white, one of whom was part of a producing partnership with a white man).

According to USC's Annenberg Inclusion Initiative, in 2018, 22.8 percent of all C-suites, boards of directors, and executive film teams at major media organizations were women, while 77.2 percent were men. Fewer than 6 percent of all those positions were held by women of color.[72]

Of the people who are in the position to decide what TV shows get made, 93 percent are white.[73]

None of that has changed since Weinstein/#OscarsSoWhite.

In spite of the mountains of data demonstrating that films by and about women (and other non-white, non-cis, non-straight, non-able-bodied men) make more money, Hollywood persists in primarily telling stories about white men. In the few instances when the story is about somebody else, the stories are still being told *by* cis, straight, able-bodied, white men.

Despite their continued near-total stranglehold on content creation, however, some men say they are feeling extremely oppressed just at present. A male Hollywood insider recently went so far as to comment off the record to a reporter that, post-Weinstein, "men are living like Jews in Germany."[74]

Indeed, many white men are starting to feel tired of this whole aggravating and uncomfortable conversation altogether. "When one notable executive creative director declared recently that he was, 'Bored of diversity being prioritized over talent,' he perhaps articulated a latent view within the industry that this whole 'gender and race thing' was a distraction at best, and at worse meant that the creative work was being compromised as a result," Rachel Pashley points out in *The New Female Tribes*.[75] "When you're a white middle-class male at the top of the industry you can afford to be bored with diversity. This ignores the fact that for an industry that thrives on the originality of its ideas, having a diverse workforce leads to a diversity of ideas."

If the white men in charge feel threatened or interfered with by this conversation, rather than doing the nuanced self-reflection to realize that they are, perhaps, missing out on a whole new landscape of storytelling by shutting out a plurality of voices, their commitment to real change is going to be tepid at best and, ultimately, will last only as long as their patience.

WOMEN'S STORIES ARE STILL NOT VALUED

Underlying all of these cultural and structural problems is the simple, persistent reality that we do not value women's stories as we do men's.

White men's stories continue to be considered Important and Universal. If the films of Quentin Tarantino, Stanley Kubrick, or Christopher Nolan don't speak to you, you are considered by other filmmakers and creatives to be a philistine of the highest order, one who is simply too ignorant to grasp the depth of their genius.

But men can hardly be expected to sit through the films of those female filmmakers most radically plumbing the depths of the female experience. After all, they are telling small and personal stories.*

Nowhere has this modern, casual dismissal of women's stories been more potently laid out than in Lili Loofbourow's astonishing essay "The Male Glance: How We Fail to Take Women's Stories Seriously."† She writes,

> "The male glance" is a narrative corollary to "the male gaze." . . . The effects are poisonous and cumulative and have resulted in a huge talent drain. We have been hemorrhaging great work for decades, partly because we are so bad at seeing it. . . . The male glance is how comedies about women become "chick flicks." . . . It tricks us into pronouncing mothers intrinsically boring and it quietly convinces us that female friendships come in two strains: conventional jealousy or the even less-appealing non-plot of saccharine love. . . . The upshot is that we still don't expect female texts to have universal things to say. We might imagine them as small or petty and domestic or vain or sassy or confessional . . . or sentimental or melodramatic or even in *Transparent* and *Girls* provocative, unflattering exhibitions. But we don't expect them to be great. We have not yet learned to see within female ugliness the possibility of transcendent art (as we have with its male counterpart). . . . We don't see complexity in female stories because we have so little experience imagining it might be there.[76]

As Loofbourow points out further, the danger of the male *glance*, unlike its more overtly sexist, old-school counterpart the male *gaze*, is that the male *glance* is "reasonable."

When we are told by our husbands or boyfriends or fathers or sons or male colleagues that the stories that kick us in our guts, grab our

---

* At what point and by whom (three guesses) was it decided that a story about war—an experience that (thankfully) only a tiny percentage of at least the Western population have recently been through—is Universal, while a story about a young mother dealing with the complicated emotional territory of raising a child—an experience that a significantly large portion of the population has gone or will go through—is small and personal?

† Which you should go and read in full on the *Guardian*'s website, because it is extremely important.

hearts, or resonate with our cells are "chick flicks"; or when those stories are dismissed with eye rolls, we scuttle away, wounded, sure that they must be right—since at least some of us have shamefully carried the secret our whole lives that we really *don't at all get* what the big deal with Tarantino is.

While part of the reason for this marginalized view of women's stories is for reasons we have already explored—such as the gatekeepers being men and the studios making their content decisions based on outdated data and ideas—there is another reason that audiences and the industry alike are not open to the true value of stories from the true female voice (i.e., by actual women), which is that doing so would require a significant and thoughtful look at how we fundamentally value stories.

Women's stories are for women only. Stories are for everyone. Except that, given the percentage breakdown of who is actually telling those stories—at least today and in recent history—what is meant by "stories" are actually "men's stories." Ipso facto, women's stories are for women and men's stories are for everyone. Men's stories are, therefore, implicitly, Big, Important, and Universal, whereas women's stories are embarrassingly small, personal, and not to be imposed on the patience of the other gender. Women are raised from a young age with the expectation that they will watch all stories, seek to empathize with whatever protagonist there is, and feign interest in, or at least sit through, even those stories that do not resonate with them. Men, in contrast, are raised to watch only stories with male protagonists and from the male perspective, and it is acceptable, even manly, to brush away as insignificant anything else. Women, trained as we have been in this same set of rules, often back off quickly, agreeing too readily with our fathers, brothers, partners that they should most certainly not be forced to endure stories about us.

In an attempt to avoid the kind of deep soul-searching that would require us to interrogate these foundations, there has instead been a great quest for a clear definition of what makes "a good story for women."

We have the Bechdel test,* a benchmark that should be so impossibly simple to reach that even the test's creator, the cartoonist and writer Alison Bechdel, has distanced herself from it, reminding us frequently,

---

* If a film has at least two female characters with names who speak to one another about something other than a man, a film "passes" the test. If it doesn't contain that, it "fails."

as in a 2015 *Vulture* article, that she wrote the test into a comic strip and that "it's not meant as a serious metric"—and, yet, it is a benchmark that a majority of films still don't meet.[77]

Given that most of the films that do pass the Bechdel test still feel unsatisfying, we women call out for more leading female characters. The industry gives us *Ghostbusters* and *Ocean's Eight*, with leading female characters, created by men.

With *Wonder Woman,* we get closer to a female cinematic perspective with Jenkins directing, but as noted, she is still surrounded on all sides by white, male creatives and executives. Worse, when Gal Godot's Wonder Woman next appears in a film, it is in *The Justice League*, directed by a man.*

Hollywood, self-satisfied with these minor and convoluted steps toward equality, wants us to be happy now. We have more female leading characters. Some of them are strong. No, we're not the original creators. No, we're not the writers. Or the directors. Most of the women who are involved are white. Most are young. All are cis. But we're supposed to be happy that we got one on the board with *Wonder Woman.*

This doozy of a question, about what makes a story good for women, means, as Deb Verhoeven says, that "we have to keep redefining what the problem is because the patriarchy keeps modulating to keep women's voices out."

The only real answer, of course, is to *let actual women tell stories*—entire stories, from beginning to end—and see what emerges.

As Pashley says in *The New Female Tribes*, "If you want to design for women, it feels pretty smart to employ women in the design, not just to know 'what women want' in the most superficial sense, but to experience and see the world as a woman."[78]

It seems clear to me that Step One would be to allow actual women to create and make the stories that they feel are true expressions of their experience and personhood. Step Two would be to consider on a cultural level that women's stories are, in fact, Universal and Important and are safe for everyone to watch. Step Three would then be to allow women

---

* If you ever wonder what it means to have a man versus a woman direct a film, compare images of Gal Gadot in *Wonder Woman* versus *The Justice League*—even her costume changed to become more sexualized and less powerful.

to create and make stories about whatever the hell they want, at which point, we could all stop banging on about it altogether.

Hollywood is at Step Zero and a Half.

In light of that, for better or worse—and I believe very much for the better—some of us women who have been beating on those doors of Hollywood for so long find ourselves unwilling to wait for the gatekeepers who are benefiting from the system to wake up and change it. And so, even as #OscarsSoWhite, Weinstein, and the #MeToo movement have forced Hollywood into a panicky, if surface-level, reckoning with itself, even as those conversations are at risk of fading away, a women in film movement that has always existed at the margins is slowly but surely emerging as a genuine force to be reckoned with.

CHAPTER 8

DAUGHTERS OF THE DUST*

There has been a women in film movement in some form or another ever since women were first unceremoniously jettisoned from the industry back in the 1930s and 1940s. Sometimes that movement has coalesced into specific and organized actions, as with the Original Six, and at other times it has simply been women in small or large groups finding ways to support one another and/or make and release their work outside of the system. Frequently, this work has been driven by women of color, who have benefited least from it and have had the greatest difficulty getting Inside. They pioneered, out of necessity, some of the most truly independent forms of production and distribution, many of which received no notice from the critical universe until white people eventually caught onto them.

But not since talkies came about has there ever been a women in film movement that could match the size, organization, and strength of what exists today.

Most people trace the opening shot of this current movement back to a weekend in a hotel room in 2000. In April of that year, after decades of collective inaction, director Allison Anders gathered more than one hundred industry women for the Women Filmmakers' Summit at the Miramar Hotel (the event would thereafter be known as "Miramar") for a weekend-long pajama party and venting session.[1] "Woman after

---

* *Daughters of the Dust* (1991), dir. Julie Dash.

woman, across three generations, told tales of hurdles and harassment and dreams dashed—situations that, until then, many had thought that they alone had experienced."

That weekend ignited something in the attendees. Shortly thereafter, activist and journalist Melissa Silverstein began Women and Hollywood, along with a weekly newsletter of films opening by and about women. That same year, 2003, Stacy Smith began her research at USC's Annenberg School for Communication and Journalism to finally provide incontrovertible data, backing long-standing claims of discrimination. Over the next ten years, alumnae of that weekend founded a historic number of groups designed to elevate, promote, and help enable the work of female filmmakers. That grassroots work began to slowly create an upward pressure on Hollywood to once again consider its "women in film problem" and on women themselves to become both filmmakers and changemakers in ever-increasing numbers.

In 2002, the Guerrilla Girls, a then seventeen-year-old activist group for gender parity in Hollywood, got together and bought billboards along the route to the 2002 Oscars ceremony that said:

> The anatomically correct Oscar.
> He's white & male, just like the guys who win!
> Best Director has never been awarded to a woman.
> 94% of the Writing awards have gone to men.
> Only 3% of the Acting awards have gone to people of color.[2]

A decade later, in 2011, the movement took another significant leap forward. Somewhat mysteriously, during that time, a huge number of women all over the country, more or less simultaneously, arrived at a decision to take their growing frustrations with Hollywood and do something about it.

Some started the process of making their first micro-budget features, some decided to become director/filmmakers after having other jobs in the business, some started writing film scripts for the first time, some abandoned trying to get bigger-budget feature films made and moved ahead with a down-n-dirty micro-budget feature instead, some launched organizations and initiatives aimed at helping other female filmmakers, and many came to the harsh awakening that the Hollywood system was never built for them.

Many of these women didn't know each other at the time, nor were they aware that their own personal revolutions were anything more than individual. When I began making *Imagine I'm Beautiful* in 2011, it felt like a completely personal and isolated decision.

Yet, that year came up so often in my interviews as such a pivotal one that I began to realize that there had to be some reason—political, socio-economic, historical, global, technological, or other—that 2011 became when a whole bunch of us thought, *Fuck it.*

After lots of digging and thinking and sourcing ideas from interviewees, here's what I believe occurred.

FILMS GET CHEAPER TO MAKE

There is a reality to filmmaking—and this has always been true—that a film costs the amount of money that you have to make it. Although making a film, unlike making a painting or writing a novel, will always cost more than ten dollars, you would be astonished how elastic film budgets are. Particularly in indie-film land, we are wizards at finding people and things for free or cheap and at wheedling companies, restaurants, and location owners into giving us things at steeply discounted rates. On the other end of that spectrum, there is no limit to the number of additional positions on set you can invent to spend money—studios, to their credit, are wizards at that.*

Coming up with a film budget, then, is almost exclusively a matter of making a set of decisions that primarily include answering the following questions:

1. What are my absolute hard costs (such as gear rental, location fees, and hard-drive purchases)?
2. How much am I going to pay my crew members?
3. How much am I going to pay my actors?

---

* Whenever I'm on a large studio or network set, I'm always amazed at the sea of individuals with a confoundingly vague set of responsibilities. It's actually kind of impressive.

4. How much can I get for free?
5. What is the size and scope of my movie?*

The answers can only be made by the film's producers in conversation with the filmmaker by somehow balancing the equation of how much money you can actually raise with the minimum quality threshold that you are willing to accept for your movie given the convergence of factors 1 through 5 above.

All of that being said, the hard costs of making a great-looking film are cheaper now than they were a decade ago. We are able to shoot on sophisticated digital cameras and not on film stock, which was incredibly expensive. When folks were shooting only on that, every minute spent filming was, in itself, a hard cost.

In the early days of digital cameras, at the end of the 1990s, things improved for independent filmmakers but not by much. Hard drives with appropriate amounts of space were prohibitively pricey, and the visual quality of the final product could never compete with the shot-on-film movies coming out of the studios. In those days, digitally shot indie films never quite escaped looking rather like a home movie.

The RED camera changed all of that. In 2007 Peter Jackson, director of *The Lord of the Rings* movies, tested two prototypes of this camera on a short film. When the camera officially launched that same year, directing/producing titan Steven Soderbergh (*Sex, Lies, and Videotape, Erin Brockovich, Ocean's Eleven*) reportedly told RED's founder, James Jannard, "I am all in. I have to shoot with this."[3] Finally, there was a digital camera that could replicate the visual quality of film† and even surpass it, since shooting digitally meant that all sorts of aftereffects could be applied more cheaply and simply, and real-time playback allowed directors and cinematographers to check shots moments after filming them.

In 2007 the price tag on those cameras was high—far out of reach from almost any indie filmmaker and definitely for an indie filmmaker trying to work in the micro-budget space. But, like all technology eventually

---

* In other words, is this a quiet family drama that more or less takes place in one location or are we making *Lord of the Rings*?
† *Nearly* replicate, as film enthusiasts will tell you, but, let's be real, it's close enough to looking like actual film to satisfy most audiences.

does, the prices eventually went down, secondhand cameras became available on the cheap as original owners upgraded, and, eventually, let's say around . . . oh, I don't know, 2011 . . . indie filmmakers started to get their hands on them.

At the same time, the cost of hard-drive storage took a nose dive, such that you could suddenly buy a high-end two-terabyte hard drive—enough space to store the entire *Lord of the Rings* trilogy twenty-two times—for less than a hundred bucks.

On a parallel track, the first widely used and fully dynamic digital-editing software, Final Cut, was slowly but surely becoming more practical for use by the independent filmmaker. Although early versions were released in the early 2000s, it wasn't until later in the decade that the price became low enough and the system's features practical enough that wide adoption grew. By 2007 the full possibilities of editing software had met the digital age.[4]

To understand how revolutionary the introduction of Final Cut was to indie film, take Lila Yomtoob, who was a young, ambitious, and just-the-right-amount-of-naïve filmmaker making her first feature film in 1999. Lila shot her film on digital a year or two before the first version of Final Cut came out. This meant that, although she was editing digitally and wasn't losing time physically cutting and taping film strips together, she was hindered by the lack of speed, space, and efficiency of early editing software, and it took her a full five years to edit the film. She edited it herself, working on it part-time while she held a full-time job. It took our *Imagine I'm Beautiful* editor, Chris Steele-Nicholson, nine months to complete the same process, working on it part-time while holding a full-time job.

By the close of the first decade of the new millennium, indie filmmakers had something they had never, ever had before: an extremely low-cost method of shooting, storing, and editing movies that, at least from a technological standpoint, could look every bit as professional to the viewing audience as what the studios were making.

CROWDFUNDING BECOMES A THING

If you have somehow not had a single artist friend over the past decade and have never been hit up for a crowdfunding campaign, (a) congratulations and (b) crowdfunding is an online method of raising sums of money by pooling the resources of a lot of different people, thus giving you a way to raise larger sums of money than you might otherwise have been able to.

This concept isn't new. Nonprofits, for instance, have almost always raised their budgets by getting smaller donors to supplement their larger donors. A few particularly enterprising individuals have even applied this concept to filmmaking in past decades. Deborah Kampmeier, who has chutzpah to spare, financed her first feature in 2002 by sending a snail-mail letter to everyone she knew asking them for $750 or, if they didn't have $750, to see whether they could find ten friends to all give $75—a method through which she raised $65,000 and earned my eternal respect.

It wasn't until IndieGoGo and Kickstarter launched in 2007 and 2009, respectively, that crowdfunding became easy (you just go to a website, pick a perk, and put in your credit card number) and even a little fun, with animated meters that measure how close the project has gotten to its funding goal with each donation. With that, it became a socially acceptable and commonly used means of raising money for a project. By 2011 crowdfunding had proven so successful a means for filmmakers and content creators to raise money that almost no indie film was getting made without running a crowdfunding campaign. This spawned the pioneering crowdfunding site Seed&Spark, dedicated exclusively to crowdfunding campaigns by filmmakers and other content creators.

This form of fundraising, like any, favors people from wealthier backgrounds. Obviously, you can raise more money if your average friend can give you $75 or $200 versus $10. But crowdfunding at least loosened the near-absolute stranglehold on independent content creation from those rich kids who, historically, had so thoroughly occupied the ranks of filmmakers. At the very least, it gave those of us who didn't have family members able to write us $100,000 checks a fighting chance at actually being able to raise the money to make some kind of movie.

THE GATEKEEPERS LOSE THEIR STRANGLEHOLD ON FILM DISTRIBUTION

YouTube was founded in 2005. Given the extent to which it is now integral to our lives, it takes a specific kind of concentration to even remember what life was like before. Cataloguing my use of YouTube *just yester-day alone*:

- My husband and I watched over breakfast The Young Turks inde-pendent news channel, getting our news information and analysis from a nontraditional broadcaster who, even though they only post their videos on YouTube, reliably get more viewers on a daily basis than most TV news shows.
- I then took a yoga class from Yoga with Adriene on YouTube for free and without having to leave my house.
- Mid-morning, a friend sent me a clip of Rudy Giuliani being a dipshit on a network news show, the clip of which I watched on YouTube.
- In the afternoon, I needed to listen to a song that the director of *Bite Me* was considering to play over the credits of our movie, so I looked it up on YouTube and listened to it.
- Before bed, my husband and I watched funny animal videos on YouTube to decompress.

Fifteen years ago none of those activities would have been possible—at least not easily or from the comfort of our own home.

Think about how the advent of YouTube has impacted independent content creators. When Lila Yomtoob finished her first feature film, *High Life*, in 2005, the best she could do was submit it to film festivals—of which there were far fewer at the time—and hope that someone from the film industry would see it, be impressed, and want to hire her as a director. Like filmmakers in decades past, she was able to build a small audience for the film in New York City through word of mouth, however, the idea that she could get the film to a wider or more significant audi-ence online was not feasible at any kind of scale.

Half a decade later, however, Lila made a short film—a piece about real-life heroes—that got picked to be on the home page of a very-early-days YouTube on Martin Luther King Day. There was such an up-roar about it from the racist conservative corner of the country that some alt-righters hacked into Lila's account and removed the video. That was not specifically the reaction Lila was going after, but, for any struggling filmmaker, getting enough views of your work to invoke a major contro-versy feels like a pretty big win.

In 2010, before I'd gotten it in my head to make a feature film, I made a silly web series that I spent zero dollars on and made no effort to market beyond posting it on Facebook. The series has, to date, had a total of 4,171 views across three episodes on YouTube. Four thousand views doesn't sound like much, considering viral videos reach into the millions. But that is a considerably larger audience than ever attends most plays in New York City. The fact that independent artists can reach that big an audience is a very recent phenomenon and wholly attributable to the internet.

It's not just YouTube that has expanded distribution opportunities. In 2005 iTunes started allowing consumers to stream and download mainstream movies and TV shows through their digital store. Over the course of the next five years, they began including a greater and greater number of independent films as well.[5]

In 2007 Netflix announced—to widespread mockery from the film industry—that it was moving its core business model away from mailing DVDs to an online streaming subscription model. This was a model it built first using indie films, since for a long time the studios and major distribution companies refused to give Netflix the rights to stream their "bigger" movies, while indie filmmakers were quite happy to have Netflix introduce people to their work. In 2010 Netflix began expanding to international markets, starting with Canada, meaning that independent films were being delivered easily, cheaply, and efficiently for the first time into the homes of an international audience.[6]

Prior to 2005, it had long been possible for independent filmmakers to *make* movies. But until the rise of online streaming platforms, there was no viable method of independently *distributing* those films on any kind of mass scale. Once you had a film, you had to hustle and hope like hell that the gatekeepers at one of the mainstream or independent distribution companies would agree to pick up the film and release it. If that didn't happen or you weren't interested in that route, you could, alternatively, release it in art house theaters, rent cinemas, and self-distribute, but you would have been hard-pressed in any of those forums to have your film seen by even the 4,171 people who watched my mediocre web series.

Also, distributing films became cheaper for indie filmmakers because they could now upload their films to YouTube or deliver them to iTunes or Netflix for the cost of a WiFi subscription. In the past, the cost of large-scale distribution was prohibitive. A film reel copy needed to be printed and made for each theater in which the movie would play. Even with VHS and DVDs, the up-front cost of printing the physical product was high.

Suddenly, truly independent, scalable film distribution was possible. That blew a giant hole in the absolute power the distribution gatekeepers had long held over what films and content were seen. This was a critical moment for women and other historically silenced voices in film. By 2009–2010, it was beginning to dawn on many of us that we could actually reach and build our own audiences for our films without having to wait for any kind of blessing from the industry.

Even more electrifying to some was the emerging possibility that doing just that—creating and releasing your own content—could get you through the industry firewall. Two web series, *Broad City* (2010) and *High Maintenance* (2012), originally made partly on crowdfunded money and self-released online, built such substantial and fervent audience bases that they were picked up, given real budgets, and turned into full-fledged TV shows by Comedy Central and HBO, respectively.

By 2011, not only could filmmakers now make content and deliver it directly to audiences, thereby building an ecosystem for ourselves as artists, but also in doing so, we might just gain the industry acceptance and validation that many of us still craved.

THE SOCIAL NETWORKS DEBUT

In 2004 Mark Zuckerberg launched Facebook at Harvard, where he was a student. The next year, the platform began being used by students at other universities and at high schools. In 2006 membership opened to everyone, and the world changed irrevocably.[7]

There are two reasons this development catalyzed the emergence of a historically broad base of indie female filmmakers around 2011.

First, social media—led by Facebook—became a powerful, free,* and scalable way to build an audience. Even for those of us at the beginnings of our careers, who had no "fan following" to speak of, social media became a simplified way of "advertising to" our extended network of friends, family, and acquaintances. That alone was revolutionary, es-

---

* Originally.

pecially in terms of crowdfunding to raise money for and eventually distributing our films.

Not only could we easily communicate to a wide group of people that we were running a crowdfunding campaign or releasing a movie, but the day-to-day update feature of the platform—particularly once Facebook's news feed launched, in 2006—allowed us to bring that same base of people along on the detailed, emotional, and fascinating journey of making a film. Finally, we had a value proposition for audiences that Hollywood couldn't provide.

Because I posted frequently about the process of making *Imagine I'm Beautiful*, countless Facebook friends who I otherwise didn't really stay in touch with, later waxed lyrical about how much they felt part of my journey and how unbelievably excited they were when the film came out, because they'd been on the ride with me.

In this way, social media became a new and powerful tool for building audiences. As filmmakers, we didn't just have to sell audience members on the film itself; the story of the *making* of the film became as useful a marketing tool as the trailer or anything else. Audiences that came along as part of the journey became a mobilized fan base for the finished projects, enthusiastically sharing the good word with their own social networks to buy or pay to see the film, since they felt a stake in and ownership of the project.

The second development social media brought to this new women in film movement was that we female and other underrepresented filmmakers began to find one other. As Melissa Silverstein, founder and publisher of *Women and Hollywood*, told me, "The isolation as a woman in Hollywood was pretty real before social media." Filmmaker Lila Yomtoob looks now at the online communities of female filmmakers, which often translate to in-person ones, that have blossomed in just the last ten years with amazement and some envy. "I just think 'Wow!'" she says. "If I could have had something like that when I was young, my life would have been really different."

HOLLYWOOD GIVES UP ON DOMESTIC AUDIENCES

Starting in 2007, Hollywood began to slowly give up on domestic audiences. Leaving aside the fact that they had pretty much only ever been making films by and for white men, the industry was about to take another dive to the bottom of artistic innovation. Driven by shifting macroeconomics—namely the rise of streaming platforms, a precipitous drop in DVD revenues, and the opening up of new international markets, such as China and Russia, to US content—studio executives began a strategy of making films to appeal to broad international audiences, films that, to their full knowledge, would quickly wear thin with US audiences.* So, by 2011, audience members, as much as artists, were starting to desperately miss the kind of juicy, risky, original films of past decades, films that could suddenly be made at far lower budgets and a higher quality than ever before by independent filmmakers.

KATHRYN BIGELOW WINS

Finally, there was the match in the tinderbox in the form of Kathryn Bigelow, becoming the first woman to ever win a Best Director Oscar, which she did in 2010 for *The Hurt Locker*, possibly, in part, due to pressure from the growing women in film movement. The impact of this event was not, I believe, that we women suddenly realized that we *could* be movie directors. We knew about Kimberly Peirce, Julie Dash, Amy Heckerling, Jane Campion, Mary Harron . . . the list goes on.

I'm not even sure that the biggest impact on us women filmmakers was that Kathryn Bigelow *won*. It's that *when* she won, almost every article covering the event included the shocking information that she was *the very first woman ever* to win a Best Director Oscar and that, at that point, only three women had even been *nominated* in that category *ever*.†

At that time, Melissa Silverstein pointed out to me, these facts were not widely known or spoken about.

In one crackling moment of collective awakening, after we all watched Kathryn give her acceptance speech and once we learned those stunning statistics, a whole lot of us seemed to say privately to ourselves, "Well, that right there is some bull*shit*. Maybe *I* should make a movie. . ." And then, over the next year, leading into 2011, a bunch of us began to do exactly that.

---

* We're going to talk way more about this in a moment, so hang on.
† Lina Wertmuller (*Seven Beauties*, 1975), Jane Campion (*The Piano*, 1993), and Sofia Coppola (*Lost in Translation*, 2003).

Like me, each of these women decided she was done waiting. And through advancements in technology, unlike every woman in the film industry who found herself in that very position since 1945, we could finagle the means to make, finance, and distribute our films entirely outside the studio system.

If you think I'm overstating the drama or impact of this moment of convergence, here is a graph of the number of independent films (shorts and features) directed by women by the year in which they were released.

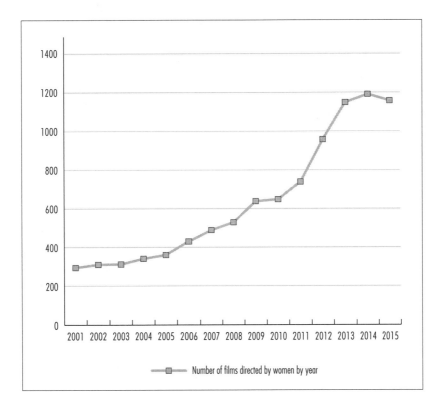

Number of films directed by women by year

Now let's look at the timeline of those stark increases in films directed by women in relation to each of the events previously discussed.

From 2001 to 2005, the number of women directing indie films rose slightly, consistent with prior trends. From 2006 to 2010, that number doubled. From 2010 to 2015, that number almost doubled again, meaning that by 2015 more than three times as many women were directing indie films as were doing so a mere ten years earlier.[8]

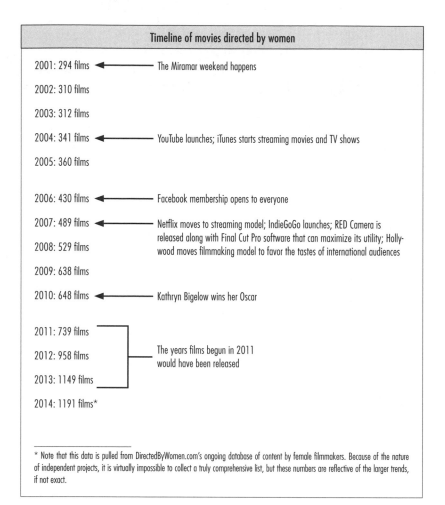

Timeline of movies directed by women	
2001: 294 films ◄———————	The Miramar weekend happens
2002: 310 films	
2003: 312 films	
2004: 341 films ◄———————	YouTube launches; iTunes starts streaming movies and TV shows
2005: 360 films	
2006: 430 films ◄———————	Facebook membership opens to everyone
2007: 489 films ◄———————	Netflix moves to streaming model; IndieGoGo launches; RED Camera is released along with Final Cut Pro software that can maximize its utility; Hollywood moves filmmaking model to favor the tastes of international audiences
2008: 529 films	
2009: 638 films	
2010: 648 films ◄———————	Kathryn Bigelow wins her Oscar
2011: 739 films	
2012: 958 films	The years films begun in 2011 would have been released
2013: 1149 films	
2014: 1191 films*	

* Note that this data is pulled from DirectedByWomen.com's ongoing database of content by female filmmakers. Because of the nature of independent projects, it is virtually impossible to collect a truly comprehensive list, but these numbers are reflective of the larger trends, if not exact.

Although few yet realized it, the modern women in film revolution had begun.

During my barnstorming time on the speechifying circuit talking about women in film, which has continued long after I was originally told by those in the industry to shut up, I have often had the good fortune to speak to rooms filled with highly successful and powerful women from other industries. I always go through my normal routine of explaining that, *yes*, there is still a women in film problem (a rather massive one, actually), why I think that it matters for the world at large, and how our continued exclusion is predicated on an idea that doesn't fundamentally make any sense to me—that audiences don't want to see films about women. In 2016, after one particular talk, a coiffed, petite, fierce-looking blonde woman in her mid-fifties came up to me.

> BLONDE WOMAN: I come from finance. I've never thought that movies mattered. You've changed my mind. This is a terrible situation. What do we do about it?
>
> ME: Oh. Well . . . basically we need money to make our movies.
>
> BLONDE WOMAN: Okay, well then there should be an investment fund that specifically drives that change through investing in female filmmakers and demonstrating returns.
>
> ME: . . . yes.
>
> BLONDE WOMAN: Well, have you spoken to the film financiers about this?
>
> ME: . . . I'm not sure you're quite grasping the depth of this problem.
>
> BLONDE WOMAN: Okay. Well, if I start a fund like that, would you start it with me?
>
> ME: . . . okay . . .

It was a ten-minute conversation and, honestly, I thought she was joking. She wasn't. She turned out to be Lois Scott, former CFO of the City of Chicago; a founder of Scott Balice Strategies, one of the largest private financial advisory firms in the country; and a thirty-year veteran of the financial services industry.

With her deep experience in and understanding of finance (though not film) and my reasonable understanding of film (though not finance), we set out on a multiyear journey, taking a crash-course-by-coffee-date in macro-film finance from anyone who would talk to us and, in short, attempting to figure out how the economics of film finance work in the first place and why women weren't getting the money.

Lois and I learned much of what I have now written in these pages with regard to the lack of funding for women's projects, but we also came to understand the bigger picture of how the film industry has landed itself in its current cycle of endless remakes, sequels, and franchises and out of the business of making anything remotely fresh.

Like clockwork, every couple of decades, the film industry goes through a major crisis as some new technology is developed, viewing habits change, and old revenue models become unsustainable. Everybody panics, lots of articles are written about the end of the film industry, and then some new innovation comes along—usually pioneered by the indie-film world first—and saves Hollywood from annihilation. This has been happening cyclically since the 1950s when TV became an audience-stealing force. So far, we still have a film industry.[9]

As Jessica Goodman, former executive at Universal Pictures, Warner Bros., and 20th Century Fox, explained to me, in the mid-1990s version of this cycle, movies were doing quite well theatrically. Whatever a movie made opening weekend, you could multiply that by five for its domestic gross, far more for overall gross, and everyone was happy. Soon, however, ticket sales fell out due to the advent of Blockbuster and VHS tapes, marketing costs soared, and soon the total gross for a movie was likely to be only two times what it grossed opening weekend.

Cue panic mode, crisis, articles, and then innovation, this time in the form of DVDs. Whereas with VHS tapes, most people likely only owned their very favorite movies, with DVDs, for whatever reason, there sprung up a whole culture of owning "collections."* Roughly 15 percent of all DVDs sold in the mid-2000s were never removed from their shrink-wrap.[10] Also with studios earning a profit of $15 per disc sold, theatrical revenues became less important and, with places like Walmart placing bins of discounted DVDs near their registers, "all but the biggest flops became profitable."[11]

This was a golden period for Hollywood profits. As Michael Lynton, chairman of Sony Pictures, said, "There was so much money swilling around in the system in [the early 2000s] you could afford to make enormous mistakes because of the safety net of the DVD business."[12]

All of that money led to the appearance of incredibly expensive new special-effects movies like *Harry Potter* (2001) at $100 million and *Spider-Man* (2002) at $139 million.[13] This marked a turning point for

---

* Possibly having to do in part with their thinner design and relatively smaller command of shelf space.

Hollywood, because budgets for these tentpole* films ballooned to enormous heights, far beyond what a film had ever cost to make in the past.

As Ben Fritz, journalist and author of *The Big Picture*, says, "Hollywood is an industry of followers, and in the wake of the success of *Spider-Man*, everyone jumped on the Marvel superhero train."[14] The fiscal flushness of the era also allowed studios to take a lot of creative swings on "lower-budget" films, in the $30–80 million range, safe in the knowledge that the tentpoles would balance out their books and that they'd likely recoup on DVDs alone on most of the smaller films, whatever their theatrical performance.

A typical yearly slate from a studio in the early 2000s consisted of about twenty-five films, of which only two or three would be tentpole films, which left plenty of room for the studio to make the smaller, smarter, original films more appealing to grown-ups. Those "smaller" films are almost all the Oscar movies from that time and, for many people, represent the totality of the films that they loved and remembered past the time the credits stopped rolling.

The studios were happy because they were making money. Audiences were happy because Hollywood was providing them with smart, original, creative fare that interested them, while also giving them the option to go out for a fun night to the theater and see explosions every once in a while.

DVDs were so successfully propping up the film market, however, that by 2007, a full 50 percent of studios' overall profits were coming from DVD sales alone.[15] Theater attendance, in the meantime, had been declining since 2001, from 1.57 billion tickets sold in the US and Canada in 2002 to 1.31 billion sold in 2016.[16]

So, starting around 2008, when the market for DVDs fell out virtually overnight, the studios found themselves in freefall. DVD sales had been upended by online piracy, by iTunes and Amazon offering movie streaming through their platforms, by Netflix switching from a DVD-rental to a subscription streaming model, and by the proliferation of services like

---

* A tentpole film is one that a studio thinks will "hold up the tent" of its yearly slate of films in terms of box-office returns—think *Harry Potter*, *Hunger Games*, superhero movies, and the like.

Redbox, which made renting DVDs easily accessible and hassle-free, all of which catastrophically affected the studios' DVD revenues.

During this period, movie consumption by audiences sky-rocketed, even though people were spending less money to watch them. People either stole them from piracy sites or paid a few dollars to rent them (as opposed to paying $15 to buy a DVD, in those golden days of yore). Home entertainment revenue, a category that includes DVD sales, plummeted from $22 billion in 2004 to half of that, $12 billion in 2016.[17]

The ease of watching films from home further depressed theatrical ticket sales and, to make matters even worse, movie stars were no longer the sure-fire audience draw they used to be. Even the biggest celebrities, like Tom Cruise, became hit or miss at the box office.[18] The studios were in full-blown panic.

One truth was now clear: it was no longer possible to domestically recoup the movie budgets that had been increasing in the ten years prior. And it seemed extremely unlikely that those kinds of domestic recoupments would ever be possible again.

In this moment, Hollywood had two options. Either cut overhead, slash budgets, and go back to making movies with reasonable budgets that *could* still recoup domestically, or commit to making movies that could sell in every territory in the entire world, thereby making up for lower domestic revenue.

Realistically, the first option was never going to happen. Studio executives like Amy Pascal (then at Sony) were making between $6.7 million and $14.2 million annually between 2002 and 2014, and they were never going to make the decision to suddenly go back to slumming it with a dramatically cut paycheck.[19] Also, in the intervening decade, the studios had institutionally forgotten how to make cheaper movies.* Finally, the studios by this time had all been purchased by corporations and now had a mandate to make as much money as possible for their shareholders.

Fortunately for the studios, international markets for American films were opening up. In an odd story involving James Cameron and the unusual release of *Titanic* in the former Soviet Union in 1997, Russia had gone from being a "nothing" market on nobody's radar to becoming in

---

* As the major Hollywood producer Lynda Obst wrote, "I wouldn't know how to make [a $100,000 movie] with a gun to my head." (Obst, *Sleepless in Hollywood*.)

five years' time one of the world's top-five film markets.[20] During this same period, censorship laws began to loosen in China, ushering in a voracious demand for once forbidden American movies. By 2014, eighteen new movie screens were being built in China *every day*. By late 2016, there were 371 IMAX screens in China, with 381 more already contracted to be built. At that stage, China was suddenly 45 percent of IMAX's worldwide screen total.[21] Latin American economies were also growing alongside China's, and in both regions, "the rising middle-class spent their newfound wealth on what was to them the novel and luxurious experience of a night out to see the latest Hollywood flick."[22]

To give you an idea of the scale of this shift, in 2001 international box office revenue was $8.6 billion. By 2016 it was $27.6 billion. The most swiftly growing market during that period was China, which went from $2 billion box office revenue in 2011 to $6.6 billion in 2016 and is at this moment pitched to surpass the US in box office revenue.[23]

During the same period, 2001–2015, domestic box office grew by (only) 40 percent, which actually represents a slight decline in attendance, when taking into account rising theater ticket prices.[24]

International revenue, in other words, swooped in to save the day.

From the 1980s to the 2000s, international revenue accounted for about 20 percent of Hollywood's total revenue. By 2008, it was 50 percent—perfectly replacing the lost DVD revenue. By 2011, international was 70 percent—an even bigger haul than DVDs. Today, international revenue is around 80 percent of studios' overall revenue, with nothing but rising trends forecasted.[25]

Hollywood has been kid-on-a-sugar-high giddy over these new revenue streams. *Harry Potter and the Chamber of Secrets* (2002), part of one of the all-time most successful franchises of the ten-year earlier tentpole model, grossed $849 million worldwide.[26] *Iron Man* (2008) grossed $585 million globally. *Iron Man 2* (2010) grossed $624 million. *Iron Man 3* (2013) grossed $1.2 *billion*. *The Avengers* (2012) grossed $1.5 *billion*. *Skyfall* grossed $1.1 *billion*. Even *Ant-Man* (2015) grossed $519 million.[27]

Meanwhile, the smart, original, interesting films for grown-ups that used to be the bulk of what Hollywood made only years earlier were *still making money*, but not nearly as much as the tentpole movie franchises. The most successful among that strata of films, like *21 Jump Street, Moneyball*, and *The Social Network*, made $40–60 million in profit.[28] Not a bad take to your average Joe, but what studio was going to be able to justify going to their shareholders on Wall Street and explaining why it was going to continue dinking around with tens of millions of dollars in profit when they could consistently return billions of dollars in profit instead by selling internationally? Nobody. That's who.

As Hollywood producer Kevin Goetz rather astonishingly chided fellow producer Lynda Obst: "Lynda, never lose yourself. Don't forget this; we're in a business. If we can make six-hundred-forty-billion-dollar rides, why would we want to make two-hundred-forty-billion-dollar rides? It's a business."[29]

And he's right. If the financial bottom line is the only metric you care about, then there is no conceivable definition of "enough." The studios made the best possible decision for their shareholders.

Except for a few Oscar bait-y movies every year, the studios got out of the business of making those mid-level movies almost entirely and focused all their resources on making this new brand of mega-blockbuster, globally selling tentpole films.

In *Sleepless in Hollywood*, Obst runs through a list of movies that would never now be made (except *mayybbbeeee* as tiny indies well outside the studio system): *Field of Dreams, Forrest Gump, The Fisher King, Driving Miss Daisy, The Big Chill, The Graduate, Moonstruck, Rain Man.* She concludes, "The more we love the movie, the less likely it would get made now."[30]

This new trend is bad for US movie lovers and anyone else who wants to watch movies with zero men in spandex, but it's not just the type of movies that has changed. The overall quality has precipitously declined. If you need a movie that will culturally translate to audiences in Cincinnati and Dubai and Shenzhen and Moscow and Sao Paulo and Jaipur, that is not an easy order. The obsessive conversations in restaurants around Los Angeles for the past decade have been various theories on what types of stories will or will not "travel."*

Comedies, for instance, are mostly untouchable since humor tends to be culturally specific. The only comedies that *could* work would be of the

---

* One interviewee for this book was horrified to overhear at a film market—where the industry goes to buy and sell films—a film buyer confidently stating to a sales agent in reference to *Twelve Years a Slave*, "Well, yes, but Russia doesn't buy black."

broadest, most basic nature and must definitely not rely on wit, nuance, or smart repartee (i.e., slipping on a banana peel is funny everywhere; wit is not). Dramas tend not to travel, since they are often also culturally specific and rely heavily on dialogue, which is less compelling when dubbed and annoying to (some) audiences when subtitled. The only movies that consistently travel well are action movies and family-friendly animated fare—both of which are easier to dub and benefit from the fact that people will apparently always pay to have their child sit quietly for a few hours in an air-conditioned room.* As a general rule of thumb, though, the more explosions and less dialogue, the better.

Another driving factor for preferred global content has been that, in countries like China, with its new middle-class emerging as the primary ticket buyers, attending these big American movies with their families became a status symbol and an opportunity for a high-flying night out. In that context, you don't want some dreary movie that's going to spend the evening provoking you to look at the darkest recesses of your soul. You want an "event." Superheroes! Capes! Explosions! Mind-blowing action sequences! Those are the movies worthy of a night on the town.[31]

An additional hurdle for the studios to this global model, and a big reason for the decline in the quality of the films, is that they had better make damn sure there's nothing in their movie that's going to turn off, offend, or unintentionally insult local audiences in any country on earth.

In talking to a screenwriter friend who writes for studio films, I expressed my frustration with the total blandness of the screenplays of these global tentpole movies. "It's not like it costs more money for a better script," I cried. He explained, "Most of the original screenplays for those movies were a lot better. But the studio execs are terrified of pissing any audiences off. If you want to offend the least number of people, you're going to end up with a screenplay that's so watered down—driven to the middle—that everything that started out in there that made it interesting is going to get stripped out by the time you get to set."

As *New York Times* film critic A. O. Scott said recently, "Good movies are [now] made as much in spite of the industry as by means of it."[32]

It gets even worse.

---

* This explains animated films' status as the last frontier of fresh, interesting content coming out of the studios.

The US population is about 5 percent of the world's population. Now studios have to market their films to the other 95 percent of the people on earth. They can't just exponentially expand their marketing budgets; otherwise, the financial equation stops working.[33] This is where franchises, sequels, prequels, and "intellectual property"* have become key.

In order to avoid having to heavily market a movie, your safest bet is to only make movies with brands that will be recognized by viewers internationally.

If you release the umpteenth *Harry Potter, Fast & Furious, Transformers, Spiderman, Star Wars*, or *Avengers* movie, the marketing spend is much lighter. Audiences who are devotees of those brands already want to see those movies, so you just have to let them know that the next one is coming out to get them to the theaters. You don't have to do the much more costly work of educating audiences about a new movie and convincing them to go see it, as you would have to do with an original concept.

As a result, studios are in a frenzy buying up rights to every conceivable globally recognized IP in existence—whether or not they even make sense as a story (see: *The Emoji Movie*). The single and only important thing is whether or not the movie is part of a brand that will be recognized in every country on earth and then whether you can then turn that series into a franchise.

In fact, as Fritz writes in *The Big Picture*, "Even franchises are old news—now it's about cinematic universes. Pioneered by Disney-owned Marvel studios, these have overarching narratives that connect multiple characters and allow story lines and characters to weave in and out of them. . . . Plot points that begin in an *Iron Man* movie can continue in *Thor* and *Captain America* and be resolved in *The Avengers* . . . and fans flock to see them all."[34]

Another important factor is whether fans will also buy related merchandise. Fritz writes, "To decide which film to make first [from its library of characters] . . . Marvel brought together groups of children, showed them pictures of its superheroes, and described their abilities

---

* In this context, "intellectual property" (IP, as it's known) refers to any big brand-name content that is seen as being internationally lucrative when turned into a movie (franchise, ideally).

and weapons. Then they asked the kids which ones they would most like to play with as a toy."

For US audiences who remember what it was like to experience movies that bore some relation to the important, cathartic, uplifting, provocative function that art and storytelling can provide, this continued talk of sequels, prequels, remakes, spin-offs, and "cinematic universes" is a major turn-off.

The thing is, Hollywood knows this.

To cite just one example, let's look at the domestic versus international performance of the *Ice Age* franchise, as shown in the following chart.[35]

	Domestic Box Office Revenue	International Box Office Revenue
Ice Age (the first)	$175M	$206M
Ice Age 2	$192M	$456M
Ice Age 3	$200M	$700M
Ice Age 4	$46M	$716M

Hollywood knows US audiences hate the path they are taking and frankly, my dears, they don't give a damn, because they are making money hand over fist on this stuff internationally.

My 2011 pivot-point coincides pretty nicely with the period of time during which Hollywood fully gave up on domestic audiences and grown-up content, and the latest spike in female independent filmmakers started to take shape. Because if I'm looking at this situation from purely a business and finance perspective—as, indeed financier Lois Scott and I were in early summer 2015—there is a clear marketplace opportunity being left open by Hollywood's abandonment of domestic audiences.

Those audiences are currently deserting movies en masse and are instead searching for replacements for the quality content they used to get consistently at the cinema. Arguably that's why Netflix, Amazon, and other TV networks producing fresh, smart, prestige TV programming have done gangbusters business in recent years. They stepped in to fill that vacuum. Their success suggests that audiences do still want quality content.

Yet in spite of the fact that Netflix heavily and algorithmically pushes their audiences' viewing habits toward serialized content (especially their own) over movies, according to an off-the-record conversation with an employee,* of their audience's overall viewing hours, movies have still never dropped below one-third. This suggests that audiences have not given up on movies entirely.

This is great news for independent filmmakers, particularly those from underrepresented demographics, like me. Because remember, those lower-budget movies the studios are no longer interested in *were still making money domestically.* For an independent producer, a cool $10 million domestic box office revenue stream—not to mention streaming licensing and purchase fees—is most definitely worth leaving your house for, even if it isn't worth it for the studios. Meanwhile, technology has improved to the point that it is now possible to produce those old $30–80 million movies for $1–20 million, without losing quality, making those movies more plausibly recoupable domestically even without the vanished DVD sales.

If I am an investor and I can't get a piece of Hollywood's billion-dollar-movie scheme, the clear place I would want to invest is in $1–20 million smart, original, grown-up content to fill the marketplace gap left by Hollywood.

Talented, savvy, women indie filmmakers with great ideas? There might be a place for us yet.

But is there an audience for our content? That is the perennial question.

The first question to ask ourselves is Where did this persistent idea that people don't want to see films about women even come from in the first place?

Four-quadrant marketing has long been the gold standard by which studios choose which films to make. The four quadrants divide by gender (men and women) and by age (older than twenty-four and younger than twenty-four).

The idea is that, before executives decide to green-light a film, they need to know exactly which and how many quadrants that film will

---

* Since, again, they release none of this information publicly.

appeal to. The "holy grail," as Lynda Obst says, is all four. "Family movies are often four-quadrant movies—*Shrek, The Lion King, Madagascar*, almost all Pixar movies"—presumably since families will often go to movies together. Four-quadrant grown-up movies are a lot harder to peg, but *Titanic*, for instance, was thought of (and indeed proved to be) a four-quadrant movie. According to the studios' somewhat limited thinking, you've got the love story for the women, the ship-sinking action for the men, the sexy scene to pull in the young people, the historical nostalgia to pull in the old farts. Badda bing, badda boom, major hit.

The vast majority of films, of course, do not reach all four quadrants, so, for executives, what to produce has always come down to knowing which quadrants you most needed to appeal to in order to turn a profit.

The studios' thinking, particularly in the late 1990s and early 2000s, has been that the male under-twenty-fours, most specifically the teenage boys, are the mother lode. These folks, to their minds, are the ones who will reliably come out to theaters on opening night or weekend—no obligations, nothing to do, in possession of some pocket money.

The male over-twenty-fours are good, too, but, according to Obst, "could rarely make a hit alone." Fortunately, it seems to be pretty easy to make films that appeal to the sensibilities of both male quadrants, in which case you have a massive hit on your hands.

Female under-twenty-fours are all right, though not as good as teenage boys, but the problem, as far as the studios are concerned, are the female over-twenty-fours. Writes Obst, women over twenty-four have been the "least frequently targeted quadrant because of our penchant for waiting until we have unloaded the dishwasher and done every other imaginable errand we have to do before we leave the house and go to the movies."

How is that for a self-reinforcing patriarchy?

The net result of this theory is that, because you can't rely on the female over-twenty-fours to come out to movies at all, you can't make hits out of movies that appeal to women overall, therefore you must keep making movies by and about men.

How convenient for them.

I had originally assumed that the four-quadrant marketing system's obsession with teenage boys as the ultimate audience member was an idea that had been based on data at some point in its genesis. Producer and former studio executive Jack Lechner informed me, however, that that may not have ever been true. He recalls having been told in the late 1980s by another studio executive that the father of modern movie research and research consultant to the studios, Joseph Farrell, had conducted a study back then and concluded that, actually, the prime audience member at that time was a fourteen-year-old girl. In other words, the golden teenage boy theory may never have been anything more than a gut feeling on the part of (almost exclusively male) studio executives, but it has nevertheless ruled Hollywood's decision-making since at least the 1980s.

Even assuming this golden teenage boy theory was ever salient, though, in these first decades of the twenty-first century, American women's personal wealth has increased substantially, giving them the financial freedom to partake in leisure activities and, presumably, freed them at least partially from time spent in front of the dishwasher.[36] We know for a fact that women are now consistently 52 percent of all movie ticket purchasers.[37] Yet studio executives remain devoted to their golden teenage boy demographic.

Obst writes, "The studios just can't give these boys up, kind of like your nutty girlfriend who won't stop stalking an old lover despite his obvious lack of interest. Every week there is an update about whether the boys' attention is finally back and, if not, what will draw them back."

Fortunately, we don't actually need a Ouija board to resolve this question, because film revenue is quantifiable and, in fact, draws a direct correlation to how many audience members paid to watch them. In other words, we have data. Here is what that data shows.

Note: Throughout this section we are primarily going to look at return on investment, or ROI—meaning, per dollar invested in the movie, how much does the investor make back. This is because, as discussed, films by and about women are almost universally given lower budgets to work with and, since gross revenue (how much in total the film makes) has a strong correlation with budget (the more expensive films tend to make more money overall), this means that films by and about men do tend to make more *gross* revenue. From an investors' perspective, however, gross revenue is not an important metric. For instance, if I invest $1,000 in a film that grosses $450 million, but due to the budget size, I only get back $1,010, that is a less good investment than if I invest in a smaller film that made only $10 million, but due to budget size, I get back $2,000. How much I get back in relation to how much money I put in is ROI and, from an investor's perspective, that is the important thing.

DATA POINT #1) FILMS *ABOUT* WOMEN MAKE MONEY.

Slated, an online film financing marketplace, teamed with FiveThirty Eight.com to study this very contention and found that films that pass the Bechdel test—again, not a serious indication of a strongly feminist film but at least a general indicator of the presence of more female characters in a film—make an average of $0.23 more in revenue per dollar spent than films that don't.[38] A study conducted by Gracenote, a Nielsen company, examining the 350 top-grossing films released between 2014 and 2017, found that, on average, female-featured films led global box-office revenue at every budget level.[39]

Oscar-nominated films with a "clearly definable female lead" were 33 percent more profitable than male-led films.[40] Despite that, only 28 percent of Oscar-nominated films *have* a female lead.

Frozen, a film about two interesting women and, currently at $1.3 billion gross revenue (before you even get to toys, merchandise, and the Broadway musical), is the biggest-grossing animated film of all time.[41]

Girls Trip (2017), a film with an ensemble black female cast—even less likely to do well by the studios' estimation, because when they are thinking about quadrants they are thinking about white quadrants—opened to $30.4 million and has earned over $135 million worldwide, "the best start for an R-rated comedy in two years," with the audience composed of 51 percent black viewers and 38 percent Caucasian viewers.[42]

DATA POINT #2) FILMS *BY* WOMEN HAVE HIGHER FINANCIAL RETURNS.

Because there was less available data on this question, Lois Scott and I commissioned Bruce Nash, from the database The Numbers, to run a study that looked at the relative profitability of films by men versus women. For this study, Bruce looked at all narrative feature films (no documentaries) that were released between 2011 and 2016 that received any kind of distribution deal whatsoever.[43] So this data covers everything from the biggest studio film all the way down to the tiniest indie that got thrown up on a streaming platform, but it does not include films that were finished but not released in any manner beyond film festivals.

The results were astonishing, even to us:

Role	ROI for Films with Male in the Role	ROI for Films with Female in the Role
Director	23%	29%
Producer	4%	23%
Screenwriter	18%	53%

In every single category the ROI is higher if the role is filled by a woman. Every. Single. One.

We're not talking about small amounts of money here. For directors, it comes out more or less evenly, with women having a bit of an edge. But if you are hiring a producer and/or screenwriter, to return to our hypothetical scenario of investing $1,000 in a movie, you definitely, *definitely* want that person to be a woman. We're talking about a difference, on the producer end, of making back $1,004 (man) versus $1,023 (woman). With a screenwriter, that's $1,018 (man) versus $1,053 (woman). Not a huge difference when you're talking about $1,000, but generally people invest a whole lot more in movies, so if it's $1 million investment, that's an added profit for you of $190,000 for a female producer and $350,000 for a female writer.

(Oh, but the teenage boys, though . . .)

DATA POINT #3) FILMS WITH DIVERSE CASTS ARE MORE PROFITABLE.

According to the 2019 UCLA Hollywood Diversity Report, which looked at the two hundred top-grossing films from 2017, films with casts featuring 31–40 percent non-white actors "enjoyed the highest median global box office" at $169.8 million.[44]

In fact, films with homogenous casts (with 89 percent or more white actors) made up a significant majority of all films made in 2017 and yet had the lowest global box office of any category.[45]

The idea, yet another one that is "well-known" in Los Angeles, that movies featuring non-white actors don't travel globally is also nonsensical on its face. There are about 7.5 billion people on the planet. According to the CIA World Factbook, the largest recognized ethnic group in the world is the Han Chinese at 1.3 billion, followed by Arabic people, then the Spanish, both at around 450 million.[46] It is a breathtaking level of arrogance to presume that those people are primarily interested in watching films about white people.

This commonsense logic is borne out by the recent international performance of films like *Moonlight* and *Hidden Figures*—despite "black doesn't travel" being one of the grossest and most commonly "known truths" in Hollywood. *Hidden Figures* generated over $230 million worldwide, on a $25 million production budget, $66 million of which was made internationally.[47] *Moonlight* actually made *more* money internationally. Made for a mere $1.5 million, it has grossed $65 million overall, of which $37 million came from foreign sales.[48] The juggernaut *Black Panther* fared almost equally well theatrically in the domestic market ($700 million) as internationally ($647 million).[49]

DATA POINT #4) OLD PEOPLE PAY TO WATCH MOVIES.

The four-quadrant schematic notwithstanding, it turns out that films about people age sixty-plus are highly profitable.

In 2016, of the ten most-profitable indie films to play in cinemas, seven were aimed strictly at adults, and many were centered on characters age sixty and over.[50]

Hello, My Name Is Doris, a comedic romp about the burgeoning sex life of an aged Sally Field, is a perfect example of this. Eric D'Arbeloff, co-president of Roadside Attractions, which distributed the movie, said, "When we bought *Hello, My Name Is Doris*, there were people saying it's cute, but it doesn't have commercial legs."[51] So far, the film has made $14.3 million, becoming the highest grossing film to have ever premiered at SXSW,* and it has done quite well for its investors, since it was made for $1 million.

In fact, one journalist writing in the *Guardian* wryly noted about the wild box-office success of *Woman in Gold* and *St. Vincent* in 2015: "Both films were tepidly received by critics, leading to the conclusion that their targeted demographics are likely to flock in droves simply because they exist. They don't even have to be that good."[52]

---

* Without having prior distribution attached.

DATA POINT #5) GENDER PARITY IN LEADERSHIP LEADS TO HIGHER REVENUE.

Disney, which has far and away the highest number of women in positions of leadership of any of the major studios, is also the most profitable.[53]

While there are myriad factors contributing to their success, the presence of women in management as a driver of success does match with a well-established trend across industries. For instance, companies with women on their boards financially outperform companies that do not. "Gender parity is correlated with increased sales revenue, more customers, and greater relative profits."[54]

DATA POINT #6) LOOK TO NETFLIX.

Netflix is the company most responsible for stealing audiences away from Hollywood content and bringing them to its own (mostly serialized) content.

As I said before, Netflix has access to a greater and more complex amount of viewership data than any other entertainment company or industry in history due to the fact that it can and does track in *minute* detail consumers' behavior on their site. Although it does not release these metrics, Netflix relies on them to make content decisions. Although we don't have access to Netflix data, we can see what it is choosing to make. The number of Netflix original films and series by and about women, people of color, and other historically underrepresented voices so far outstrips what Hollywood is doing that watching only Netflix content is like living in a parallel universe (a universe that looks a whole lot more like the world we live in than Hollywood's).*

What this means is that the people who are most intimately familiar with audiences' viewing habits know, at least by now, that the old four-quadrant marketing is garbage.

DATA POINT #7) THE WORLD HAS CHANGED.

All of these viewing and revenue trends make sense if you take into account that the demographics and behaviors of audiences are not the same as they were twenty years ago.

---

* They are still not at parity in front of or behind the camera with women or any other marginalized group, but they are closer.

As Tim Haslam, co-founder of Embankment, points out, today's women "make for strong audiences. They leave the theaters and get on their phones. They're emotionally engaged. We can do all of that without explosives and huge budgets."[55]

Non-whites accounted for the majority of ticket sales for five of the ten top-grossing films in 2016, with Latinx millennials as the biggest spending block overall now in the US.[56]

These are trends that will only continue as the underlying factors continue to shift. Non-whites, currently 40 percent of the US population, are expected to become the majority within a few decades.[57]

The *Economist* called female economic empowerment "the most profound social change of our times." Women in the US get more college and graduate degrees than men. We currently control more than 80 percent of US consumer spending.[58] And it is estimated that by 2030, women will control two-thirds of our nation's wealth.[59] If women are already buying the majority of movie tickets now, imagine how much more this percentage will increase over the next decade.

I am not just talking about US women. The idea that the new global model of movie sales means that we have to retrench ourselves in white male cinema is wrong-headed. "It's estimated that by 2020 the female economics of India and China will be worth $5 trillion."[60]

To boot, in a global survey of eight thousand women, ages seventeen to seventy, across nineteen countries, over 70 percent of women were interested in seeing more women in leading roles, yet over half of women said that they found it difficult to relate to female characters on-screen, and slightly over 60 percent of women surveyed said they felt there weren't enough older women on screen, with similar numbers agreeing there isn't enough racial diversity of women on-screen.[61]

More than a third of women "claimed to have stopped watching a film, TV programme or advert that they felt was stereotyping them, and a resounding 85 percent of women felt that media and culture were blind to how much they stereotype women, indicating that they feel the industry as a whole has a huge blindspot."

Women are becoming the dominant financial drivers, and we see you, Hollywood. We're sick of your crap.

From a purely economic perspective—assessing the market gaps, opportunities, and data—if I look to future trends, just as Hollywood is doing with its rampantly globalizing markets, the only logical conclusion I can come to is that the best investment is in films by and about women, people of color, and other historically underrepresented voices. The evidence points to the fact that this is where the appetite, dollars, and market lie. In fact, looking at the convergence of the shifting cinematic macroeconomic trends with audience and spending transformation as an investor, my logical conclusion is that the new "holy grail" is a $15 million film, written, directed, and produced by women and centering on the story of a sixty-plus-year-old Latina disabled woman.

Where's the movie for that lady?

CHAPTER 9

WONDER WOM(E)N*

O ver the course of learning all of these macroeconomic factors, Lois Scott and I recognized that there was a dire need for more funds specifically dedicated to financing narrative feature films by female directors, as well as a clear marketplace opportunity for investors to do the same.[†] We were outraged that the "women in film issue" continued to be spoken about as a charity case when, to the contrary, it was actually a good business opportunity that was being summarily ignored. Determined to take action, we joined ranks with my *Imagine I'm Beautiful* producer and now distribution expert, Caitlin Gold; acclaimed indie producer Lindsay Lanzillotta; and Jessica Goodman, former executive from Universal Pictures, Warner Bros., and 20th Century Fox, whose films at the same time had generated over $2 billion in revenue, in an attempt to put together The 51 Fund, a private equity fund that would finance films by female directors with budgets between $500,000 and $15 million.

I'd always found the whole "nobody wants to see films about women" premise iffy at best. After studying the numbers, I felt vindicated. Women have the most buying power, purchase 52 percent of all movie tickets, yet have the fewest movies made for them. Our plan to fill that marketplace void was clearly golden and backed by cold, hard data.

---

* *Wonder Woman* (2017), dir. Patty Jenkins.
† At that time there was only one, Gamechanger Films.

My 51 Fund partners and I triumphantly marched back to Los Angeles, armed with this—we thought—irrefutable evidence. *Surely, people will listen to us now.*

Not even close.

We were brushed off, stonewalled, and derisively called "feminists." Meeting after meeting we were met with, "I don't know. That just doesn't sound right to me." Followed by the infinitely more condescending, "Hollywood is a profit-driven *business*. If what you're telling me is true, they would be financing films by and about women."*

Occasionally someone would say, "Yeah, we know. But we just can't do anything about it because 'we can't find good enough projects by women,' 'the women themselves aren't qualified enough to finance,' 'Y film by Z woman just flopped, so obviously . . .'" and so on.†

My team and I were not the only data-armed group shouting at the industry about the business case for women in film. The articles written about it by major and minor media publications, companies trying to be started, and studies done about the lack of women in film and the business case for hiring and financing more of them—most especially between 2013 and the Weinstein meltdown—numbered in the hundreds. The powers that be swatted each of us away like flies.

I found myself over and over, once again, in the disorienting position of, on some days, regularly giving speeches to up-and-coming filmmakers or non-film-industry folks and showing them the data and statistics and receiving mind-blown and outraged responses—"How did we not know about this?" "Why aren't they doing anything about this?" "What can *we* do to help?" And then, on other days, meeting with the people who actually *are* in a position to do something about it and getting the

---

* In trying to work out why, in spite of data to the contrary, the studios are *not* financing more films by and about women, the best explanation I have found was the response of one former studio executive who told me, "I worked for the studios for twenty years. In no meeting ever did someone look up and say, 'What's a market opportunity we're missing? What haven't we tried yet?' Instead the mind-set is always one of, 'How can we replicate as closely as possible what was successful last time?'"

† Daniel Melnick, one of Hollywood's leading producers, was quoted in 1964 as saying, "I think that as an industry, we have very often shown the instinct of lemmings." As everything changes, everything stays the same. William Goldman, *Adventures in the Screen Trade* (New York: Hachette, 1984).

cold shoulder or the even more infuriating, "Yeah. I really can't help you. But if you do manage to raise your funds, I've got four or five projects that I'd *love* for you to take a look at to consider financing."

By 2016, after a year of trying to get The 51 Fund off the ground and three years into speaking and writing nonstop about the experience of women in Hollywood,* I was feeling demoralized and frustrated. More than anything, though, I was becoming incensed. I wasn't even so much incensed for myself or for other women or for people of color or for other underrepresented colleagues (although I was). I was incensed most of all for film audiences. The public was demanding more representative content and stories, proving over and over again that they will support this kind of work though they are consistently being force-fed the same adolescent, white, male diet.

My outrage was abundant. So, when I was invited in the spring of 2015 to give a TED Talk on the subject, I accepted the opportunity. I was nervous about how the film industry would respond, of course. TED Talks provide a global platform, and the film industry gatekeepers I had been trying to woo for so many years and through so many rounds of spreadsheets would hear about the talk eventually. But I had to do it—no question. A blanket industry silence had allowed this discrimination to go unchecked for too long, and regardless of whatever personal career risks existed, I was not willing to be part of maintaining their cover.

As the day of my talk neared, I grew so nervous that I developed physical symptoms. I couldn't seem to settle my stomach. I did the only thing I could do. I took a shot of whiskey and went back to the data. I looked at what has happened to the career of woman after woman in this industry—even the most successful ones. "The inexorable zero"; the hurdles around financing, production, festivals, and distribution; the lineage of generations of brilliant voices never given wings or light; and the irrefutable and yet-refuted profit advantages. That was clarifying enough for me. *Fuck it*, I thought, once again.†

I wasn't the only woman feeling that way, of course.

---

* Which, it's important to note, is decades less than many other fierce women have been banging on about this.

† I listened to "Defying Gravity" on repeat no fewer than twelve times before I was brave enough to walk onstage.

In the decade and a half since Miramar, organizations, companies, collectives, and initiatives formed by activists and changemakers were springing up left, right, and center, each trying a different approach to at long last move the needle. So much so that, as of today, there are at least 130 such efforts actively working on everything from the grassroots to the corporate level. That there is such a broad base of organizations, initiatives, for-profit companies, and individual activists makes the current women in film movement different and (hopefully) more impactful and lasting than in any previous era.

The movements' fronts are sixfold: Study, Make, Hire, Fund, Disrupt, and Watch.*

STUDY

Data is crucial in this work. Until the Original Six dug through the hiring records and were able to prove that only 0.5 percent of directing jobs were going to women, their claims of discrimination were written off as hysterical.

The Geena Davis Institute on Gender in Media, led by Caroline Heldman; the USC Annenberg research team, led by Stacy Smith; Martha M. Lauzen and her team at the Center for the Study of Women in Television and Film; and the team at the UCLA College of Social Sciences have been and continue to be vital, picking up where the Original Six left off, providing the cold, hard facts about representation, both behind and in front of the camera, facts that the rest of us have been able weaponize and use to incite action. I have heavily relied on their data throughout this book and in all my work.

MAKE

There are important organizations working directly with female filmmakers to get their films made at the indie level, to whatever possible extent, without having to wait for the say-so of the gatekeepers.

Many of these efforts take the form of collectives, in which women can build community, engage in peer-to-peer knowledge sharing, hear

---

* Please note that, although I reference various groups here as examples of each front, it is impossible in the context of this book to give proper due to every group doing good work. For a more complete resource list, please look at the Resource List beginning on p. 242.

from outside speakers and experts to provide training and workshops, and, hopefully, find mentorship and in-the-trenches tips from other members who may be slightly ahead of them on their career paths.

Institutions like Women in Film and their location-specific chapters have been doing this work since 1973. But the sudden swell of female creatives that occurred as the twenty-first century began its second decade has engendered smaller, grassroots-based communities and collectives such as the Latino Filmmakers Network, Blue Collar Post Collection, Cinematographers XX, Black Filmmakers Group, CAPE (Coalition of Asian Pacifics in Entertainment), NYC Women Filmmakers, Women of Color UNITE, Film Fatales, the FilmmakeHers, and countless others. These groups provide women and other historically underrepresented voices not only with practical skills, information, and networking but also, often, with the emotional sustenance and support needed to navigate an industry that continually works against them.

There have also been labs created that work to usher specific and vetted projects into production. The Sundance Catalyst Lab matches investors with individual film projects from underrepresented filmmakers, as does Tribeca All Access. The far-more-grassroots, but impressively effective, From Script to PreProduction works with eight female filmmakers each year over a six-month period in a weekly intensive to help them develop the tools they need to get their films from script to preproduction. Several of their alumnae are now financed and in production.

HIRE

Then there are endeavors that specifically work to make it easier and more enticing for the existing system and industry to hire greater numbers of women, while putting continual pressure on them to do so.

To combat the executives' and agents' common excuse of "We'd love to hire women and people of color, but we just can't find any," several databases featuring lists of women and people of color looking to be hired have been created. Cheryl L. Bedford has launched the JTC List, a database of women of color ready to be hired across a multiplicity of entertainment jobs. April Reign, the creator of #OscarsSoWhite, is now at work on Akuarel, a digital repository of talent (behind and in front of the camera) and journalists. A former agent at CAA, Christy Haubegger has started the Amplify Database, a searchable directory of more than eight hundred writers of color in TV.[1]

Many groups that started off as collectives, such as the JTC List, Film Fatales, and Cinematographers XX, are now also being tapped by the industry as key places to "find" female talent. Bedford says that what began as a Google doc "just sort of exploded." The JTC List started in February 2018 when Cheryl invited one hundred women of color to join. The list now includes hundreds of women of color with the training and experience to be hired in positions ranging from writers and directors to department heads and production assistants. She has had regular requests from studios, networks, and independent producers for recommendations and introductions.

Jen McGowan, seeing the need to take the databases a step further, founded Film Powered in 2015, since renamed Glass Elevator. It allows pre-vetted female creatives to create online profiles and anyone to post jobs, which the women can then apply to directly. As this book goes to print, Glass Elevator has over 3,500 members—everyone from union Local 399 Teamster drivers to executives, directors, actors, visual effects artists, composers, writers, and everything in between. Many members have won or been nominated for Emmys, Oscars, and NAACP Awards, and Jen sees women booking work off the site every week.

Transgender Talent, started and run by Ann Thomas, serves as a management company for its members and works to get them hired both in front of and behind the camera. In recent years, this work has gathered much steam, and 2019 brought a big win, as Ann and her team managed to provide the opportunity for Zach Barack to be cast in a role in *Spider-Man: Far From Home*. Zach is the first openly trans person in history to play a speaking role in a blockbuster superhero movie.

One of the most hopeful and, if the outcome is substantial, truly game-changing steps in the work of getting the system to hire more women is the legal conclusion of the EEOC investigation, which was ignited by Maria Giese in bringing her case and story to the American Civil Liberties Union in 2013. If the EEOC finds, as the ACLU did, that the studios and networks are in legal violation of discriminatory hiring practices under Title VII, the EEOC would have the legal power—either via mediation or a lawsuit—to mandate that the studios and networks meet certain hiring requirements, and it would have jurisdiction to pursue further legal actions, including fines, if those requirements are not met. The EEOC investigation began in October 2015 as a result of the ACLU's findings. By February 2017, the EEOC had reportedly filed a Commissioners Charge—for hiring discrimination—against all six major studios, networks, mini-majors, agencies, and unions. No formal legal action has yet been taken publicly, but it seems hopeful that something concrete will emerge. Although the effectiveness of these legal actions has a checkered history, it is indisputable that the failed suit of the Original Six led to the biggest jump in the hiring of women since the silent era. I'm optimistic that this investigation will lead to the same and, hopefully, more significant and lasting efforts.

FUND

Outside the studio system, a critical point of action lies in getting women's films financed. As in many industries—and mirroring the world of start-ups and venture capital—the bottom line remains that women trying to get their films made have less access to the capital required to do so, are historically given smaller budgets when they do get capital, and are chronically the subjects of unconscious biases when it comes to trying to attract investors.

Actress and producer Reese Witherspoon notably has put up her own money for her production company, Hello Sunshine, with a commitment to create female-centric content.[2] Abigail Disney has put up the money for a partnership with Killer Content to create Level Forward, a start-up studio venture aiming to back projects driven by women and people of color.[3] A number of other private equity funds are currently working to get off the ground. The 51 Fund is, of course, right there among them. We are all walking a path littered with the bones of other women in film funds that have been tried and have failed, but the fundraising temperature seems to have improved during Donald Trump's presidency and Harvey Weinstein's downfall. The stakes feel higher, and at the same time it feels like we have nothing to lose.

DISRUPT

Critical to lasting change are start-up, for-profit companies that are seeking to disrupt the antiquated mechanisms of Hollywood's funding and distribution models in a way that capitalizes on the possibilities of technology;

innovates into the future faster than Hollywood has the agility to do; and, thus, are democratizing the means of film production and distribution, such that women and other underrepresented populations gain the power to more directly reach and benefit from their audiences.

Chief among the innovators in this space is Seed&Spark, founded in 2012 by Emily Best and which has since become the world's top crowd-funding platform for TV and film. Due largely to their commitment to educational efforts and filmmaker support, 80 percent of all crowdfunding campaigns on their site meet their fund-raising goals (their closest competitor, Kickstarter, is 37 percent). At the time of this writing, their site has been used to raise more than $20 million for over 1,500 projects and has served as a mechanism for legions of women, people of color, and LGBTQ+ creators, who would in any other epoch of film had their voices systematically silenced, to fund their content fully outside the system. Seed&Spark also gives audiences (as crowdfunders) the ability to green-light the projects they are interested in, rather than any gate-keeper green-lighting the projects they *think* audiences will be interested in.

A plethora of other wonderful tech start-ups, such as Kitsplit, which bills itself as the Airbnb of gear rental and allows indie filmmakers to rent gear and equipment more cheaply from one another and also earn revenue off their own gear and equipment when they're not using it, are further breaking down and democratizing access to the ability to make films in a truly independent and self-empowered fashion.

WATCH

Although films by and about women are already demonstrating higher returns, the more that audiences are aware of these issues—by voting with their dollars and eyeballs—the more pressure will increasingly be put on Hollywood to create more inclusive, fresh, and diverse content.

Melissa Silverstein is at the vanguard of these efforts with Women and Hollywood, founded in 2007, which, both through a website and newsletter, directs audiences to find out about the latest films by women and educates them on the intricacies of women in film issues through journalism.

Hollywood's Black Renaissance and Film Inquiry focus on amplifying the work of black and otherwise underrepresented filmmakers, respectively, and expand the ease with which audiences can find and appreciate cinema that might be flying under the radar.

Sites like Grademymovie.com and PictureParity.com, and initiatives like the ReFrame Stamp, provide rating systems of current and past movies and TV shows to help audiences and parents know the gender/racial perspective of the content before they watch it (and/or take their kids to see it).

Ava DuVernay has launched Array, an independent film distribution and resource collective dedicated to the amplification of independent films by people of color and women filmmakers globally.[4]

A proliferation of perspective-specific film festivals, such as the Athena Film Festival (films celebrating women and leadership), Urbanworld Film Festival (films representing the "broadest lens of diversity"), LA Skins Fest (films from indigenous filmmakers), and ReelAbilities Film Festival (films promoting awareness and appreciation of people with different disabilities), have sprung up to provide audiences interested in seeing content from underrepresented communities a physical place to find it.

A tranche of tech companies are exploring ways to make sure that streaming customers are provided with the means and platforms to find content by women and other historically underrepresented voices. The female-founded Blue Fever has created an empathetic AI that messages with teen girls to curate the internet, like a big sister, and, based on her emotional needs of that moment, will recommend content based on crowdsourced feedback from their community. And Seed&Spark, having helped democratize film financing, is now tackling the other end of the equation with a pay-what-you-can subscription streaming service. It is currently the only streaming platform to feature 50 percent content by female creators, and it is focusing its efforts on helping viewers who feel overwhelmed by Netflix's and Amazon's browsing algorithms and are tired of spending hours simply trying to find something to watch.

For those of us who are actually rolling up our sleeves and engaging in the work of the revolution, we are facing the sticky realities that activists and movement builders have always faced: change is hard, nonlinear, exhausting, and frequently painful.

There are difficult truths that must be recognized in trying to enact a demographic shift as seismic as what we are fighting for.

In any discussion of parity or fight for equality, we must acknowledge that all historically marginalized groups within the film industry (in this case, everyone other than white, cis, straight, able-bodied men) have individual and unique needs that must be met. Those needs are not all the same. There are groups who sit at certain intersections that, if we are not careful and inclusive enough at every stage, are more likely to be left out of our larger movement. Social justice movements like these tend to benefit white women and men of color the most, while women of color (who have the short end of both the race and gender privilege sticks) are most likely to be left out. White, cis, straight, able-bodied women in our movement, as in many movements, have frequently been guilty of thinking we're fighting for all women, when our work does not address the specific needs of women of color and, even, perhaps unwittingly, shuts them out. Often, even in instances where we manage to be inclusive of race, other groups, such as disabled women, are forgotten. A rising tide for women has *never* lifted all boats. In this current women in film movement, it is absolutely essential for us to remember this and to finally get it right—to find ways to fight truly for all of us at the same time.

Struggling to rectify where others have so often failed requires difficult conversations and a willingness to walk into discomfort, serious introspection, and self-questioning. I am proud of the ways in which I see my fellow activists and movement-builders engaging with these questions. I am proud of the ways in which I think we are doing better at repairing these bridges than in past movements. But I constantly see the ways in which we, myself included, still badly screw up. Again, inclusiveness at every stage is what will help us all.

Another nuanced question we find ourselves in the midst of trying to collectively answer is that of who is allowed to tell what stories. Jessica Chastain got a huge amount of heat in 2018 for hiring a male director for a film she was producing, in spite of her public advocacy for more female storytellers.[5] The 2019 Best Picture Oscar winner, *The Green Book*, has been resoundingly criticized—though not to an extent that swayed voters from awarding it Best Picture—for its team of white, male creators turning the fascinating story of Don Shirley into a movie that, in the words of *The Root*, "spoon-feeds racism to white people."[6] Steven Spielberg and Lena Dunham caught a lot of well-deserved flack when, presumably in a move Spielberg thought was progressive on the women front, he hired Dunham to adapt a story about a Syrian refugee.[7] The subject of ownership over telling specific communities' stories has been raised over the years, but never with the fervor it is receiving now.

But the conversation is no more fervent than its stakes. It matters who gets to tell stories. It has *always* mattered. Obviously, there are instances in which directors and writers are allowed to tell the stories even if they have no personal experience with the topic or the theme. Stanley Kubrick made *2001: The Space Odyssey* without ever having been to space. I'm reasonably certain that no one involved in a single one of the *Harry Potter* movies even once attended a wizarding preparatory school. My most recent film is about the real-life community of people who believe they are vampires, although I am not myself a member of that community.

But we cannot conflate fantastical or niche groups with sizeable communities whose voices have been historically and systematically omitted from our cultural narrative and whose very images have been flattened into degrading stereotypes.

Not everyone in the movement agrees on what the answer to this question is. Some, like trans filmmaker Ariel Mahler, feels that it can be important for those to whom society gives a platform to use that platform to tell untold stories, but Ariel also believes that the situation is not so straightforward. "The best option is always to hire someone from that actual community to tell the story," Ariel says. "But there is also a responsibility of people with privilege to amplify other voices. I think it's okay for people to be interested in telling stories that aren't from their own community. In those cases, it's about doing the work and paying people for their input, making sure there are [paid] people on the team who can speak to that issue from an authentic place." You also have to go in ready to be uncomfortable, Ariel says. "You're probably going to fuck up, and that's okay. How you respond to criticism is so important. You have to really do your best to make sure that you get as much right as you can."

Others take a harder line and say that, at this point, there is no excuse for the privileged telling the stories of unrepresented or underrepresented populations.

Sarah Springer, a producer and founder of Advocates for Inclusion Media, writes, "No one can articulate a story better than the person who lived and experienced it firsthand. The moment we think we are the ones who can tell someone else's story better than they can is the moment we lose the truth of the narrative and add our own ideas of 'other' to the information being relayed."[8]

For my part, I believe that, for the time being and probably a great long while after this, substantial emphasis should be placed on ensuring that those voices behind the camera that have been systematically and historically excluded should be given a chance to tell their own stories in their own voices. Why not embark on the radical experiment of allowing women filmmakers to tell women's stories, Latinas to tell Latinas' stories, and so forth? There is a balancing of the scales that must be done to rectify the past century of cinema; deep work on all our parts will be required to investigate what it's like to understand different populations through their own authentic voices and not solely through the white men's prism. This does not mean that all of us should not endeavor to make our own films more reflective of the world, more inclusive of characters that are like us and not like us. We should do that too. But those of us with privilege, white men most of all, but even those of us with the privilege of white womanhood, need to know when historically under-heard voices need to be the loudest voices in the room.

Like most movements that grow out of the pain of the intense lack of access, resources, and visibility experienced by the oppressed and which carry with them as much electric charge as this movement does, there is an often damaging amount of pressure placed on those few who are first lifted up and given a platform to speak on behalf of a population that is, of course, diverse in its own experience.

A number of trans folks I interviewed spoke about repeatedly watching members of their community make one mistake publicly and then be eviscerated and ousted—or, using the latest parlance, "canceled"—from the community. What I heard over and over again is that because trans people and culture are so badly underrepresented in the media, and because there is so much stigma and misinformation about them, there is intense pressure put on trans people by other trans people to present their experiences on-screen in a way that feels true, authentic, and mistake-free. Frequently, I heard the outcome of this isn't optimal.

According to Ariel, "There's still a culture of scarcity where it feels like there can still only be one trans creator, which creates a false sense of competition within the community."

That pressure can create vitriol toward those who first make it through our ranks. Lena Dunham, for instance, has been, in a multiplicity of ways, an unfortunate candidate to receive the platform she did, ostensibly speaking on behalf of all millennial women in the wake of the success of *Girls*. I will not stand here and defend much of what she has done and said. However, the amount of contempt that has been leveled at her over the past decade, most frequently by women themselves—often far more viciously than those attacks they have aimed at the worst white, male offenders, even the likes of Harvey Weinstein—has made me wince more than once.

As we are beginning to finally achieve sets and spaces that we are able to shape ourselves, we are exploring ways to try to navigate this collective pain of being unseen and unheard that has built up in our populations for so long.

Ariel spoke to me about working on a film recently with an almost entirely trans cast and crew. "Let's assume good intentions," the director encouraged the team on the first day of filming and most days thereafter. It was a startling but meaningful recommendation. "It shifted the feeling on set," Ariel recalled. "People were kinder to each other and less quick to leap to judgment."

Like any activism, like any social justice work, this work is exhausting, and the hopes of too many tends to rest on the shoulders of too few. Particularly in the time since the Weinstein scandal and #MeToo brought the world's attention to our cause, it has often felt like drinking from a fire hose of attention after a long drought. I worry as I see the weight of fatigue settle in on the faces of my compatriots—and feel it on my own.

The work that is and will be required for this women in film movement to achieve the future we envision is *work*. It's not the fun "work" of sending out press releases or giving award acceptance speeches, which earn you public applause, nor is it a straightforward series of hurdles that we must collectively link hands to overcome. This work is complicated, murky, and uncomfortable, and it demands at least as much internal scrutiny and vigilance as the exterior workload demands.

It can be painful to look at the rich white men benefiting from this system as it exists—those who are in no way being forced to do this same level of difficult work—and not ache to throw in the towel and simply cast your lot with a lottery system that might, maybe, someday pluck you and you alone out of this *work* of accountability and into the world of glitter and little gold men. While you know in your soul that it is unlikely that you will be chosen, that things will continue on as badly as they are forever if you do, hoo boy, some days that temptation does call mightily.

I doubt a single one of us on the ground fighting for this doesn't have those moments of weakness, of wishing we could just walk away—probably at least once a week.

As my friend Lynne Marie Rosenberg says, "Sometimes I need to not fight that day and just sit at home and do a jigsaw puzzle."

But it is a testament to the passion, dedication, courage, and sheer belief in the importance of this that all of these women and men beside me battle on as we surely do.

I have felt an increase in outside support for out movement over time. My 51 Fund team and I spent a year and a half running full throttle into brick walls trying to get the fund off the ground. I knew other women were facing their own brick walls: refusals to believe there was a problem, "yeah, but's," and, worst, outright indifference. For The 51 Fund, everyone would pat us on the head and say they thought it was a worthy idea, but no one was willing to get out their checkbooks. I'd spent the previous five years writing, teaching, and speechifying about the plight of women in film and the ways in which we all needed to rally together to change it, and I got really good at lighting individual rooms of people on fire about it. But I have to say that it felt most of the time like screaming into the wind.

Then the Weinstein story broke. Twelve days later, my TED Talk went online. Over the next three months, it was viewed over one million times by people all over the world. I received thousands of emails and social media messages from women *and men* sharing their stories of pain, struggle, survival, and finding ways around systems. Many pledged to join the women in film revolution or at least to seek out films by women. Many asked how they could commit money to the cause. From their impassioned generosity and belief in the work we were doing, in the course of about ten days, I raised the rest of the financing I needed to finish my second feature film. We raised our pre-seed round of financing for The 51 Fund. Major financial institutions began calling *us* to see whether they might be able to incubate that fund and help us raise even more money. I got an email from Mark Gottlieb at Trident Literary Agency asking me if I wanted to write this book. I said of course. Rakia Clark at Beacon Press bought it. I have written this book and you are reading it.

In many ways, researching and writing this book has been both devastating and liberating for me, personally. After six years spent on a day-to-day basis, in deep thought and active engagement with issues against women in the film industry, I thought nothing could shock me. I have lived and experienced the harassment, the casual dismissals, the closed doors, the patronizing head-pats, the blatant sexism, the indifference toward women in film for over a decade. I have studied the data and numbers—understood the depth of the systemic discrimination. I had begun to think that there wasn't very much about this that could take my breath away anymore.

Then I started doing the interviews and listening to the stories of women up and down the industry, spotting the career-flattening patterns, digging deep into the numbers, listening to the pain in women's voices over the potential that may forever be lost. Over many months, as I laid all of the facts and stories and numbers down on the table and onto these pages, the magnitude of it knocked me to my knees all over again.

What I saw is that the problem we are talking about is so foundational that it is cellular. What few attempts to fix it now feel crushingly minor against the most toxic forms of white male patriarchy, which replicates itself through this industry—and our larger society—like a sickness.

Janet Grillo was the first person to bring up the DNA metaphor in her interview, and she pointed out that what we need to do is mutate the genes of those cells during the replication process. At first this seemed like an exciting prospect. (*Yes! That's* exactly *what we need to do.*) But months later, it dawned on me that what she's talking about is evolution. What further dawned on me, is that evolution is not a short-term project. It is the work of millennia. I'm already thirty-two years old. I can't wait millennia to be given a fair shot.

This series of realizations has radicalized my thinking. Buying into the idea that I have to accept incremental progress? No, thank you. Not anymore.*

Happily, I am not alone. And here's where things get really exciting. Along with evidence of the systemic patterns of discrimination that emerged from the interviews I conducted with women filmmakers, so, too, did I see the emergence of a new, collective attitude. After Trump, after Weinstein, after mostly limp efforts of change following the tsunami of #MeToo, a huge number of the women I spoke to no longer have a single fuck left to give. They are in the process of transforming—hopefully transforming the industry, yes—but maybe even more importantly, transforming themselves.

> The post-Weinstein shift has been mainly in myself. In July 2017, I began thinking about systems of power and how they're built to keep white men powerful. In January 2018, I was scheduled to go out to LA and pitch a TV series and then I thought, "Why would I go to LA and pitch? This industry doesn't know its arse from its elbow." It's not fucking changing because the arrogance of power is blinding them—Shakespearean level hubris. At that point, I finally felt, "Fuck you guys. I'm going to build my own castle." Coming out the other side of that pain and agony, I have found my truest voice, learned and fought to trust it, and now I want to use it. Deciding that the industry is rigged has actually been liberating. I just feel like there are no actual rules. Which means, I get to make up the rules, because the rules we were told are bullshit.
>
> —LISA TIERNEY-KEOGH, writer, soon-to-be-director

Before #MeToo, I was told by a woman executive, "Oh, wow. You're a Latina woman and you like directing comedy? You have 0 percent chance of working in the film industry." I can't even tell you how much

---

* If this evolutionary process of getting women into Hollywood got us from 0.5 percent from 1945 to 1979 to 5 percent from 1995 to 2018, well . . .

that hurt, how much it crushed me. But I'm still here. And, okay, maybe I won't work for that network, so instead, I'll work on creating my own so that I can prove to people that I can do the same thing that dude over there can do. All those no's and all those terrible things that have been said to me in my career, I just continued growing and learning and experiencing and creating and trying to figure things out. Now it's finally blossoming. I wish this happened a long time ago, but it is happening now. I'm doing my work and I'm helping to create opportunities for my community to do the same.

—MAYLEN CALIENES, actress, director,
founder of Latino Filmmakers Network

My mother, from the time I was born, told me I had one job: to make the world a better place for the next generation. That's the one job. And the *only* way to make things better for the next generation is to make things better for this generation right here right now. That's what I get up and work on every day. That's what motivates me.

—CHERYL L. BEDFORD, producer, founder
of the JTC List/Women of Color UNITE

We are on the verge of a whole bunch of revolutions that are going to happen. I feel on the verge of a personal revolution about letting go of fear around expressing myself and just being who I am and letting the rest of the world deal with that. The same thing is happening at a macro level—a lot of work is happening intersectionally across communities that have been historically marginalized that are just on the verge of exploding. I see the outspokenness of what you [the author] are doing on social media and that makes me braver. That's happening all over. I want to be part of this revolution that's about to happen.

—ARIEL MAHLER, filmmaker

At the grassroots level—so Outside that the Inside doesn't yet realize we're even coming—bursting through the cracks and crevices of this industry, women, people of color, and other historically shut-out filmmakers are finding each other, nourishing communities, and managing to tell their stories however and in whatever ways they can. That there is a formidable, ever more organized women in film movement growing to meet them is the greatest reason for hope of them all.

Looking at the progress of my own career since that rainy day bus arrival in New York City, there are things that haven't changed a decade later. I still can't get meetings in Hollywood. I still can't get put up for Inside writing jobs or acting jobs to save my life. But I am in and among and a part of an army now—a mob at the castle gates. I am no longer screaming into the wind. I have a platform to be heard, to share my message, to use my voice and my hands and my skills to help bring to the world stories it needs from voices that matter.

Like many of the other women I interviewed, there's been a change in me too. Something's been unleashed within. It's made me take myself seriously, made me understand that I, like the other women standing beside me, don't need to keep looking for Hollywood studios to give us a big break. We are the leaders we have been seeking for all along.

CHAPTER 10

ME AND YOU AND EVERYONE WE KNOW*

"My impression is that people believe in this notion of 'creeping incrementalism,' that things are getting a little better every year and that, eventually, this is an issue that will take care of itself. But there is no evidence that that is the case," said Martha Lauzen in a 2018 interview.[1] Lauzen is the executive director for the Center for the Study of Women in Television and Film and an expert on the employment of women in Hollywood.

Her observation bears repeating. *But there is no evidence that that is the case.*

Creeping incrementalism is a dangerous notion. It lets everyone off the hook from being immediately accountable for their little corner of the industry and allows us to coast without action. And that very lack of accountability—that lack of conscience—plays into the Hollywood system that the women in film movement is trying to dismantle.

There are concrete actions that anybody interested can do to help. But first, two necessary frameworks are important to understand and accept.[†]

---

* *Me and You and Everyone We Know* (2005), dir. Miranda July.
† Borrowed heavily from Robin DiAngelo's framing of racist structures in *White Fragility* because it's brilliant and I'm not going to come up with anything better. P.S., All white people reading this book, please go read *White Fragility* afterward (it's also a Beacon Press book, but that's not why I'm saying this).

FRAMEWORK #1: WE ARE ALL SEXIST—IT JUST DEPENDS TO WHAT DEGREE WE MANAGE TO COMBAT THAT IN OUR THOUGHTS AND BEHAVIORS. THIS IS A MOVEABLE POINT EVERY DAY. We live in a sexist society (just as we live in a racist and heteronormative and ableist society). Partly through the movies we watch and media we consume; partly through witnessing the behaviors of people around us; partly through subtle teachings in school; partly through our life experiences that elevate and applaud the actions of white men; and partly through the erasure, invalidation, and dismissal of women and non-white men, most of us have been socialized to value white men's stories, bodies, and actions more than anybody else's. All of us have a baseline level of sexism.

The degree to which we are able to actively combat that baseline over time determines how sexist our thoughts and behaviors are at a given point in time. This is not a static metric, as it can fluctuate with each thought and action. It's also not a personality trait, which is great. Because poor behavior can be corrected. With *work*. And with intention.

FRAMEWORK #2: OUR INSTITUTIONS ARE SEXIST. Institutions are made up of two things: rules/structures and the people who run them. White, cis, able-bodied men created the rules/structures for Hollywood as we know it and, for the most part, they are still in charge of those structures today. These men who run Hollywood were raised in and live in a sexist society, as we all do. They bring that sexism to the institutions and industry they run.

Hollywood is not the only industry where this is true. Corporations, whole governments, and basically everything conceived under the umbrella of our modern, patriarchal culture are sexist at a structural, foundational, and practical level.

The result of frameworks 1 and 2 is that white men benefit from sexism, while everyone else is held back by it to varying degrees, depending on race, able-bodied-ness, and other factors. Having a different president does not change this. Having a lot of conversations does not change this. Having a record-shattering hit with a female lead and/or a racially diverse cast does not change this. White male filmmakers have trouble getting films made does not change this. The sexism is baked into the fabric of the film industry. It is, in fact, there by design. That is why the system has been so hard to change.

One of the biggest hurdles to making the film industry less sexist is people refusing to recognize that these two frameworks exist. So, recognize them. And let's get to work.

What agents/studio employees/production companies and those inside the system can do

The Hollywood system isn't built to find non-white men, and it won't magically find them all of a sudden now. But there are consultants who do this work full-time. Hire one. Let them help you figure it out. Let them walk you through how to do this. After all, companies hire consultants all the time for help.

Anna Serner, head of the Swedish Film Institute, is confounded that this hasn't already occurred. "Any studio/agency/production company can put up a change target. That's what you would do with any other change management. If you were a large corporation and you were changing office spaces, you would hire a consultant to help you figure out the best possible new space. So why are the studios throwing up their hands on the issue of a lack of women in film like they're totally helpless here?"

That is a most excellent question.

What else can insiders do?

- Finance women's movies.
- Attach your A-list actors to those movies.
- Call John Landgraf over at FX. He probably has some ideas he can share with you.
- Take risks on women.*
- Bet on them.†
- Stick your neck out and say, "I know this woman doesn't meet x, y, or z benchmark, but I think she's really good."‡
- Be prepared to fall on your face when, inevitably, sometimes she doesn't succeed.§

Then take all those same actions all over again with other women.

----

* Just like you do for men.
† Just like you do for men.
‡ Just like you do for men.
§ Just like you do for men.

What famous actors and actresses can do

We plebeians do love it when the big stars speak out about the women in film issue during their acceptance speeches and write articles and op-eds about it. It was groovy when you all wore black to the Golden Globes in 2018 and stood in solidarity on the steps at Cannes. But we actually only need you to do one thing right now, and it's *super* simple.

Big, famous stars: call your agents and tell them that you just read this really fantastic book and that, going forward, 50 percent of your slate of projects must have female directors.*

That's it!

If you're feeling nervous, you could even soften the blow a little bit and say something like, "I understand that it may take you a minute to fix your systems to find these female directors, so for the next year, I'll settle for 25 percent female directors. By year two, though, it's 50 percent or bust."

If you all did that, (a) you would get *great* publicity, and (b) the entire system would change within a year.

And we get it. It's gonna be a little scary at first. Actors are wholly at the mercy of their directors, and this situation may require that you stick *your* neck out for a newer female director and star in her movie. But a veteran female filmmaker wanted me to pass along a message to you: "Directing is hard, but it's not brain surgery. What's the worst that can happen? You make a bad movie. People make bad movies all the time. If you're not willing to make a bad movie to create change, then you don't actually care that much about change."

Films get financed based on the level of talent attached to them. Attach yourselves to women's projects, and our films will get financed.

Amazing. So simple. Thanks *very* much.

What our white, male film industry colleagues can do

First of all, breathe. This is all going to be okay. I promise. There are times when it's going to be uncomfortable. If it is uncomfortable, consider why. Realize that there really is a long, long way for us to go before you're an

---

* Send them this book! Flag this page!

oppressed class of people. No one's gunning for you. So, breathe. And then advocate for your female colleague in five ways.

1. *Support equal jobs and pay.*

    There's a wonderful recent example of Jessica Chastain discovering that Octavia Spencer was going to make less money on a film they were doing together. Horrified, Jessica went to the film's producers and, using her privilege as a white woman, tied her salary to Octavia's so they would each make the same amount. This increased Octavia's salary five times over. Imagine what would happen if men tied their salaries to women's in a similar fashion.

    Be vigilant as you move through your own work for instances of women, especially women of color, getting paid less for equal work or not getting considered for jobs or representation. Send your talented female colleagues' materials to your agent with a personal recommendation. Then follow up with your agents and make sure they've actually paid attention to them. Follow up with them again. Agents are notoriously hard to pin down.

    Remember that you are more likely to have access to the gatekeepers in the first place, and you are on safer ground standing up to them and acting as an advocate.

2. *Call out sexist acts when they are happening.*

    If a colleague makes an inappropriate comment about your female colleague's appearance or body, interrupts her when she's speaking, or ignores a really good point she made, speak up. Don't be patronizing about it or turn it into a federal case, but remember that women have to stand up to these sorts of things every day, and it gets exhausting and can sometimes be dangerous, and it can be really awesome sometimes when someone else stands up for us instead.

3. *Sponsor a female colleague.*

    There's a large body of research suggesting that "sponsorship" is the single most effective tool to combat career sexism and can help level the playing field for women in their careers.[2] Sponsorship is like mentorship, except that it demands concrete action from the sponsor. So, instead of just giving career advice or reading your sponsee's scripts (although do that, too, if it's helpful to her), actively work to help her get jobs and opportunities through your own connections. Stick your own neck out for her, remembering, once again, that you have greater and firmer access to gatekeepers than she likely does.

Jack Lechner, producer of *Blue Valentine* and *The Fog of War* among much else, has been an incredible sponsor for me. Throughout the time that I have known him, he has always been available for advice and information, and he has generously read and given notes on my scripts (and this book). Even more importantly, he has now twice put his own reputation on the line for me: once to get me hired at *The New Yorker Presents* and, later, close to one hundred times in investor meetings to get my second feature film, *Bite Me*, financed. I am 100 percent sure that I would not be as far along in my career as I am without his mentorship *and* sponsorship. That's what real advocacy looks like.

A couple of quick notes on being a sponsor, because I have observed from my interviews and life experiences that these things can sometimes take a turn for the worse. Do not mansplain, patronize, or talk down to your sponsee. She is not there to make you feel amazing and smart. You are there to *help* her. Listen to what she needs and then provide that information/help if you can. Definitely do not make sexual comments or try to sleep with her ever under any circumstances. There is almost nothing as demoralizing in a career as having a perceived and trusted mentor/sponsor suddenly flip the tables on you. It is catastrophic to one's self-esteem, and it is deeply painful. If you really, really, really think that a human attraction may have grown up between you and your sponsee in the natural course of things and you want to explore it, discuss the entire situation with at least four female friends before making any move. Do it only with their universal consensus. Even then, be careful.

4. *Think long and hard about what stories you're choosing to tell.*
Jessica Hinds, creator of the Meditative Writing method, finds that her writing students often sigh and say, "Well, I don't want to write

anything political. I just want to write a scary horror movie/silly comedy/action flick. I'm not trying to send any kind of message."

Every story is political. Especially right now. But, also, always.

Movies that seem to be just for fun are, in some ways, even more political than so-called political films. The less-overt choices you make in terms of who the main versus minor characters are, what agency they have/don't have, what happens to those characters and the choices they make, are less likely to be consciously evaluated by your viewing audience and are much more likely to be shot directly, unprocessed, into the slipstreams of their unconscious. Which film is likely to have greater sway in writing our neural pathways? *Citizen Kane*? Or that romantic comedy you watched precisely seventy-four times between the ages of twelve and seventeen?

You are *always* sending a message. With every script you write and every film you make, you are *always* either upholding societal views, values, and tropes, or you are disrupting them. The decision of every single choice, decision, moment, frame, and shot matters.

5. *Commit to making good decisions.*
   Let me help you get started.

   When first deciding what story you want to tell, seriously assess whether you are the best person to tell that story. If the story is, say, about a young Colombian woman risking her life, safety, and sacrificing everything to illegally cross the US border in hopes of a better life and you are a hot-shot screenwriter guy who grew up in Seattle and has spent the last decade in Los Angeles, possibly the answer to that question is "no." If you are captivated by the story of that young woman and feel passionately about getting it out into the world, that's terrific. Use your white, male privilege to lift up someone who could more authentically tell that story if they had the same access to resources you have. Work with her to get that movie made. That would be excellent.

   Naturally, you, too, will go on writing screenplays as you always have—we certainly don't expect you to stop. Sometimes you might be hired to write a film that centers on a female character's experiences even though you are not a female. In that case, advocate strongly with the producers to have a female director brought on board—even go so far as to say that you are only comfortable signing on to the project if there is a female director.

In those instances, and also in other instances when you are writing authentically from your own experiences, here are some guidelines:

- Commit to making sure after you've finished a draft of each script that your characters (major, minor, and background) are reflective of the actual human population. I'm not saying that you have to have precisely 51 percent female characters or precisely 17 percent Latinx characters—you're not going to get it perfect every time—but make sure that you're at least in the region of the real world.

- Commit to checking your script for stereotypes and tropes every couple of drafts. We all fall into them. Hell, how could we not? We've been watching them in movies since we could see. But do better. If you don't trust yourself to recognize the tropes/stereotypes, CastAndLoose (www.castandloose.com) is a valuable tool to educate yourself on the types of characters and storylines that are overworked and problematic. Don't reinforce stereotypes, disrupt them. You'll end up with more interesting characters and help change the world.

- Commit to checking your blind spots. If you are a white man writing about an Indigenous woman, make sure to have an Indigenous woman read your script regularly throughout the process. There are corners of her experience that you will not even know that you don't know about. Pay these women for their feedback. Do not burden the already underpaid with additional free labor. Just like you'd pay a real scientist to consult on a script about nuclear physics about which you have a limited understanding, pay one or more members of the relevant community to help you expand your understanding and spot check your work.

- When you fuck up, admit it, then do better the next time. You're human. You are going to have moments you're not proud of. People may be really upset at or disappointed in you. It will feel terrible. Please don't retreat to inaction. Please continue the difficult work the rest of us are doing. Due to a truly random series of lotteries of birth and genetic coding, you entered this world with a great deal of privilege. Weaponize it to make the world a better place.

What film schools can do

Don't kid yourselves, film schools. You are where it all begins. You bear a great responsibility in the causes and potential for change on this issue. Here are some suggestions for how to do better:

1. Revise your "Films to Watch" lists to substantially include films by/about women and other historically marginalized filmmakers—not a few of them—a *whoooole* lot of them.
2. Get something approaching gender parity among your faculty.
3. Mandate a section in every single screenwriting class that explicitly addresses representation, tropes, and historical cinematic biases/stereotypes. Make sure your screenwriting teachers are actively watching for those things in their students' work and that they use those instances as teaching moments for the whole class about how to stop making sexist/racist movies.
4. Mandate one section in all directing classes that teaches them how to run a safe and inclusive set; one section that *specifically* teaches them how to direct sex scenes and intimate moments with a strong emphasis on how to responsibly get consent from their actors at each moment (without unconsciously or consciously pressuring them). They should also be required to take the screenwriting class from #3.
5. Make this book mandatory reading for every single student before they graduate.
6. Even better, create a semester-long class that is a requirement for all film students that addresses the historic oppression and exclusion of women and POCs in our industry. Explicitly explain to both the male and female students the ways in which this industry will be harder to navigate for the female and POC students, give them tools to navigate those hurdles and teach the white male students how to be the best allies they can be.

What financiers/investors can do

Finance films by female filmmakers.

You will make money and change the world.

Talk is fine. "Support" is good. But where the cash hits the bank account is where change actually occurs.

If you're still feeling "iffy" at a gut level about investing in women, even at this stage in the book, in the face of all of my excellent data, you're not alone. Case in point:

> A 2014 [Wharton] survey of more than 1,000 executives found that business leaders relied most often on gut instinct, beating out data and the advice of others. The results are often disastrous, predictable and persistent as data coming out of angel and venture investment firms now attests. To figure out how investment decisions are being made, Wharton's Laura Huang planted her research team for two years inside five investment firms and watched, blow by blow, how they made decisions. She discovered that investors consciously grouped their areas of attention into two categories: the first was data . . . the second area they focused on was their perception of the entrepreneur him or herself. . . . Intuition trumped any business data they had.[3]

In *The New Female Tribes*, Rachel Pashley offers advice to combat this unconscious sexism:

> Investors should intentionally seek out and spend time with successful female entrepreneurs, making these role models more instantly available to their intuitive process. Rather than ignore the data that exposes the flaws of their industry, and looks like a threat to their unquestioned genius, they should see it as a treasure map to uncovered opportunity. And perhaps most importantly, they should bring far more female partners onto their decision-making teams.[4]

If your gut is still telling you that investing in women and their stories just doesn't "feel right" or you find yourself endlessly intoning, "Well, I'd *love* to invest in women's films, but I just can't find any that are good enough/interesting/being led by experienced-enough women," you, too, maybe suffering from a patriarchal bout of unconscious sexism. Employ the measures suggested by Pashley above to help avoid these pitfalls.

Find female filmmakers and invest in their movies. If you don't want to bother with that, The 51 Fund will gladly include your investment in our slate.

If you don't have big dollars, but want to help anyway, I love you. Thank you. You can always find a crowdfunding campaign for a female filmmaker's project at Seed&Spark (https://www.seedandspark.com/fund /category/women). Every single dollar really does help a female filmmaker tell her stories.

What lawyers can do

Sue the living daylights out of the studios, agencies, and production companies. They are in clear, cold violation of Title VII.

There are at least fourteen different class action lawsuits that could be formed.

Given that the Original Six's lawsuit, even though it failed, resulted in the only real movement in the percentage of female directors in the last seventy-two years, this option should be pursued to the full extent of the law.

What government officials can do

Most US states (and many countries around the world) offer tax incentives of one form or another to productions that film and/or complete post-production in their locale. They do this because the revenue that a film production brings to the community is so enormous that it is actually worth the government turning around and writing a check back to that production for, often, 25–30 percent of money spent as a rebate.

Crazy, right? Yet true.

A couple of states are exploring the possibility of having those tax credits facilitate hiring and pay equity on the sets of those productions. One option would be that a film can't get access to those credits at all without having demographic equity among the cast and crew. The other (probably easier) option would be to offer an added bonus of, say, an additional 5 percent rebate to those productions that achieve parity.

Money always talks, but the film industry pays particularly close attention to the intricacies and benefits of those tax incentives. What else could have Hollywood's production hopping from New Mexico to Louisiana to Georgia like a crazed frog?*

If you linked your tax incentives to parity, Hollywood would have to shape up.

You'd also get some pretty great publicity to boot. . . .

What everyone who watches movies, TV, or any kind of entertainment media can do

Pay attention.

Now that you know we're in *The Matrix*, so to speak, start by noticing. Notice whether the film you're watching was directed, written, and produced by men or women. Notice how women and people of color are portrayed on-screen. Notice which cultural stereotypes the film is propagating or disrupting. Notice how often women are getting raped and/or are wearing far less than their male counterparts. Notice who has agency (makes decisions that affect their fate) in the story and who doesn't. Notice which characters the filmmaker chooses to put at the center versus the periphery of the stories.

Pay attention.

Once you're doing that, have a good hard think about what kinds of stories you want shaping your neural pathways. If you have children, definitely have a good hard think about theirs.

Then . . .

Vote with your dollars.

I'm not saying that you have to be in 100 percent agreement with me about what stories you want influencing your brain. But just know that every time you purchase a movie ticket, stream a TV series, pay $2.99 on Amazon, *the industry is watching*.

The greater pressure that you help put on their bottom lines and pocketbooks, the quicker they're going to have to get with the program and shift the kind of content they're making.

Even the most powerful Hollywood executive is at the mercy of the viewing audience.

Supporting a film by buying a theater ticket on opening weekend (even if you can't go) sends the biggest message of all.

---

* Aside from some stunningly regressive civil and human rights decisions.

Seek out films by female filmmakers and films about complex female characters and watch them. Pay to watch them wherever possible.

In fact, if you would do something for me, commit to watching at least one film by a female filmmaker per month. Surely you can do at least that, can't you? Yes, you can. Isn't this an amazing revolution? You get to change the world by watching movies that will show you perspectives and stories that you have never seen on-screen before.

If you need help finding those movies—and, believe me, you might, given the anemic marketing budgets our movies so often get—the title of each chapter in this book is one of my very favorite films and each is by a female director. Check them out! In addition, here are some great further resources:

- Seed&Spark (seedandspark.com), in addition to being the best crowdfunding site for film and TV projects available,* has a pay-what-you-can† streaming subscription platform that is sort of like Netflix for indie films and is currently the only streaming platform with gender parity among the directors of its content. Subscribe to them to find great indie content you won't find anywhere else, discover cool new voices before anyone else, and support independent content by historically underrepresented creators.
- Women and Hollywood (https://womenandhollywood.com) is a great resource for all things women in film and, if you sign up for their newsletter, you'll get a weekly email listing all new releases by female directors.
- Hollywood's Black Renaissance (http://hollywoodsblackrenaissance .com) is "dedicated to highlighting the achievements of women of the African diaspora in film and television" and is a wonderful resource for finding great content to watch.
- The ReFrame Stamp "serves as a mark of distinction for projects that have demonstrated success in gender-balanced films." A list of recipients can be found at https://www.reframeproject.org/stamp.
- Grademymovie.com provides grades for films based on how well they achieved gender and race parity in key cast and crew

---

* According to me and also anyone who knows anything.
† Yes, you read that right.

positions. These grades are published before the films open so that "you can use your consumer dollars on opening weekend to choose films that are inclusive." The grades thereafter remain in a searchable database on their site.

- Picture Parity (http://www.pictureparity.com) rates current and past movies and TV shows based on how well women are represented in front of and behind the camera. Their website has a searchable database, and their Instagram account will keep you up-to-date on current content.
- Moviesbyher.com is a user-friendly database of feature films by female directors searchable by genre!
- Blue Fever is a subscriber service targeted primarily at teenage girls that will send videos "for whatever you're going through in your life." They do this through their "Glow guide Blue who text messages with you whenever you need."[5]

What female filmmakers can do

Okay, ladies. I'm really hoping that the people in some of these other categories are going to help us, but we cannot count on that happening fast enough, in our lifetimes, or at all. We must make this change happen for ourselves.

Here's how this is going to have to go.

RULE #1: Find a way to make your movies/serialized shows/media content and get it to audiences however you can.

That is the first, most, and ultimately only important thing.

If you can get your stuff made inside the system, great. If you can't, find a way to make it outside the system and rejoice in the fact that you are part of the first generation of filmmakers to actually have the ability to finance, make, and distribute content to global audiences without ever needing a gatekeeper to say "yes."

There is not one single good excuse to wait a day longer to begin making your next project. It doesn't matter where you're starting from. Start wherever you are.

As you should understand by now, this process will be harder for you. I'm not going to sugarcoat it. Because you are a woman, and especially if you are a woman of color or a disabled woman or a trans woman, you will have to work several times as hard, be several times as excellent, be several times more persistent. It is unfair, but please keep at it.

It is your civic, global, and humanitarian responsibility to tell your stories and get them to the audiences who so desperately need (and want) to see them. By whatever means necessary.

RULE #2: Participate in the system to whatever extent it is helpful to you, but never, ever forget that it is foundationally stacked against you and never give them the power to tell you your worth.

Reread this book every time you get knocked to your knees by the failure of the system to recognize or give appropriate accolades or opportunities to your work. Have it handy every time they try to gaslight you into believing something that you know in your bones isn't true.

Their value system is not as unimpeachable as they try to make us believe. Determine your own value system and believe in it.

RULE #3: Dare to be radical.

Be radical in your approach to your career.

Given Rule #2, question everything you have and will be told by the film industry about what the "right" way to have a career is, what value systems you should subscribe to, and what success looks like.

In fact, the more successful you become within the system, the more you're going to have to continually remind yourself to stay suspicious. As Virginia Woolf wrote in *A Room of One's Own* almost a century ago, it can become amazingly easy to buy into the rules of a patriarchal system once it is taking care of one's basic needs.[6]

There are three reasons, in particular, that we should all remain constantly vigilant against the little-girl-dreaming promises of engaging with the Hollywood system and be radical in our thinking instead:

1. *There will almost certainly continue to be a pipeline problem for women within our lifetimes:* Even if we take the current moves toward change at face value and assume that they will continue and are in earnest, the number of women and people of color that "diversity programs" and the top festivals can elevate in a given year are paltry and will not, within my lifetime certainly, get us anything close to parity within the system as it exists.

2. *It actually may not be that great Inside:* It is at this point a cliché to say that Hollywood is a place that routinely consumes, sucks the soul out of, and then discards talented humans of all stripes, but that makes it no less true. Of the most successful and most Inside-y people I interviewed for this book, the majority of them were trying to figure out how to get back out of the system because it was destroying their brains, lives, and happiness.

3. *The castle roof might be about to cave in:* To say that this is an unstable time for the entertainment media industry is a laughable understatement. The whole industry is teetering somewhere between soul-irradiating corporate commercialism and middle-of-a-civil-war-battle chaos. I have often thought that we women are in the process of expending a hell of a lot of energy trying to get inside a castle and that we may just make it inside in time for the roof to collapse on our heads.

There is profound liberation in walking away from their games, in refusing to invest in their value systems, in deciding to imagine our own. Dare to be radical enough to imagine a time and industry in which Hollywood is not the epicenter at all. What would that look like? What would you chase and build then?

What are you waiting for? Build those things now.

Also, be equally radical in your storytelling.

As Woolf, who really did know a thing or two about being a female artist in a male-dominated art form, also wrote:

> Women have served all these centuries as looking-glasses possessing the magic and delicious power of reflecting the figure of man at twice its natural size. . . . That serves to explain in part the necessity that women so often are to men. And it serves to explain how restless they are under her criticism; how impossible it is for her to say to them this book is bad, this picture is feeble, or whatever it may be, without giving far more pain and rousing far more anger than a man would do who gave the same criticism. For if she begins to tell the truth, the figure in the looking-glass shrinks; his fitness for life is diminished. How is he to go on giving judgment, civilizing natives, making laws, writing books, dressing up and speechifying at banquets, unless he can see himself at

breakfast and at dinner at least twice the size he really is? . . . Hence, the enormous importance to the patriarch who has to conquer, who has to rule, of feeling that great numbers of people, half the human race indeed, are by nature inferior to himself. It must indeed be one of the chief sources of his power.[7]

There, Virginia cuts to the true core of why men have worked so hard for so long to keep women's voices out of the most impactful storytelling form of our lifetimes; why they are tying themselves into pretzels to ensure that when stories about women *are* told, they are told by men, or at least kept well-contained by the structures, conception, and note giving of men. The idea of all of womankind's bodies, voices, and experiences taking up the full, expansive, shimmering space that is our life-given right is nothing short of terrifying.

Century after century, decade after decade, the patriarchy has morphed, transfigured, and disguised itself infinitely to prevent the full-throated unleashing of that female voice—of our stories, our experiences, our joys, our pain, and, most definitely, our desires.

This vocal strangling has been so effective, the force-fed universal consumption of the white male gaze so complete, that we have to seriously confront as artists that we actually, even at this supposedly progressive, uber-modern moment, don't have any real idea what the female cinematic voice even is.

Certainly, we have seen flickers of what it might be throughout cinematic history, past and present. If we look back to those days of silent movies, there's a nerve-cracklingly radical vein in their storytelling: there were women making films about birth control, lesbian and bisexual relationships, cross-dressing, abortion, and, even with some frequency, nudity through the female director's own gaze.[8] There we begin to see what might be so alarming about allowing us our say.

But there has never been a time when a substantial number of women, properly unfettered by white male control, were making films at the same time and—like the halcyon Spielberg/Lucas/Coppola/etc. days—experimenting, inventing new forms, watching each others' work, and pushing each other to greater heights of imagination, structures, and discovery.

Well, never, that is, until now.

Quite by accident, through that 2011 convergence of crowdfunding, technological advancements, video streaming, and Kathryn Bigelow's Oscar, you and I, those of us making films today, find ourselves in that female-voice primordial ooze at this very moment. Yes, it's at the grass-roots level. Yes, it's on the fringes. No, we haven't gotten the notice or sanctification of those golden men of Hollywood,* but we are making our stuff. We are watching and working on each other's stuff. We are getting it to audiences and learning from their reactions. A lack of resources is forcing us to different and new creative forms. Most importantly, down in that ooze, the tight budgets and practicalities are our only restrictions. There is no one standing over us telling us what stories we can tell or how we can tell them.

I see in myself and my colleagues, and I hope soon in you, too, the burgeoning possibility, that slowly, with ever-tantalizing quivers of brilliance, we might finally have the space to discover our cinematic voices for the first time.

I urge you to join me in getting radical about finding it.

And what do I mean exactly by that? What *is* the female gaze?

Well, that's just the point. I have no idea. No one does!

We have to get into the mucky, messy, gleeful creative goo together, make stuff, inspire each other to greatness, and allow it to emerge.

I want you to go out and make a movie or a TV show or a web series and show me something I have never seen before. I want you to make something that will make me ache with jealousy because of how good it is, that will make me show up at my desk and push myself harder and more daringly because I want to match your heights. I want you to prove me wrong and prove me right and bathe us all in the shattering fullness of your voice. I want you to make something that will scare the living daylights out of the white patriarchy. I want you to become the voice their structures are designed to suppress.

And here's the truth: we're going to make some bad movies, probably even some terrible ones along the way. That's what happens when you swing high. But who gives a shit? That's what the white men have

---

* Which, for these intents and purposes is probably a good and necessary thing.

been getting to do for years. Dare boldly enough that you make a terrible movie. Because along the way, before and after and in between any bad movies . . .

We're going to blow people's minds with our truths and originality, and change the world with images and stories that people have never been fortunate enough to see before on-screen.

CONCLUSION

ENOUGH SAID*

Writing *The Wrong Kind of Woman* between March 2018 and August 2019 has been a bit like trying to report from the inside of a washing machine. The story and the headlines were constantly moving, and it remains unclear where any of it will land long term. *"X Woman Got Hired to Direct Y Blockbuster or TV Series!" "Famous White Dudes Make Another War Movie Where They Also Get to Avenge the Rape of a Woman Who Is in the Movie Only So There Will Be a Rape to Avenge." "Executives Say They're Really Getting Tired of Everyone Complaining and They Really 'Just Have to Hire the Best Person' for the Job."* And on and on it goes. It is wholly unclear whether the small increases we're seeing in the percentage of women behind the camera and improved representation on camera are aberrations of a PR moment or early indicators of lasting upward trends. Meanwhile, almost none of the dozens and dozens of men credibly accused of sexual assault and violence (including Harvey Weinstein himself) have been sent to prison.[1]

As the entertainment industry continues to reckon with itself post-Weinstein and #MeToo, it is simultaneously facing a second reckoning, seeking new distribution and revenue models to avoid a spectacular collapse. This sort of reinvention in response to changing consumer and cultural tastes and technological advances happens like clockwork once or twice a generation in Hollywood, but I'll venture to say that

---

* *Enough Said* (2013), dir. Nicole Holofcener.

we are in the midst of the most seismic of those transformations since talkies came on the scene.

It is, therefore, unwise to assess where we now stand with the women in film question without examining the broader context of this transformation, a moment in which unprecedented power has been consolidated by an unprecedented few, while the grassroots of change continue to grow quickly.

Let us look first at the state of the studios. Overall, the news there is bleak. Domestic movie ticket sales continue to nose-dive—presumably as a result of some combination of unlimited quality content streaming to our couches and the ever-more-inane fare Hollywood seeks to lure us back with. Those foreign audiences the studios traded us in for are, meanwhile, showing warning signs of going elsewhere. For the studios, this is disaster time. Every studio, that is, except Disney. In March of 2019, Disney, which alone has been thriving this past half decade, bought 20th Century Fox in one of the biggest acquisitions in Hollywood history, adding them to their stable, which includes Pixar, Marvel, and Lucasfilm. Even as every studio around them founders, Disney's five films released so far in 2019 had, as of June, already made over $5.61 billion worldwide, meaning the studio will likely earn more this year than its 2018 yearly total of $7.33 billion, a record, save for Disney's 2016 best of $7.61 billion.[2] In short, Disney finds itself peerless and indeed more powerful than any other studio in the history of the industry.*

Meanwhile, in streaming land, Amazon and Netflix continue to keep all competitors far at bay. The powerhouse subscription services lure ever more viewers to stay home, consuming more content than ever, while persistently training those same viewers that they should expect great and expensively budgeted content for free (or what feels free because of the easy-to-forget monthly subscription fee that comes off their credit cards). This training has long made the industry nervous, given that great-and-expensive-content-for-free is not exactly the sort of rock-solid economic model likely to be endorsed by Harvard Business School. But recently, those nerves have been borne out, as even Netflix, the

---

* With the possible exception of MGM in its early-industry heyday, though, given the mass globalization of content, Disney is now more powerful and far-reaching than that studio ever was.

streaming industry groundbreaker and leader, is seeing the first har-
bingers of disaster. During the second quarter of 2019, its growth rates
dropped precipitously, gaining only half of its projected 5.5 million new
subscribers for the quarter, and in its largest drop to date, actually losing
around 130,000 US subscribers during the same period. The reversal in
Netflix's fortune and the resulting next-day 10 percent drop in its stock
does not suggest immediate catastrophe. But it does indicate that we are
likely headed toward the revenue and distribution-model floor dropping
out on us yet again.[3]

The monolithic domination by Disney, Amazon, and Netflix of market and decision power in the entertainment industry is unprecedented.
Looking through the prism of the lack of women in film, this is either
terrific or catastrophic news.

If, on the one hand, the power brokers at Disney, Amazon, and
Netflix—with John Landgraf/FX–style vision and determination—set
themselves the goal of achieving hiring parity behind and in front of the
camera, they now have the reach to shift the industry-wide percentages
in a matter of years and, virtually single-handedly, bring about gender
parity (and intersectional parity) in film and television.

If, on the other hand, they take a pass on that lucrative and righteous
possibility, and/or if they lack the personal or institutional strength to
sufficiently implement real change, there will be precious little any of us
can do to force companies of that heft to do so.

Before those gates close, we must push harder than ever before. We
must appeal equally to the better angels of their natures and to their
greed. We must vote with our dollars and argue with their bottom lines.
We must pursue legal avenues to force their hand. We must use the lever-
age point of the rapidly changing tastes and habits of our viewers that
threaten even the most powerful institutions to argue that women and
people of color and the LGBTQ+ and disabled creators stand as the Hail
Mary solution to their problems, not as an irrelevant annoyance to be
flicked away. We must force them to look beyond their own limited visions and to pick up the money they are leaving on the table.

While that jury of powerful decision-makers deliberates, however, I
stand unprepared to leave our destiny tied up in their hands. I continue
to place my hope—and I do feel full of hope—in women filmmakers
and on audiences who, when presented with the option, are delighted to

watch their work. There is a real and growing grassroots sensibility attached to making the change I want to see happen. I believe in that brand of disruption, even when the opposition is a Goliath getting bigger every year. The grassroots movement that motivated me and that I am now a part of is not letting up. I continue to invest my efforts in that direction.

To wit, in the summer of 2019, while Hollywood was spinning itself into a jumble, I set out to release my second feature film, *Bite Me*. Underwhelmed as I—along with virtually every other filmmaker I knew—had been in our past experiences with distributors and figuring that in this current landscape nobody really knows what the hell is going on anyway, my teammates and I decided to take matters into our own hands and try something different. Feeling sure that there was an audience out there for a female-created, subversive, romantic comedy about a vampire and the IRS agent who audits her, we decided to find that audience. My team's thinking was that, given the current difficulty in getting people to put on pants, leave their homes, and pay to watch a film in a theater, we filmmakers needed to give them some added incentive to do just that. So I packed up my life, threw it all in an RV, drove a complete loop around the contiguous United States, putting on fifty-one screenings of our film in forty cities over three months. The fact that I, as the film's writer/star/producer, was in attendance at each screening gave the audience an added incentive to attend. They met me and got to participate in a Q&A discussion after the film. Further, after almost every screening, we threw a Joyful Vampire Ball—part costume party, part community-building celebration of uniqueness—which offered audiences a chance to dress up and, in total, promised them a real night out.

After some initial research, we began cold-calling independent theaters and alternative event spaces around the country. We pitched this idea, fully expecting to get blown off. But so many venues said yes that we eventually had to start turning them down because we could not fit more than fifty-one screenings into our schedule. Even better, many of them said, "Yes, and . . ." As in, "Yes, and, how about we create a 'Vampires in Summer'-themed costume contest?" "Yes, and what if we hand-painted you a sign covering one entire exterior of our building to advertise the event?" "Yes, and, what if we did a Joyful Vampire Yoga Class before a screening?" What seemed initially like a vaguely madcap idea became the Joyful Vampire Tour of America, which began in New York City on May 6, 2019, with three sold-out screenings and, after 13,001 miles driven in an RV,* ended back in New York City on August 5, 2019.

We set out to innovate a new kind of distribution model for film—one that would empower content creators, venue owners, and audiences to reach each other directly to build community and conversation through tour-driven, event-based screenings, and to use those screenings to push digital sales of a film. In removing layers of mostly male, mostly white gatekeepers, we wanted to see if we could widen the cracked door through which everybody who's not male and white is currently trying to squeeze, and if we could, in fact, build a different door altogether.

The in-person tour itself was successful in ways we could not even have imagined, though that did not result in matching digital sales. (We see you, Netflix, and your promise of great, free content.) So on this current tour, we did not crack the precise revenue model for a new brand of distribution. But because we gathered and then shared our journey, data, lessons, and triumphs with radical transparency in a YouTube docu-series called *The Joyful Vampire Tour of America*, audiences and filmmakers all over the world are now building on what we uncovered. Our summer tour ignited new ideas for my team and dozens of others who are now experimenting with similar direct-to-fan models. We are all closer to a solution now than we were before. So of course, I am going to keep innovating, trying new models, working on constructing that brand-new door.

One thing I've learned from my women in film work is that no one person or team of people working at the grassroots level can solve the industry's problems. But I continue to believe that big change begins with small change, and small change often happens at the fringes, where the powers-that-be aren't paying attention.

The most transformational part of my RV summer, touring film across America, however, even as we looked up at the terrifying new levels of power of the gatekeepers in Hollywood, was meeting and talking to thousands of people around the country after they had watched our movie. I giggled wildly with a gothic queen in Wichita, debated Christianity in America with a woman in Ohio, and held a man in Vicks-

---

* Well, two RVs to be precise. Our first RV's transmission crapped out in Ohio.

burg, Mississippi, as he wept, feeling newly seen—all reactions invoked by the story we had put up on a screen. I was reminded, more vividly than ever before, of the truly awesome power of storytelling. To create them is a breathtaking amount of power and a breathtaking amount of responsibility.

It is damaging to all of us when that power is limited to the same kind of voices and perspectives time and time again. For all of the words in this book, it really is as simple and as overwhelming as that.

What are the voices we are not hearing? Who are the heroines we have not yet even imagined? Which little-known or forgotten histories are ripe for cinematic revelation? Do the creators of that work look like people you're not used to seeing behind the camera? Maybe they should.

It is not acceptable that voices of more than 51 percent of our population are missing from our cultural narrative. It never was acceptable, and it sure as hell is not acceptable now.

Fight for them with me.

Because if there is one thing I learned this summer, over the course of writing this book, in my work in this lifetime so far, it is that the citizens of this country and planet most urgently need to see stories from the wrong kinds of women.

ACKNOWLEDGMENTS

I would like to thank the academy . . . just kidding. Academy, get your shit together.

In the meantime, I would like to most sincerely thank the following people . . .

My masterful editor, Rakia Clark, who saw what this book should be before I did, walked with and guided me as I navigated how to do it, and without whom this book very simply would not be what it is. My agent, Mark Gottlieb, who called me up one Saturday and said, "I think you have a book in you. Would you like to write it?" and then sold the idea so that I could. Everyone at Beacon Press for turning it into an actual book! You are magicians.

All of those who let me interview them for this book. I could not have understood or shared what I came to know without your stories. The researchers who gave me the data and those thinkers from whose articles and books I was able to pull the threads with which to weave the bigger picture.

Those early readers who sent notes, feedback, and encouragement to keep going, most especially my sister warriors who also let me ask endless questions about the history of the movement, Jennifer Dean, Jan Eliasberg, Rachel Feldman, Victoria Hochberg, and Maria Giese.

My yellow-brick road colleagues in the film projects that make up my own experiences in this book: Meredith Edwards times two, you are a visionary and a goddess, and I am infinitely grateful for our partnership; Joanna Bowzer for helping us figure out how to make a movie in the first place; Caitlin Gold for agreeing to at least two of my more madcap ideas and rolling up your sleeves to make them realities; Sarah Wharton, I don't have the words, I hope you feel the depth of this thank-you; Joanne Zippel, for believing in me enormously, helping me locate my vision, and then build the wings to make it fly; and Jack Lechner, for being a shining example of how successful men can use their power to lift women up, giving the best notes ever, lending your encyclopedic brain to this book, and, generally, being the menschiest of all the mensches.

To The 51 Fund team—Lois Scott, Caitlin Gold (again), Lindsay Lanzillotta, and Jessica Goodman—for working so hard and so long with me to try and make the Big, Bold, Important thing happen.

To Theater Masters and Brad Moore for prompting me to write my first lines of dialogue and then convincing me that I might have a knack for it, and to Julia Hansen for quietly making sure I started and continued, providing mentorship, support, and opportunities at every turn.

To everyone who has invested in or donated to one of my films. You are the only reason that I have been able to lift myself around and out of a system that has trapped women for nearly a century. Thank you for your extraordinary belief and willingness to put your literal money on the table in support of that belief.

To every person who has been part of my journey this far. It is genuinely overwhelming to think of the number of people who have helped, guided, lifted, and shaped me so that I could get as far as I've gotten in the face of the odds outlined in these pages. It would take a whole other book to thank you all individually, but I am weak with gratitude for every action and moment, large and small.

To my assistants, Hilary Adams and then Marlee Newman, for being excellent and keeping me sane through the last few years. To Joanna Pickering for being my unofficial mathematical consultant for this book (any errors and looseness with mathematical concepts are mine).

To the members of my lady tribe who have given me the kind of strength, love, and good advice that allowed me to keep finding and believing in my own voice ever a little bit more: Katie Morrison and my Threadbare Women: Mara Lileas, Mia Romero, Gwenevere Sisco, and Elspeth Turner.

To my parents, Paul Jones and Claire McDougall, who gave my siblings and me a richly creative environment to grow up in, insisted that we follow our passions, and have never once flagged in their belief that we are capable of anything, nor wavered in their support. Whatever else I have faced, you stacked the deck permanently in my favor from the beginning.

To my siblings, Obadiah and Talitha, for gamely participating in the earliest productions and being ballasts in the ocean since. You both inspire me with your talents and hearts.

To Veronica, my best reader always, for making me feel seen, heard, and safe no matter where each of us has been in the world and for talking through practically everything with me for as many hours as I wanted for the past twenty years.

To Stephen, for being the kind of husband who agrees to move into an RV for three months in an attempt to invent a new model for independent film distribution, for making me laugh every single day, for reminding me what a real artist is every time you play, and for your good advice, brilliance, kindness, and heart.

To all women in film, past, present, and future, for inspiration, hope, and different kinds of stories. In solidarity.

LIST OF INTERVIEWS

- Lynne Marie Rosenberg, phone interview, March 14, 2018
- Katie Morrison, phone interview, March 14, 2018
- Heidi Miami Marshall, phone interview, March 14, 2018
- Makia Martin, phone interview, March 17, 2018
- Jennifer Morrison, New York, NY, March 18, 2018
- Nate Washburn, phone interview, March 19, 2018
- Cuyle Carvin, phone interview, March 20, 2018
- Michelle Hendley, phone interview, March 21, 2018
- Alexandra Turshen, phone interview, March 21, 2018
- Christian Coulson, phone interview, March 22, 2018
- Gwenevere Sisco, phone interview, March 23, 2018
- Jennifer Dorr White, phone interview, March 23, 2018
- Carly Zien, phone interview, March 23, 2018
- Sonja O'Hara, phone interview, March 23, 2018 and June 26, 2018
- Caitlin Gold, phone interview, March 28, 2018
- Susan Wands, phone interview, March 28, 2018
- Mahira Kakkar, phone interview, March 29, 2018
- Matthew Murumba, phone interview, March 29, 2018
- Nicole Coulon, phone interview, March 29, 2018
- Jacqueline Pereda, phone interview, April 2, 2018
- Katya Martin, phone interview, April 3, 2018
- Ally Beans, phone interview, April 4, 2018
- Katherine Kahrs, phone interview, April 5, 2018
- Jessica Goodman, Los Angeles, CA, April 11, 2018
- Michelle Hurd, Los Angeles, CA, April 12, 2018
- Jack Lechner, email interview, May 5, 2018

- Will Sullivan, phone interview, May 16, 2018
- Sarah Wharton, phone interview, May 30, 2018
- Jen McGowan, phone interview, May 31, 2018
- Denise di Novi, phone interview, May 31, 2018
- Caytha Jentis, phone interview, June 1, 2018
- Lila Yomtoob, phone interview, June 2, 2018
- Janet Grillo, phone interview, June 4, 2018
- Rachel Feldman, phone interview, June 4, 2018
- Victoria Negri, phone interview, June 5, 2018
- Ariel Mahler, phone interview, June 5, 2018
- Maria Giese, phone interview, June 7, 2018, accompanied by follow-up email interviews
- Jessica Hinds, New York, NY, June 8, 2018
- Michael Mitnick, phone interview, June 8, 2018
- Jan Eliasberg, phone interview, June 8, 2018
- Gabrielle Hawkins, phone interview, June 9, 2018
- Leah Meyerhoff, phone interview, June 11, 2018
- Gabriella Moses, phone interview, June 13, 2018
- Bat-Sheva Guez, phone interview, June 14, 2018
- Lisa Tierney-Keough, phone interview, June 14, 2018
- Jaclyn Gramigna, phone interview, June 16, 2018
- Deborah Kampmeier, phone interview June 17, 2018
- Victoria Hochberg, email interview, June 20, 2018
- Anu Valia, phone interview, June 26, 2018
- Catherine Eaton, phone interview, June 29, 2018
- Sarah Adina Smith, phone interview, July 3, 2018
- Melissa Silverstein, New York, NY, July 20, 2018
- Emily Best, phone interview, August 17, 2018
- April Reign, phone interview, August 29, 2018
- Rachel Watanabe-Batton, phone interview, August 30, 2018
- Deb Verhoeven, phone interview, August 31, 2018
- Christina Campagnola, phone interview, September 3, 2018
- Anna Serner, phone interview, October 8, 2018
- Karyn Kusama, Los Angeles, CA, October 25, 2018
- Cheryl L. Bedford, phone interview, June 9, 2019
- Maylen Calienes, phone interview, June 11, 2019

- Marilee Talkington, phone interview, July 5, 2019, accompanied by a follow-up email interview on July 30, 2019
- Sarah Springer, email interview, July 7, 2019
- Annie Doona, email interview, July 9, 2019
- Jenni Gold, phone interview, July 12, 2019

A large number of people I interviewed asked that their names not be included in the book in any form out of concern for their ongoing careers in the film industry. Out of respect for their wishes, I have omitted their names from this list as well as from the main text of the book.

RESOURCE LIST OF ORGANIZATIONS WORKING TOWARD INTERSECTIONAL PARITY IN US ENTERTAINMENT MEDIA

Although I tried to be thorough, I am sure that this is not a complete list of all the incredible organizations working in this space. To those that I have accidentally omitted, my most sincere apologies.

5050by2020	www.5050by2020.com
Accessible Hollywood	www.accessiblehollywood.com
ACLU of Southern California	www.aclusocal.org
Advocates for Inclusion Media	www.aimcoalition.org
AFI Directing Workshop for Women	www.afi.com/dww
Alliance for Women Film Composers	www.theawfc.com
Alliance of Women Directors	www.allianceofwomendirectors.org/board-of-directors
Allies in Arts	www.alliesinarts.org
Arthouse Convergence	www.indiewire.com/2018/01/art-house-convergence -arthouses-sundance-2018-diversity-theaters-1201919138
Asian American Women Media Makers	www.facebook.com/AAWMM
Asian Cinevision	www.asiancinevision.org
Avenida Productions	www.avenida.tv
Black Filmmakers Group	www.facebook.com/groups/blackfilmmakers
Black Public Media	www.blackpublicmedia.org
Black Women Animate	www.blackwomenanimate.com
Blue Collar Post Collective	www.bluecollarpostcollective.com
Blue Fever	www.bluefever.com
Brown Girls Doc Mafia	www.feedbackloopfilms.com

CAPE (Coalition of Asian Pacifics in Entertainment)	www.capeusa.org
Centre for the Study and Research of African Women in Cinema	www.africanwomenincinema.org
Cherry Picks	www.cherrypicksreviews.com
Chicana Director's Initiative	www.chicanadirectorsinitiative.org
Chicken & Egg Pictures	www.chickeneggpics.org
Cinefemme	www.cinefemme.net
Cinema Touching Disability Film Festival	www.ctdfilmfest.org
CinemAbility Foundation	www.cinemability.org
Cinematcher	www.cinematcher.com
Cinematographers XX	www.cinematographersxx.com
DGA West — Women's Steering Committee	www.dga.org/The-Guild/Committees/Diversity/Women.aspx
Divas with Disabilities, Inc.	www.divaswithdisabilities.com
Easterseals Disability Film Challenge	www.disabilityfilmchallenge.com
Film Fatales	www.filmfatales.org
Film Festival Alliance	www.filmfestivalalliance.org
Film Independent Project Involve	www.filmindependent.org/programs/project-involve/
Film Inquiry	www.filminquiry.com
Film Lab	www.film-lab.org
Film Launch	www.filmlaunch.online
FilmRev	www.filmrev.org
Final Girls	www.finalgirls.org
Firelight Media	www.firelightmedia.tv
Frameline	www.frameline.org
Free the Bid	www.freethebid.com
From Script to Pre-Production	www.fs2p.org
Geena Davis Institute on Gender in Media	www.seejane.org
Getting Played: Symposium on Equity in the Entertainment Industry and Awards	www.kantonia.wix.com/symposium2019
Glass Elevator	www.glasselevate.com
GlobalGirl Media	www.globalgirlmedia.org
GradeMyMovie	www.grademymovie.com
GreenLight Women	www.GreenLightWomen.org

Hawai'i Women in Filmmaking	www.hawaiiwomeninfilmmaking.org
imagineNATIVE Film + Media Arts Festival	www.imaginenative.org
Indiefemme	www.indiefemme.com
Indigenous Media Freedom Alliance	www.imfreedomalliance.org
International Collective of Female Cinematographers	www.ICFCfilm.com
Kid Opal	www.kidopal.com
Kitsplit	www.kitsplit.com
LA Skins Fest	www.laskinsfest.com
Latino Filmmakers Network	www.latinofilmmaker.org
Level Forward	www.levelforward.com
Los Angeles Women's Film Collective	www.lawomensfilmcollective.com
Media Access Awards	www.mediaaccessawards.com
Moms-in-Film	www.momsinfilm.org
National Association of Latino Independent Producers (NALIP)	www.nalip.org
National Association of Latino Arts and Cultures (NALAC)	www.nalac.org
NBC Universal TIPS	www.nbcunitips.com
NewFest: New York's LGBT Film & Media Arts Organization	www.newfest.org
NYC Women Filmmakers	www.nycwomenfilmmakers.org
NYU Graduate Film Program Women's Initiative	www.tisch.nyu.edu/grad-film
New York Women in Film and Television (NYWIFT)	www.nywift.org
#OscarsSoWhite	www.ReignOfApril.com
Pacific Islanders in Communications	www.piccom.org
PGA East Women's Impact Network	www.facebook.com/PGAWomen
Picture Parity	www.pictureparity.com
POV/American Documentary	www.amdoc.org
Prime Latino Media	www.facebook.com/groups/PrimeLatinoMedia
Queer Producers Collective	www.queerproducers.com
ReelAbilities Film Festival	www.reelabilities.org/newyork
ReFrame	www.reframeproject.org

RespectAbility	www.respectability.org
SAG-AFTRA National PWD Committee	www.sagaftra.org
Scriptd	www.scriptd.com
See Jane Do	www.seejanedo.com
Seed&Spark	www.seedandspark.com
Sundance Film Institute	www.sundance.org
Superfest Disability Film Festival	www.superfestfilm.org
Tangerine Entertainment	www.tang-ent.com/about
Tanji	www.tanji.mobi
The 51 Fund	www.the51fund.com
The Black TV & Film Collective	www.blacktvfilmcollective.org
The Black List	www.blcklst.com
The FilmmakeHers	www.thefilmmakehers.com
The Representation Project	www.therepresentationproject.org
The Writers Lab	www.thewriterslab.nyc
Times Up — Entertainment	www.timesupnow.com
Times Up — NextGen	www.timesupnow.com
Transgender Talent LLC	www.transgendertalent.com
Tribeca Film Institute	www.tribecafilminstitute.org
Vision Maker Media	www.visionmakermedia.org
WGA — Committee of Women Writers	www.wga.org/members/committees/women-writers
Woman of Her Word	www.womanofherword.com
Women and Hollywood	www.womenandhollywood.com
Women in Animation	www.womeninanimation.org
Women in Film	www.wif.org
Women in Media	www.womennmedia.com
Women Independent Producers	www.womenindependentproducers.org
Women Make Movies	www.wmm.com
Women of Color Unite/The JTC List	www.thejtclist.com
Women's Media Summit	www.womensmediasummit.org
Women's Voices Now	www.womensvoicesnow.org
Women's Weekend Film Challenge	www.womensweekendfilmchallenge.com

NOTES

INTRODUCTION: BEYOND THE LIGHTS

1. Susan Faludi, "The Patriarchs Are Falling. The Patriarchy Is Stronger Than Ever," *New York Times*, December 28, 2017, https://www.nytimes.com/2017/12/28/opinion/sunday/patriarchy-feminism-metoo.html.

CHAPTER 1: IT FELT LIKE LOVE

1. Cara Kelly, "She Wanted a Hollywood Career. Her Agent Wanted Sex," *USA Today*, March 22, 2018, https://www.usatoday.com/story/life/people/2018/03/22/she-wanted-hollywood-career-her-agent-wanted-sex/403413002.

CHAPTER 2: DANCE, GIRL, DANCE

1. Martha M. Lauzen, *It's a Man's (Celluloid) World: Portrayals of Female Characters in Top Grossing Films of 2018* (San Diego: Center for the Study of Women in Television and Film, 2019), https://womenintvfilm.sdsu.edu/wp-content/uploads/2019/02/2018_Its_a_Mans_Celluloid_World_Report.pdf.

2. Darnell Hunt, Ana-Christina Ramon, and Michael Tran, *Hollywood Diversity Report 2019: Old Story, New Beginning* (Los Angeles: UCLA College Social Sciences, February 2019), https://socialsciences.ucla.edu/wp-content/uploads/2019/02/UCLA-Hollywood-Diversity-Report-2019-2-21-2019.pdf; US Census Data, July 1, 2018, https://www.census.gov/quickfacts/fact/table/US/PST045216.

3. "CDC: 1 in 4 US Adults Live with a Disability," press release, Centers for Disease Control, August 16, 2018, cdc.gov/media/ releases/2018/p0816-disability.html.

4. Danny Woodburn and Kristina Kopic, "The Ruderman White Paper: On Employment of Actors with Disabilities," July 2016, http://rudermanfoundation.org/wp-content/uploads/2016/07/TV-White-Paper_7-1-003.pdf.

5. "Hollywood Inequality Is 'Entrenched,' Study Suggests," *BBC News*, September 7, 2016, https://www.bbc.com/news/entertainment-arts-37294932; Frank Newport, "In U.S. Estimate of LGBT Population Rises to 4.5%," Gallup, May 22, 2018, https://news.gallup.com/poll/234863/estimate-lgbt-population-rises.aspx.

6. Jeanne Joe Perrone, "Gender Inequality in Film Infographic," New York Film Academy, March 8, 2018, https://www.nyfa.edu/film-school-blog/gender-inequality-in-film-infographic-updated-in-2018.

7. Frank Pasquine, "Gender Inequality in Film Infographic," New York Film Academy, November 25, 2013, https://www.nyfa.edu/film-school-blog/gender-inequality-in-film.

8. Naomi Wolf, *The Beauty Myth: How Images of Beauty Are Used Against Women* (New York: Morrow, 1991).

9. Ruth Penfold-Mounce, "How the Rise in TV 'Crime Porn' Normalises Violence Against Women," *The Conversation*, October 24, 2016, https://theconversation.com/how-the-rise-in-tv-crime-porn-normalises-violence-against-women-66877.

10. American Academy of Family Physicians, "Violence in Media and Entertainment," position paper, 2016, https://www.aafp.org/about/policies/all/violence-media.html.

11. Martha T. S. Laham, "The Film Industry's Problem of Gender Inequality Is Worse Than You Think," *Huffington Post*, August 17, 2016 (updated August 18, 2017), https://www.huffpost.com/entry/the-celluloid-ceiling-tru_b_11389544.

12. Lauzen, *It's a Man's (Celluloid) World.*

13. Laham, "The Film Industry's Problem of Gender Inequality Is Worse Than You Think."

14. Lauzen, *It's a Man's (Celluloid) World.*

15. Perrone, "Gender Inequality in Film Infographic."

16. Lauzen, *It's a Man's (Celluloid) World.*

17. Shrikanth Narayanan et al., *The Reel Truth: Women Aren't Seen or Heard* (Los Angeles: Geena Davis Institute on Gender in Media, September 2016), https://seejane.org/research-informs-empowers/data.

18. Amy Blumenthal, "How Central Are Female Characters to a Movie?," USC Viterbi School of Engineering, August 1, 2017, https://viterbischool.usc.edu/news/2017/08/central-female-characters-movie.

19. Hannah Anderson and Matt Daniels, "Film Dialogue from 2,000 Screenplays, Broken Down by Gender and Age," *Pudding*, April 2016, https://pudding.cool/2017/03/film-dialogue/index.html.

20. Anderson and Daniels, "Film Dialogue from 2,000 Screenplays, Broken Down by Gender and Age."

21. Anderson and Daniels, "Film Dialogue from 2,000 Screenplays, Broken Down by Gender and Age."

22. American Academy of Family Physicians, "Violence in Media and Entertainment."

23. "Q3 2018 Nielsen Total Audience Report," Nielsen, March 19, 2019, https://www.nielsen.com/us/en/insights/news/2019/us-consumers-are-shifting-the-time-they-spend-with-media.html.

24. Chris Isidore, "These Are the Top US Exports," CNN.com, March, 7, 2018, https://money.cnn.com/2018/03/07/news/economy/top-us-exports/index.html.

25. Wolf, *The Beauty Myth.*

26. Elaina Zachos, "Why Are We Afraid of Sharks? There's a Scientific Explanation," *National Geographic*, June 27, 2019, https://news.nationalgeographic.com/2018/01/sharks-attack-fear-science-psychology-spd.

27. Jon Nathanson, "The Economics of Product Placements," Priceonomics, December 4, 2013, https://priceonomics.com/the-economics-of-product-placements.

28. Caroline Heldman, "New Study from Geena Davis Institute Finds Archery Catches Fire Thanks to Inspiring Hollywood Images," Geena Davis Institute on Gender in Media, August 4, 2016, https://seejane.org/gender-in-media-news-release/new-study-geena-davis-institute-finds-archery-catches-fire-thanks-inspiring-hollywood-images.

29. Tabitha Blaisdell, "Can Romantic Comedies Improve Your Marriage? Recent Research Says Yes," *PsychCentral*, July 8, 2018, https://psychcentral.com/blog/can-romantic-comedies-improve-your-marriage-recent-research-says-yes.

30. K. J. Dell'Antonia, "Disney Princesses Do Change Girls—and Boys, Too," *Well* blog, *New York Times*, June 27, 2016, https://well.blogs.nytimes.com/2016/06/27/disney-princesses-do-change-girls-and-boys-too.

31. Penfold-Mounce, "How the Rise in TV 'Crime Porn' Normalises Violence Against Women."

32. LS, "Violence Against Women in the Media," *WomanStats Blog*, June 20, 2013, https://womanstats.wordpress.com/2013/06/20/violence-against-women-in-the-media.

33. Maureen Ryan, "The Progress and Pitfalls of Television's Treatment of Rape," *Variety*, December 6, 2016, https://variety.com/2016/tv/features/rape-tv-television-sweet-vicious-jessica-jones-game-of-thrones-1201934910.

34. Josh Dickey, "Everyone Is Altered," *Mashable*, December 1, 2014, https://mashable.com/2014/12/01/hollywood-secret-beauty-procedure.

35. Wolf, *The Beauty Myth*, 83

36. Katty Kay and Claire Shipman, *The Confidence Code: The Science and Art of Self-Assurance—What Women Should Know* (New York: Harper Business, 2014).

37. Dickey, "Everyone Is Altered."

38. Pasquine, "Gender Inequality in Film Infographic."

39. Lauzen, *It's a Man's (Celluloid) World.*

40. Pasquine, "Gender Inequality in Film Infographic."

41. Judith Vonberg, "Jennifer Lawrence: I Was Treated in a Way That Now We Would Call Abusive," CNN.com, February 28, 2018, https://www.wsls.com/entertainment/jennifer-lawrence-i-was-treated-in-a-way-that-now-we-would-call-abusive.

CHAPTER 4: BRICK LANE

1. Transcript from Academy Awards Acceptance Speech Database, Halle Berry, Best Actress acceptance speech, March 24, 2002, http://aaspeechesdb.oscars.org.

2. Transcript from Academy Awards Acceptance Speech Database, Cate Blanchett, Best Actress acceptance speech, March 2, 2014, http://aaspeechesdb.oscars.org.

3. Janice Williams, "Meryl Streep Once Called Harvey Weinstein a 'God,' Now Actress Is Calling Him Disgraceful," *Newsweek*, October 9, 2017, https://www.newsweek.com/meryl-streep-harvey-weinstein-harrassment-680643.

4. Rebecca Keegan, "Why the Second Movie Is the Biggest Hurdle to Becoming a Filmmaker—Especially for Women and Minorities," *Los Angeles Times*, July 7, 2016, https://www.latimes.com/entertainment/movies/la-et-mn-sophomore-slump-diverse-filmmakers-20160617-snap-story.html.

5. Ben Fritz, *The Big Picture: The Fight for the Future of Movies* (Boston: Houghton Mifflin Harcourt, 2018).

6. Melody Bridges and Cheryl Robson, eds., *Silent Women: Pioneers of Cinema* (Twickenham, UK: Supernova Books, 2016).

7. Box office data for *Boys Don't Cry* (1999) from The Numbers, Nash Information Services, June 2, 2019, https://www.the-numbers.com/movie/Boys-Dont-Cry#tab=summary.

8. *Boys Don't Cry* entry, IMDb, https://www.imdb.com/title/tt0171804/?ref
_=nv_sr_1?ref_=nv_sr_1, accessed August 5, 2019.

9. Keegan, "Why the Second Movie Is the Biggest Hurdle to Becoming a Filmmaker."

10. Box office data for *Wayne's World* (1992) pulled from The Numbers, Nash Information Services, June 2, 2019, https://www.the-numbers.com/movie/Waynes -World#tab=summary.

11. Emma Saunders, "Female Directors Need to Be 'Shameless,'" BBC.com, May 21, 2018, https://www.bbc.com/news/entertainment-arts-44320687.

12. Keegan, "Why the Second Movie Is the Biggest Hurdle to Becoming a Film-maker"; "Gina Prince-Bythewood," IMDb, https://www.imdb.com/name/nm0697656, accessed June 29, 2019.

13. Lindsay Bahr, "The Challenges Female Filmmakers Face Post-Sundance," Associated Press, January 27, 2017, https://www.apnews.com/346cd92eea5a4473 b7232701d926c68d.

14. Saunders, "Female Directors Need to Be 'Shameless.'"

15. Gavin Edwards, "We Shall Overcome: Ava DuVernay on Making 'Selma,'" *Rolling Stone*, January 5, 2015, https://www.rollingstone.com/movies/movie-news /we-shall-overcome-ava-duvernay-on-making-selma-237237.

16. Melena Ryzik, "Female Cinematographers Not Content to Hide Behind the Camera," *New York Times*, June 1, 2016, https://www.nytimes.com/2016/06/02 /movies/female-cinematographers-not-content-to-hide-behind-the-camera.html.

CHAPTER 5: MUDBOUND

1. US Census Data, July 1, 2018, https://www.census.gov/quickfacts/fact/table /US/PST045216.

2. Stacy L. Smith, Katherine Pieper, and Marc Choueiti, *Inclusion in the Director's Chair? Gender, Race & Age of Film Directors Across 1,000 Films from 2007–2016* (Los Angeles: Annenberg Inclusion Initiative, February 2017).

3. Collated from four sources: Smith et al., *Inclusion in the Director's Chair?*; Martha M. Lauzen, *The Celluloid Ceiling: Behind-the-Scenes Employment of Women on the Top 100, 250, and 500 Films of 2017* (San Diego: Center for the Study of Women in Television and Film, 2018), https://womenintvfilm.sdsu.edu/wp-content /uploads/2018/01/2017_Celluloid_Ceiling_Report.pdf; 2010 Statistics, "Women Behind the Scenes," Women and Hollywood, https://womenandhollywood.com /resources/statistics/2010-statistics; and my interview with Victoria Hochberg.

4. Lauzen, *It's a Man's (Celluloid) World*.

5. Smith et al., *Inclusion in the Director's Chair?*

6. Perrone, "Gender Inequality in Film Infographic."

7. Perrone, "Gender Inequality in Film Infographic."

8. Analysis commissioned by The 51 Fund and done by Bruce Nash of Nash Information Services, October 2016.

9. Smith et al., *Inclusion in the Director's Chair?*

10. Jessica P. Ogilvie, "How Hollywood Keeps Women Out," *LA Weekly*, April 29, 2015, https://www.laweekly.com/news/how-hollywood-keeps-out-women-5525034.

11. A. O. Scott and Manohla Dargis, "Hollywood on the Brink," *New York Times*, January 3, 2018.

12. "The 'Inexorable Zero,'" *Harvard Law Review* 117, no. 4 (2004): 1215–35, https://www.jstor.org/stable/4093368.

13. Cara Buckley, "A.C.L.U., Citing Bias Against Women, Wants Inquiry into Hollywood's Hiring Practices," *New York Times*, May 12, 2015, https://www.nytimes.com/2015/05/13/movies/aclu-citing-bias-against-women-wants-inquiry-into-hollywoods-hiring-practices.html.

14. Laham, "The Film Industry's Problem of Gender Inequality Is Worse Than You Think."

15. Analysis commissioned by The 51 Fund and done by Bruce Nash of Nash Information Services, October 2016.

16. Kerry Hannon, "Are Women Too Timid When They Job Search?," *Forbes*, September 11, 2014, https://www.forbes.com/sites/nextavenue/2014/09/11/are-women-too-timid-when-they-job-search/#63e1406a411d.

17. Kay and Shipman, *The Confidence Code*.

18. Stacy L. Smith, Marc Choueiti, Hannah Clark, and Katherine Pieper, *Sundance Institute: Artist Demographics in Submissions & Acceptances* (Los Angeles: USC Annenberg Inclusion Initiative, January 2019), http://assets.uscannenberg.org.

19. Rachel Pashley, *New Female Tribes: Shattering Female Stereotypes and Redefining Women Today* (London: Virgin Books, 2018).

20. Pashley, *New Female Tribes*.

21. *The Big Wedding* (2013), IMDb, https://www.imdb.com/title/tt1931435.

22. Martha M. Lauzen, *Indie Women: Behind-the-Scenes Employment of Women in Independent Film, 2017–18* (San Diego: Center for the Study of Women in Television and Film, 2018), https://womenintvfilm.sdsu.edu/wp-content/uploads/2018/07/2017-18_Indie_Women_Report_rev.pdf.

23. Darnell Hunt et al., *Hollywood Diversity Report 2018: Five Years of Progress and Missed Opportunities* (Los Angeles: UCLA College of Social Sciences, 2018), https://socialsciences.ucla.edu/wp-content/uploads/2018/02/UCLA-Hollywood-Diversity-Report-2018-2-27–18.pdf.

24. Buckley, "A.C.L.U., Citing Bias Against Women, Wants Inquiry into Hollywood's Hiring Practices."

25. Smith et al., *Inclusion in the Director's Chair?*

26. Jonah Sachs, "If Investors Really Listened to Data, They'd Be Investing in Women," *Fast Company*, May 7, 2018, https://www.fastcompany.com/40568407/if-investors-really-listened-to-data-theyd-be-investing-in-women.

27. *ReFrame Culture and Change Handbook* (2018), https://static1.squarespace.com/static/58a204bfb3db2b8884d8c01f/t/5c0719da21c67cc385165e1a/1543969276544/ReFrame+Culture+Change+Handbook_11–2018.pdf.

28. Pashley, *New Female Tribes*.

29. Rebecca Sun, "Study: Films Directed by Women Receive 63 Percent Less Distribution Than Male-Helmed Movies," *Hollywood Reporter*, June 29, 2016, https://www.hollywoodreporter.com/news/study-films-directed-by-women-907229.

30. Sven Mikulec, "A Discussion with William Friedkin," *Cinephilia & Beyond*, 2016, https://cinephiliabeyond.org/a-discussion-with-william-friedkin.

31. William Goldman, *Adventures in the Screen Trade: A Personal View of Hollywood and Screenwriting* (New York: Hachette Book Group, 1984).

32. Bridges and Robson, *Silent Women*.

33. Dana Goodyear, "Can Hollywood Change Its Ways?," *New Yorker*, January 1, 2018, https://www.newyorker.com/magazine/2018/01/08/can-hollywood-change -its-ways.

34. Stacy L. Smith, Marc Choueiti, Angel Choi, and Katherine Pieper, *Inclusion in the Director's Chair: Gender, Race, and Age of Directors Across 1,200 Top Films from 2007 to 2018* (Los Angeles: Annenberg Inclusion Initiative, January 2019).

35. Clara Guibourg, "Oscars 2018: Female-Led Oscar Films 'More Profitable,'" BBC, March 1, 2018, https://www.bbc.com/news/entertainment-arts-43146026.

36. Smith et al., *Inclusion in the Director's Chair?* (2017).

37. Q&A presentation following an advance WGA screening of *Selma* with Ava DuVernay, New York, NY (AMC Loews Nineteenth St), December 9, 2014.

38. David Welch and Joey Scoma, "How Star Wars Was Saved in the Edit," You-Tube, December 7, 2017, https://www.youtube.com/watch?v=GFMyMxMYDNk &feature=youtu.be.

39. Amy Zimmerman, "Catherine Hardwicke Broke Records with 'Twilight.' Then Hollywood Labeled Her Difficult." *Daily Beast*, October 1, 2018, https://www .thedailybeast.com/catherine-hardwicke-broke-records-with-twilight-then -hollywood-labeled-her-difficult.

40. Andy Greene, "Flashback: Shelley Duvall and Stanley Kubrick Battle over 'The Shining,'" *Rolling Stone*, November, 17, 2016, https://www.rollingstone.com /movies/movie-news/flashback-shelley-duvall-and-stanley-kubrick-battle-over -the-shining-188549.

41. Maureen Dowd, "This Is Why Uma Thurman Is Angry," *New York Times*, February 3, 2018, https://www.nytimes.com/2018/02/03/opinion/sunday/this-is -why-uma-thurman-is-angry.html.

42. Sun, "Study: Films Directed by Women Receive 63 Percent Less Distribution Than Male-Helmed Movies."

43. Sun, "Study: Films Directed by Women Receive 63 Percent Less Distribution Than Male-Helmed Movies."

44. Smith et al., *Inclusion in the Director's Chair?*

45. ReFrame Culture and Change Handbook.

46. Sun, "Study: Films Directed by Women Receive 63 Percent Less Distribution Than Male-Helmed Movies."

47. Rebecca Sun, "Film Critics Even Less Diverse Than Films, Study Finds," *Hollywood Reporter*, June 11, 2018, https://www.hollywoodreporter.com/news/film -critics-diverse-films-study-finds-1118659.

48. Box Office data pulled from The-Numbers by Nash Information Services on July 15, 2019, https://www.the-numbers.com/movie/Jennifers-Body#tab=summary

49. Smith et al., *Inclusion in the Director's Chair?*

CHAPTER 6: SONGS MY BROTHER TAUGHT ME

1. Mike Miller, "Angela Lansbury on Working with a Female Director for the First Time at 92," *People*, May 3, 2018, https://people.com/movies/angela-lansbury -working-female-director-first-time-92.

2. Sarah Whitten, "Listen Up Hollywood: Women Want to See More Female Ensembles and Filmmakers," CNBC, March 8, 2019, https://www.cnbc.com/2019 /03/08/women-want-to-see-more-female-ensemble-films-and-filmmakers.html.

3. ReFrame Culture and Change Handbook.

4. Kay and Shipman, *The Confidence Code.*

5. Kay and Shipman, *The Confidence Code.*

6. Nina Menkes, "Sex and Power: The Visual Language of Oppression," 50th Anniversary celebration of *The Deutsche Film- und Fernsehakademie Berlin* (DFFB), March 2017.

7. Tori Telfer, "How Do We Define the Female Gaze in 2018?," *Vulture*, August 2, 2018, https://www.vulture.com/2018/08/how-do-we-define-the-female-gaze-in-2018.html.

8. Alicia H. Clark, *Hack Your Anxiety: How to Make Anxiety Work for You in Life, Love, and All That You Do* (n.p.: Sourcebooks, August 2018).

9. Jacob Gershman, "Is the Depiction of Law & Order on 'Law & Order' Influencing Jurors?," *Wall Street Journal*, September 6, 2013, https://blogs.wsj.com/law/2013/09/06/is-the-depiction-of-law-order-on-law-order-influencing-jurors.

10. Stock cited in Wolf, *The Beauty Myth.*

11. Robin DiAngelo, *White Fragility: Why It's So Hard to Talk to White People About Racism* (Boston: Beacon Press, 2018).

12. Pashley, *New Female Tribes.*

13. Perrone, "Gender Inequality in Film Infographic."

CHAPTER 7: ONE WAY OR ANOTHER

1. Cari Beauchamp, "100 Women, One Hotel, and the Weekend Retreat That Presaged Time's Up by 18 Years," *Vanity Fair*, 2018, https://www.vanityfair.com/hollywood/2018/01/women-directors-miramar-women.

2. Kristin Chirico, "Did You Know That Most Hollywood Screenwriters Used to Be Women?," *Buzzfeed*, July 30, 2013, https://www.buzzfeed.com/kristinchirico/did-you-know-that-most-hollywood-screenwriters-use-bwwj.

3. Bridges and Robson, *Silent Women*; Chirico, "Did You Know That Most Hollywood Screenwriters Used to Be Women?"

4. Chirico, "Did You Know That Most Hollywood Screenwriters Used to Be Women?"; Bridges and Robson, *Silent Women.*

5. Bridges and Robson, *Silent Women.*

6. Bridges and Robson, *Silent Women.*

7. Bridges and Robson, *Silent Women.*

8. Bridges and Robson, *Silent Women.*

9. Pashley, *New Female Tribes*; Rebecca Sun, "Female Indie Filmmakers Should Aim Higher in Their Budgets, Says Women Financing Panel," *Hollywood Reporter*, April 18, 2017, https://www.hollywoodreporter.com/news/female-indie-filmmakers-should-aim-higher-budgets-says-womens-financing-panel-995292.

10. Bridges and Robson, *Silent Women.*

11. Bridges and Robson, *Silent Women.*

12. Bridges and Robson, *Silent Women.*

13. Bridges and Robson, *Silent Women.*

14. Bridges and Robson, *Silent Women.*

15. Bridges and Robson, *Silent Women.*

16. Bridges and Robson, *Silent Women.*

17. Bridges and Robson, *Silent Women*; Pashley, *New Female Tribes.*

18. Hochberg interview.

19. Buckley, "A.C.L.U., Citing Bias Against Women, Wants Inquiry into Hollywood's Hiring Practices."

20. Hochberg interview.

21. Hochberg interview.

22. Hochberg interview.

23. Hochberg interview.

24. https://twitter.com/ReignOfApril, January 15, 2015.

25. Marshall interview.

26. Martin interview; Hendley interview.

27. Beans interview.

28. Guibourg, "Oscars 2018: Female-Led Oscar Films 'More Profitable.'"

29. 2018 Statistics, "Women Onscreen," Women and Hollywood, https://womenandhollywood.com/resources/statistics/2018-statistics.

30. Buckley, "A.C.L.U., Citing Bias Against Women, Wants Inquiry Into Hollywood's Hiring Practices."

31. Goodyear, "Can Hollywood Change Its Ways?"

32. Tre'vell Anderson, "A Look at Women Directors at the Summer Box Office the Year After Patty Jenkins' 'Wonder Woman,'" *Los Angeles Times*, April 26, 2018, https://www.latimes.com/entertainment/movies/la-ca-mn-sneaks-women-directors-20180426-story.html.

33. Mike Fleming Jr., "Cathy Yan Is Warner Bros' Choice to Direct Margot Robbie in Harley Quinn Film," *Deadline*, April 17, 2018, https://deadline.com/2018/04/harley-quinn-margot-robbie-cathy-yan-birds-of-prey-warner-bros-dc-entertainment-bat-girl-christina-hodson-1202365866.

34. Brian Welk, "Women Who Have Directed Movies with $100 Million Budgets," *Wrap*, March 8, 2019, https://www.thewrap.com/9-women-who-have-directed-movies-with-100-million-budgets-photos.

35. Stephanie Zacharek, "Hollywood Is Suddenly Serious. That's Exactly What America Needs Right Now," *Time*, March 1, 2018, https://time.com/5180705/hollywood-suddenly-serious-thats-what-america-needs-right-now.

36. Anderson, "A Look at Women Directors at the Summer Box Office the Year After Patty Jenkins' 'Wonder Woman.'"

37. Maane Khatchatourian, "Academy Invites Record 928 New Members," *Variety*, June 25, 2018, https://variety.com/2018/film/news/academy-new-members-2018-record-1202856702.

38. Laura Bradley, "The Academy's Female Membership Just Climbed to a Whopping 32%," *Vanity Fair*, July 1, 2019, https://www.vanityfair.com/hollywood/2019/07/new-film-academy-members-invitees-2019.

39. Lindy West, "We Got Rid of Some Bad Men. Now Let's Get Rid of Bad Movies," *New York Times*, March 3, 2018, https://www.nytimes.com/2018/03/03/opinion/sunday/we-got-rid-of-some-bad-men-now-lets-get-rid-of-bad-movies.html.

40. Hunt, Ramon, and Tran, *Hollywood Diversity Report 2019*.

41. Hunt, Ramon, and Tran, *Hollywood Diversity Report 2019*.

42. Zacharek, "Hollywood Is Suddenly Serious."

43. Nellie Andreeva, "Yes We Can: Female Broadcast Drama Directors Excel with Better Pilot-to-Series Batting Average Than Male Helmers," *Deadline*, May 13,

2018, https://deadline.com/2018/05/female-broadcast-drama-directors-pilots-liz -friedlander-julie-plec-1202389553.

44. Andreeva, "Yes We Can."

45. Cara Buckley, "As TV Seeks Diverse Writing Ranks, Rising Demand Meets Short Supply," *New York Times*, September 2, 2018, https://www.nytimes.com/2018 /09/02/arts/television/tv-writers-diversity.html

46. Buckley, "As TV Seeks Diverse Writing Ranks, Rising Demand Meets Short Supply."

47. ReFrame Culture and Change Handbook.

48. ReFrame Culture and Change Handbook.

49. Mark Olsen, "Five Female Directors, Many Stories," *Los Angeles Times*, August 30, 2018, https://www.latimes.com/entertainment/movies/la-ca-mn-sneaks -female-filmmakers-netflix-20180830-story.html.

50. Smith et al., *Inclusion in the Director's Chair?* (2017).

51. Lauzen, *The Celluloid Ceiling*.

52. Ryan, "The Progress and Pitfalls of Television's Treatment of Rape."

53. Matthew Fogel, "'Grey's Anatomy' Goes Colorblind," *New York Times*, May 8, 2005, https://www.nytimes.com/2005/05/08/arts/television/greys-anatomy-goes -colorblind.html.

54. Goodyear, "Can Hollywood Change Its Ways?"

55. ReFrame Culture and Change Handbook.

56. Bethanie Butler, "Why Ava DuVernay Hired Only Female Directors for Her New TV Show 'Queen Sugar,'" *Washington Post*, September 15, 2016, https://www .washingtonpost.com/news/arts-and-entertainment/wp/2016/09/15/why-ava -duvernay-hired-only-female-directors-for-her-new-tv-show-queen-sugar.

57. Keegan, "Why the Second Movie Is the Biggest Hurdle to Becoming a Film-maker"; ReFrame Culture and Change Handbook.

58. Sun, "Female Indie Filmmakers Should Aim Higher in Their Budgets."

59. Scott and Dargis, "Hollywood on the Brink."

60. David Canfield, "Hollywood Is Finally Catching Up to Karin Slaughter," *Entertainment Weekly*, August 14, 2018, https://ew.com/books/2018/08/14/karin -slaughter-pieces-of-her.

61. Scott and Dargis, "Hollywood on the Brink."

62. Goodyear, "Can Hollywood Change Its Ways?"

63. "Film Studio Fox Seeks Female Blockbuster Directors," BBC, September 16, 2016, https://www.bbc.com/news/entertainment-arts-37385322.

64. Laura Berger, "Research: New DGA Study Shows Lack of Opportunity for Women and Minority Feature Directors," *Women and Hollywood*, June 22, 2018, https://womenandhollywood.com/research-new-dga-study-shows-lack-of -opportunity-for-women-and-minority-feature-directors.

65. Buckley, "As TV Seeks Diverse Writing Ranks, Rising Demand Meets Short Supply."

66. Nicole Sperling, "CAA Launches Writers Database to Help Fix Hollywood's Diversity Problem," *Vanity Fair*, June 28, 2018, https://www.vanityfair.com /hollywood/2018/06/christy-haubegger-launches-amplify-database-at-creative -artists-agency-to-promote-hollywood-diversity.

67. This tweet has since been taken down.
68. Smith et al., *Inclusion in the Director's Chair?*; Lauzen, *The Celluloid Ceiling.*
69. Berger, "Research: New DGA Study Shows Lack of Opportunity for Women and Minority Feature Directors."
70. Hunt, Ramon, and Tran, *Hollywood Diversity Report 2019.*
71. Scott Roxborough, "Meet the 25 Players Who Can Actually Get an Independent Movie Made," *Hollywood Reporter*, May 3, 2018, https://www.hollywood reporter.com/lists/meet-25-players-who-can-actually-get-an-independent-movie -made-1107479.
72. Smith et al., *Inclusion in the Director's Chair?*
73. DiAngelo, *White Fragility.*
74. Dana Goodyear, "Can Hollywood Change Its Ways?" *New Yorker,* January 1, 2018, https://www.newyorker.com/magazine/2018/01/08/can-hollywood-change -its-ways.
75. Pashley, *New Female Tribes.*
76. Lili Loofbourow, "The Male Glance: How We Fail to Take Women's Stories Seriously," *Guardian*, March 6, 2018, https://www.theguardian.com/news/2018 /mar/06/the-male-glance-how-we-fail-to-take-womens-stories-seriously.
77. Jonathan Shia, "Alison Bechdel: The Bechdel Test 'Has Been a Very Strange Turn in My Life,'" *Vulture,* April 20, 2015, https://www.vulture.com/2015/04 /bechdel-test-creator-surprised-by-its-longevity.html.
78. Pashley, *New Female Tribes.*

CHAPTER 8: DAUGHTERS OF THE DUST
1. Beauchamp, "100 Women, One Hotel, and the Weekend Retreat That Presaged Time's Up by 18 Years."
2. Bob Pool, "Feminists' Ire at Academy on Display," *Los Angeles Times*, March 16, 2002, https://www.latimes.com/archives/la-xpm-2002-mar-16-me-girls16 -story.html.
3. Michael Behar, "Analog Meets Its Match in Red Digital Cinema's Ultrahigh-Res Camera," *Wired*, August 28, 2008, https://www.wired.com/2008/08/ff-redcamera/.
4. "Final Cut Pro," Wikipedia, https://en.wikipedia.org/wiki/Final_Cut_Pro.
5. "iTunes," Wikipedia, https://en.wikipedia.org/wiki/ITunes.
6. "Timeline of Netflix," Wikipedia, https://en.wikipedia.org/wiki/Timeline _of_Netflix.
7. "Timeline of Facebook," Wikipedia, https://en.wikipedia.org/wiki/Timeline _of_Facebook.
8. Barbara Ann O'Leary, Directed By Women, database of projects with female directors, directedbywomen.com.
9. Goldman, *Adventures in the Screen Trade.*
10. Fritz, *The Big Picture.*
11. Fritz, *The Big Picture.*
12. Lynda Obst, *Sleepless in Hollywood: Tales from the New Abnormal in the Movie Business* (New York: Simon & Schuster, 2013).
13. Obst, *Sleepless in Hollywood*; Fritz, *The Big Picture.*
14. Fritz, *The Big Picture.*

15. Obst, *Sleepless in Hollywood*.

16. Fritz, *The Big Picture*.

17. Fritz, *The Big Picture*.

18. Obst, *Sleepless in Hollywood*.

19. Fritz, *The Big Picture*.

20. Obst, *Sleepless in Hollywood*.

21. Fritz, *The Big Picture*.

22. Fritz, *The Big Picture*.

23. Fritz, *The Big Picture*.

24. Fritz, *The Big Picture*.

25. Obst, *Sleepless in Hollywood*.

26. "Harry Potter and the Chamber of Secrets," Box Office Mojo, https://www.boxofficemojo.com/movies/?id=harrypotter2.htm, accessed June 29, 2019.

27. Obst, *Sleepless in Hollywood*.

28. Fritz, *The Big Picture*.

29. Obst, *Sleepless in Hollywood*.

30. Obst, *Sleepless in Hollywood*.

31. Fritz, *The Big Picture*.

32. Scott and Dargis, "Hollywood on the Brink."

33. Obst, *Sleepless in Hollywood*.

34. Fritz, *The Big Picture*.

35. Obst, *Sleepless in Hollywood*.

36. "Daily Chart: Women's Wealth Is Rising," *Economist*, March 8, 2018, https://www.economist.com/graphic-detail/2018/03/08/womens-wealth-is-rising.

37. Sun, "Female Indie Filmmakers Should Aim Higher in Their Budgets."

38. Soraya Nadia McDonald, "Movies with Women Make More Money," *Washington Post*, April 3, 2014, https://www.washingtonpost.com/news/morning-mix/wp/2014/04/03/movies-with-women-make-more-money.

39. "Female-Led Films Outperform at Box Office for 2014–2017," Gracenote, December 2018, https://shift7.com/media-research.

40. Guibourg, "Oscars 2018: Female-Led Oscar Films 'More Profitable.'"

41. Obst, *Sleepless in Hollywood*.

42. ReFrame Culture and Change Handbook.

43. Analysis commissioned by The 51 Fund and done by Bruce Nash of Nash Information Services, August/September 2016.

44. Hunt, Ramon, and Tran, *Hollywood Diversity Report*.

45. Hunt, Ramon, and Tran, *Hollywood Diversity Report*.

46. CIA World Factbook, https://www.cia.gov/library/publications/the-world-factbook, accessed July 15, 2019.

47. *Hidden Figures* entry, Box Office Mojo, https://www.boxofficemojo.com/movies/?id=hiddenfigures.htm, June 29, 2019.

48. *Moonlight* entry, Box Office Mojo, https://www.boxofficemojo.com/movies/?id=moonlight2016.htm, June 29, 2019.

49. *Black Panther* entry, Box Office Mojo, https://www.boxofficemojo.com/movies/?id=marvel2017b.htm, June 29, 2019.

50. Nigel M. Smith, "Ignored by Youth-Obsessed Hollywood, Older Audiences Flock to Indie Films," *Guardian*, July 2, 2016, https://www.theguardian

.com/film/2016/jul/02/youth-focused-blockbusters-older-audiences-independent-films-arthouses.

51. Smith, "Ignored by Youth-Obsessed Hollywood, Older Audiences Flock to Indie Films."

52. Smith, "Ignored by Youth-Obsessed Hollywood, Older Audiences Flock to Indie Films."

53. Paul Bond and Georg Szalai, "Studio-by-Studio Profitability Ranking," *Hollywood Reporter*, February 23, 2018, https://www.hollywoodreporter.com/news/studio-by-studio-profit-report-disney-reigns-viacom-stems-losses-1086505.

54. Anna Marie Valerio and Katina Sawyer, "The Men Who Mentor Women," *Harvard Business Review*, December 7, 2016, https://hbr.org/2016/12/the-men-who-mentor-women.

55. Scott Roxborough, "AFM: Why Female-Centric Films Outnumber Male-Skewing Action Movies," *Hollywood Reporter*, November 3, 2016, https://www.hollywoodreporter.com/news/afm-2016-why-female-centric-films-outnumber-male-skewing-action-movies-943781.

56. Hunt, Ramon, and Tran, *Hollywood Diversity Report 2019*; Parker Morse, "How the U.S. Hispanic Market Is Changing This Year," *Forbes*, January 25, 2019, https://www.forbes.com/sites/forbesagencycouncil/2019/01/25/how-the-u-s-hispanic-market-is-changing-this-year/#2a891d0264fc.

57. Perrone, "Gender Inequality in Film Infographic."

58. Kay and Shipman, *The Confidence Code*.

59. Caroline Fairchild, "For Women, Being Rich Is Not a Priority," *Fortune*, November 13, 2014, https://fortune.com/2014/11/13/women-rich-financial-planning.

60. Pashley, *New Female Tribes*.

61. Pashley, *New Female Tribes*.

CHAPTER 9: WONDER WOM(E)N

1. Sperling, "CAA Launches Writers Database to Help Fix Hollywood's Diversity Problem."

2. Pashley, *New Female Tribes*.

3. Cynthia Littleton, "Abigail Disney, Killer Content Partner to Launch Female-Led Level Forward Studio," *Variety*, January 13, 2018, https://variety.com/2018/biz/news/killer-content-abigail-disney-level-forward-studio-1202664003.

4. "About Story," Array, http://www.arraynow.com, June 29, 2019.

5. Jason Guerrasio, "Jessica Chastain Explains Why She Chose a Man to Direct Her Upcoming Female-Led Movie," *Business Insider*, June 26, 2018, https://www.businessinsider.com/jessica-chastain-explains-why-a-man-will-direct-her-all-female-spy-movie-355-2018-6.

6. Andrew R. Chow, "What to Know About the Controversy Surrounding the Movie *Green Book*," *Time*, February 24, 2019, https://time.com/5527806/green-book-movie-controversy.

7. Matt Donnelly, "Lena Dunham to Adapt Refugee Survival Story for Steven Spielberg, J. J. Abrams," *Variety*, October 29, 2018, https://variety.com/2018/film/news/lena-dunham-steven-spielberg-abrams-hope-more-powerful-than-the-sea-1202992793.

8. Springer interview.

CHAPTER 10: ME AND YOU AND EVERYONE WE KNOW

1. Anderson, "A Look at Women Directors at the Summer Box Office the Year After Patty Jenkins' 'Wonder Woman.'"

2. Valerio and Sawyer, "The Men Who Mentor Women."

3. Sachs, "If Investors Really Listened to Data, They'd Be Investing in Women."

4. Pashley, *New Female Tribes.*

5. See https://www.bluefever.com.

6. Virginia Woolf, *A Room of One's Own* (1929) (Mansfield Centre, CT: Martino Fine Books, 2012).

7. Woolf, *A Room of One's Own.*

8. Bridges and Robson, *Silent Women.*

CONCLUSION

1. Andrew Dalton, "#MeToo Movement Sends Hollywood Figures into Exile, Not Jail," *AP News*, October 6, 2018, https://www.apnews.com/f89d2ab1b59c48d4b 9c3ae0d7a41d0bc.

2. Adam B. Vary, "Disney Won. Now What?," *Buzzfeed News*, July 3, 2019, https:// www.buzzfeednews.com/article/adambvary/disney-hollywood-20th-century-fox -marvel-outlook.

3. Natalie Jarvey, "Netflix Subscriber Growth Sharply Slows During Second Quarter," *Hollywood Reporter*, July 17, 2019, https://www.hollywoodreporter.com /news/netflix-subscriber-growth-sharply-slows-second-quarter-1224957.

IMAGE CREDITS

1: Martha M. Lauzen, *It's a Man's (Celluloid) World: Portrayals of Female Characters in Top Grossing Films of 2018* (San Diego: Center for the Study of Women in Television and Film, 2019).

2: Lauzen, *It's a Man's (Celluloid) World*; US Census Data, July 1, 2018, https://www.census.gov/quickfacts/fact/table/US/PST045216.

3–4: US Census Data, July 1, 2018.

5–9: Stacy L. Smith, Katherine Pieper, and Marc Choueiti, *Inclusion in the Director's Chair? Gender, Race & Age of Film Directors Across 1,000 Films from 2007–2016* (Los Angeles: Annenberg Inclusion Initiative, February 2017).

10: Smith, Pieper, and Choueiti, *Inclusion in the Director's Chair?*; US Census Data, July 1, 2018.

11: Smith, Pieper, and Choueiti, *Inclusion in the Director's Chair?*; Martha M. Lauzen, *The Celluloid Ceiling: Behind-the-Scenes Employment of Women on the Top 100, 250, and 500 Films of 2017* (San Diego: Center for the Study of Women in Television and Film, 2018), https://womenintvfilm.sdsu.edu/wp-content/uploads/2018/01/2017_Celluloid_Ceiling_Report.pdf; email interview with Victoria Hochberg, June 20, 2018; *Women and Hollywood*, https://womenandhollywood.com/resources/statistics/2010-statistics.

12–15: Lauzen, *It's a Man's (Celluloid) World*.

16: Smith, Pieper, and Choueiti, *Inclusion in the Director's Chair?*

17–18: Analysis commissioned by The 51 Fund; done by Bruce Nash, Nash Information Services, October 2016.

19–20: Smith, Pieper, and Choueiti, *Inclusion in the Director's Chair?*

21: Darnell Hunt, Ana-Christina Ramon, and Michael Tran, *Hollywood Diversity Report 2019: Old Story, New Beginning* (Los Angeles: UCLA College Social Sciences, February 2019), https://socialsciences.ucla.edu/wp-content/uploads/2019/02/UCLA-Hollywood-Diversity-Report-2019-2-21-2019.pdf.

22–23: Barbara Ann O'Leary, Directed By Women, database of projects with female directors, https://directedbywomen.com.

24: Lynda Obst, *Sleepless in Hollywood: Tales from the New Abnormal in the Movie Business* (New York: Simon & Schuster, 2013).

25: Analysis commissioned by The 51 Fund; done by Bruce Nash, Nash Information Services, August/September 2016.

0404